TEACHING
AT UNIVERSITY

'. . . knowledgeable and thought-provoking . . . blissfully free of jargon and rebarbative "education-speak". Written by a National Teaching Fellow and one of the History community's most innovative and reflective pedagogues, Alan Booth's book sets a new standard for accessible guidance on how history students actually learn.'

Eric Evans, Lancaster University

'This is a very stimulating book, by an experienced educator in history. The tone is tolerant and encouraging, while working steadily toward better teaching practice and offering, correctly, a central focus on historical understanding as the key goal. Discussions of student perspective, with some great quotes, complement attention to teaching approaches and assessment. I found myself jotting frequent notes about how to do this or that differently when I plan my undergraduate course for next semester.'

Peter N. Stearns, George Mason University

'Alan Booth's *Teaching History at University* is without question the definitive work available for university teachers of history. There is no other book like it. Scholars of historical pedagogy will begin – and could even end – with Booth.'

Peter Frederick, Wabash College

Teaching history is a substantive, intellectual task. As a form of scholarship it is as complex, challenging and creative as historical research, and it is vital to the future of the discipline.

Teaching History at University examines how high-quality history teaching and learning can be achieved in today's universities worldwide. Alan Booth draws on a wide range of international research as well as the reflections and experiences of university historians, linking theory and practice. He provides a wealth of practical ideas and strategies for the classroom. The key to improvement, he argues, lies in understanding students and in reflection on teachers' own educational beliefs, values and assumptions.

This is an essential resource for university teachers and all those who are responsible for ensuring the quality of teaching and learning policies and practices within their institutions.

Alan Booth is Reader in History at the University of Nottingham and Co-Director for History in the Learning and Teaching Support Network (LTSN) Subject Centre for History, Classics and Archaeology. His previous publications include *The Practice of University History Teaching* (Manchester University Press, 2000), co-edited with P. Hyland.

TEACHING HISTORY AT UNIVERSITY

Enhancing learning and understanding

Alan Booth

Routledge
Taylor & Francis Group

LONDON AND NEW YORK

First published 2003
by Routledge
11 New Fetter Lane, London EC4P 4EE
Simultaneously published in the USA and Canada
by Routledge
29 West 35th Street, New York, NY 10001

Routledge is an imprint of the Taylor & Francis Group

© 2003 Alan Booth

Typeset in Bembo by
Rosemount Typing Services, Barjarg Tower, Auldgirth
Printed and bound in Great Britain by
Biddles Ltd, Guildford and King's Lynn

British Library Cataloguing in Publication Data
A catalogue record for this book is available
from the British Library

Library of Congress Cataloging in Publication Data
Booth, Alan, 1946–
Teaching history at university : enhancing learning and
understanding / Alan Booth.
p. cm.
Includes bibliographical references and index.
1. History–Study and teaching (Higher) 2. History–Methodology. I.
Title.
D16.2.B66 2003
907' .1'1–dc21
2003002186

ISBN 0–415–30536–5 hbk
ISBN 0-415-30537-3 pbk

CONTENTS

ACKNOWLEDGEMENTS

This book has benefited greatly from the experiences and ideas of students and colleagues at the University of Nottingham, and those of historians at departmental and national seminars and conferences held throughout the United Kingdom under the auspices of History 2000 and the LTSN Subject Centre for History, Classics and Archaeology. Colleagues involved in the Subject Centre also helped me to think more systematically about the most effective ways of enhancing teaching and learning in a disciplinary context. Particular thanks are due to Paul Hyland, Peter Frederick and Richard Blackwell, whose insightful comments on various drafts were invaluable in helping me to clarify my ideas and structure the text more effectively. Their generosity and enthusiasm for this project have been greatly appreciated. Finally, Jeanne Booth was involved at all stages of the research and writing; listening patiently to my attempts to make sense of a vast array of material, and providing encouragement and support at times when writing seemed more a test of endurance than a labour of love.

1

INTRODUCTION

> Active research and fresh historical insight are necessary to
> keep a history school and its teaching alive; but equally
> necessary is the realisation that the teaching of history is as
> honourable, as useful, as arduous, a task as historical research
> and the writing of history books.
>
> (Kitson-Clark 1973)

For most historians in higher education, teaching is an activity to
which they devote the greater part of their time and energies on a
day-to-day basis. It is a task undertaken not merely out of contractual
obligation; it also provides the opportunity to share a love of the
subject and to see students develop as historians, learners and
individuals. In a survey of over a thousand historians conducted by
the Organization of American Historians in 1993, a significant
number reported that interaction with students constituted a
particular satisfaction. For many, the desire to teach had been an
important factor in drawing them into the profession, and the 'joy in
seeing young people come alive to history' and 'watching students
grow and mature' was a principal source of personal reward (Thelen
1994: 945). Teaching offered the opportunity to help others to
connect more deeply to their past and to themselves and develop
both subject and life skills. As one historian put it: 'I hope that
through my teaching I can open young people's eyes about our
nation's past and encourage them always to ask, "Why is X the way it
is? How did X get to be so?" If I can do that, I've helped train a
generation of inquisitive, curious minds which will be able to pursue
achievement in a variety of fields' (Shrock and Shrock 1994: 1098).
Similarly, responses to an annual survey of university history
departments in the United Kingdom since 1994, conducted by the

magazine *History Today*, testify to the strength of historians' professional and personal commitment to high-quality teaching and learning (see, for example, Fitzgerald and Hingley 1996; Barker 1997).

As one historian comments, reflecting the views of colleagues in all types of institution: 'Despite the RAE [Research Assessment Exercise] and our research mission, the bulk of our resources continue to be derived from and directed towards the provision of high-quality teaching' (Bates 1999: 56).

As the above quotation indicates, such surveys of professional opinion also reveal frustration at the distorting effects of recent trends within higher education. Thus one historian remarks that 'the academic reward system encourages historians to write for academic audiences, especially other historians, and discourages them from reaching out to multiple audiences. It also discourages them from trying to be good, effective teachers. They don't get rewarded to do this' (Thelen 1994: 939). Most criticism, however, is reserved for the subjection of history programmes to an accounting mentality in which everything is regarded as measurable and comparable, an approach widely linked in the minds of historians with a managerialism that runs counter to traditional academic values of autonomy, integrity and collegiality (see Ramsden 1998; Adams 2000; Newton 2000). The growth of student numbers on a dwindling unit of resource creates further resentment, not least because it threatens to erode the relationship between teachers and students considered integral to high-quality learning and teaching in the subject (Fitzgerald and Hingley 1996; Evans 2003). Thus W. Thompson (2000: 74) detects a trend throughout the Western world

> towards the commodification of higher education and its subjection to managerial and quasi-market forces . . . tutors will be under intense pressure to accommodate the maximum number of students with the minimum expenditure of resources, and their mode of teaching and assessment will inevitably be affected – the tendency will indeed be to teach history as a finished body of knowledge to be absorbed mechanically, with only the most cursory gestures to the complexities of historical understanding, in a fashion that makes for ease of assessment.

In a system of mass higher education, history undergraduate students are more heterogeneous in terms of age, personal and cultural background and level of preparedness for study; they are also commonly obliged to engage in part-time employment to fund their studies. The reduction in the time available for studying, the pressure to obtain employment in order to pay off accumulated debt and the prospect of a competitive employment market inevitably lead some to adopt a more strategic approach to studying. Though hardly a new phenomenon, the prioritization of effort towards assignments that count towards final grading, at the expense of preparation for non-assessed work, is widely perceived to be increasing. In addition, many students in history classes are no longer history majors, a trend intensified in modular programmes. In a meeting of representatives from the history departments of seven of the eight Indiana University campuses in 1997 to discuss the undergraduate programme, participants made it plain that their greatest concern was teaching non-history majors. 'From the smallest departments to the largest, most of the undergraduate students they taught were not majors . . . Most of the students in history classes are business or education majors' (Schreiber 1998; Bender 1994). Put starkly, history teachers can no longer count on their students possessing significant, if any, prior historical knowledge. Yet, whilst this suggests the need for greater attention to be paid to student learning, teaching increasingly competes with the need to demonstrate high-quality research output for career advancement, and with a proliferation of administrative tasks and paperwork associated with demands for quality assurance and 'transparency'. Throughout Western higher education, the academic workload is increasing rapidly, and the sense of personal control over work – once regarded as compensation for modest salaries – has all but disappeared (see Boys *et al.* 1988; Maassen and Van Vught 1996; Ramsden 1998; Knight 2002). Whilst historians can appreciate the need to ensure that undergraduate programmes are effectively managed and standards maintained, there is also suspicion that this represents a growing culture of compliance and control within higher education. From the complex paper trails necessary to introduce and monitor new courses and degree programmes to the mechanistic listing of skills outcomes, there is concern that administrative rather than educational goals have become the drivers of behaviour in the history classroom.

The practical consequence of such trends is that history teachers today are expected to design courses and teaching strategies that deliver high-quality learning to more numerous and more diverse students than ever before, in a context of multiple demands on their time. The challenges have never been greater. Moreover, if, as W. Thompson (2000: 75–6) maintains, 'keeping the principal aim and purpose of a history education in view amidst the swirl and pressure of these impositions and distractions requires a considerable degree of resolution and determination', this task is not made easier by the fact that the objectives of a history education are themselves a matter of contention. The expansion of new fields and approaches since the 1960s, and related theoretical developments such as feminism, multiculturalism and postmodernism, have all challenged traditional historical epistemology and led to considerable curricular diversity of aims, content and approaches (see Novick 1988; Wilson 1993; Frank *et al.* 1994; Jenkins 1996; Lubelska 1996; Lewis and Theoharris 1996; Joyce 1998; Jordanova 2000). What subject matter (if any) is essential to an undergraduate history education, what constitutes the optimal balance between content and skills, what should be the role of teacher and students in the learning process and how historical knowledge, skills and understanding are best assessed are all contested issues. Ultimately, of course, what individual historians or history departments define as their key objectives and priorities, and thus how they choose to structure and deliver their courses, will differ according to their own particular circumstances and needs, and those of their students. There is no single way to teach history. However, whether the goal is to provide a broad, liberal education, to train future historians, to develop skills for future employment, to promote lifelong learning, or to foster personal or social emancipation, a commitment to high-quality student learning is vital.

How historians can foster such learning constitutes the principal focus of this book. It is founded upon several overlapping premises: first, that teaching history is an important activity, an endeavour which extends far beyond producing employable graduates and can change students as historians, learners and individuals in potentially profound ways; second, that teaching should be regarded as scholarly work, as intellectually demanding, creative and rewarding as research; third, that taking time to think about what is done in the history classroom is even more necessary in the context of the challenges faced by teachers of the subject; and fourth, that finding ways to bring history alive to students, whatever their background knowledge and interests, makes the experience of teaching and learning easier, more rewarding and more fun. Although it has a practical focus, the approach adopted in this book is founded upon some well-established educational principles which represent the results of at least three decades of educational research on student learning in higher education, and the findings of a growing body of enquiry into classroom experiences in history. Whilst these propositions are considered in the following chapters, they are outlined briefly below in order to provide a sense of the approach adopted and of some recurrent themes.

High-quality learning is about changing understanding

In a history education, the acquisition of understanding is regarded as a principal objective and a key indicator of the quality of learning. Fostering the intention to understand has also been at the core of educational research and of development activities to promote 'deep' learning among students in higher education. Understanding and its associated analytical and interpretative skills are not easy to define precisely, and as a result have become suspect in the eyes of those who would reduce the complexity of learning to a list of precisely measurable learning outcomes. Yet for historians understanding is generally represented as a deep grasp of past situations and societies, a form of knowing that reaches beneath the surface of events and actions to reveal underlying structures, patterns and principles. In the process of deepening their understanding, students gain insight into their subject, themselves and the world around them by questioning established notions, considering diverse views and building independent judgements. Such learning is at once critical, reflective and imaginative, and enhances historical skills, employability and the ability to act purposefully in a world of rapid and complex change. Learning for understanding is both subject-specific and transferable to other situations, for when underlying structures and principles are understood, and an attentive approach to historical procedures developed, the chance of skills transfer is greater than if material has simply been memorized. Here the possession of information is necessary but not sufficient. Rather, understanding, as represented by history students and tutors, involves the application of knowledge to historical problems in a connective fashion: a process in which multiple pieces of information, ideas and personal experience are integrated, in ways congruent with generally accepted disciplinary modes of investigation, to form a mental representation of an event, situation or problem in the past that is satisfying in its perceived wholeness, if inevitably provisional. This sense of connected knowing is encapsulated by the following second-year history undergraduate reflecting on a course undertaken on twentieth-century Japanese society:

I felt the course really helped me to understand Japan in this period, especially by the end of the course when everything came together. There was a combination of all factors, social, economic and political, and I was able to pull all the strands together.

Understanding demands not only the acquisition of knowledge (as 'facts', historians' opinions or historiography), but the ability to structure it in increasingly complex ways. Nor is this perceived by students as a purely individual process. Rather, many feel confident that they really understand a topic when they can explain it to others. As one first-year student puts it: 'When I can talk about a topic to other people and can explain it to them confidently, then I realise I have understood it.' Understanding, then, involves a qualitative and progressive shift in learning, a change in how one sees events in the past, the nature of historical practice, the discipline itself and at its highest levels the relationship between subject, self and the world around. As understanding deepens, both subject and student are transformed.

Understanding is a holistic process

Understanding is an integrative process involving intellect and emotions, knowledge and the ability to apply it in increasingly sophisticated ways. Whilst some disciplinary conventions foreground detached approaches to the subject in the interests of dispassionate judgement, imaginative engagement is as essential to high-level learning as it is to serious historical writing. All historical material needs to be organized into meaningful patterns, and the incomplete and often fragmented nature of evidence about the past compels the historian to ask imaginative questions, intuit connections and follow hunches if an event or episode is to be adequately explained or represented, just as attempting to understand what motivated people in the past involves some empathetic engagement with their lives as a whole. The practice of history is therefore inherently creative, and, whilst the imaginative must be grounded in a critical and sceptical approach to sources, subject and self, it possesses a quasi-sensory dimension that can be seen, for example, when historians speak of a 'feel' for a period which is difficult to define precisely but goes beyond a purely cognitive engagement with the past.

Establishing a personal connection to past events is at the heart of many history undergraduates' rationale for studying the subject. For them, linking historical issues to their own concerns and values makes history relevant, inspires interest and generates the motivation that lies behind a deep approach to learning. It is no coincidence that the topics in the history curriculum most attractive to history undergraduates are those involving issues of civil, political and human rights, for these connect directly to issues of personal identity and provoke emotional as well as intellectual responses. Nor is it surprising that a 'passion' for the subject is regarded by many history students as a key characteristic of the effective history teacher. Although it does not feature in quality assurance documents, a love of the subject is fundamental to high-quality learning. So too, as all classroom teachers appreciate, feelings of self-confidence and self-esteem, and emotions such as fear, anxiety and boredom, as well as excitement and enthusiasm, lie at the heart of student experiences in the history classroom. The creation of a supportive yet intellectually challenging learning environment conducive to self-expression is essential to motivation. In the history classroom learning is not compartmentalized; rather the emotional and cognitive are interactive.

Understanding involves active learning

Understanding is not something that can be done to students, but something they must work on themselves. One historian, commenting on the need to integrate content and skills in history teaching, underlines this:

> What is the relationship between faculty teaching and student learning? If we assume a complex epistemology, where subjective processing of experience affects what people know at least to some degree, then what faculty teach is not identical to what students learn. There is no objective transfer of knowledge from the mind of the faculty member to the mind of the student. The data that faculty have reflected upon and transformed into knowledge, through their scholarship, can be experienced by students as a more refined data set – but it will not become knowledge until students transform it into knowledge themselves.
>
> (quoted in Mentkowski 2000: 319)

Students must be encouraged to take responsibility for their own learning, reflect critically upon it and connect new experiences and ideas with what they already know, in order to construct their own historical narratives. This does not mean that they can or should be simply left to their own devices. Indeed, it requires teachers to fulfil a variety of roles, not least in devising the intellectual and social context and conceptual scaffolding that can support student progress towards more sophisticated conceptions of their subject.

Promoting active learning in history is most commonly associated with teaching methods emphasizing participation, collaboration and independence. These include activities in seminar groups, projects and research dissertations, all of which provide opportunities for students to develop and demonstrate a particularly wide range of academic, personal and interpersonal skills through 'doing' history themselves. Collaborative learning not only facilitates the development of qualities demanded by employers (such as the ability to communicate effectively, leadership skills, self-awareness and sensitivity to others), but also creates conditions in which students can develop critical skills and independent judgement by encountering a diversity of approaches, views and perspectives (see Matthews 1996; Johnson, Johnson and Smith 1994, 1998). As Barker *et al.* (2000: 63–4) comment: 'communication skills and group work can be seen as the basis for the development of critical abilities. Learning to debate informally with others; to pursue and complete demanding tasks collaboratively; and to select and present ideas formally with clarity and cogency will all contribute to the high order cognitive skills necessary for undergraduate study of history.' The variety of activities evident in active-learning classrooms also helps teachers to address the diverse learning styles, abilities, interests and backgrounds of students. Such methods can, however, be daunting for new undergraduates. Thus Shrock and Shrock (1994: 1094–5) observe: 'many students come to us from high schools that emphasize memorization and passive learning. Students are primed to take notes, to memorize, to ask only immediately relevant questions ("Will this chapter be on the test?"). They may be uncomfortable, unable to actively engage with the assumptions or argument of an author, and uninterested . . . Students are asked to master content, but we chiefly emphasize the appreciation of history as a distinctive way of knowing.'

Some historians are also uncomfortable with the perceived dilution of content implicit in active learning. Thus, for example, in role play some reduction of coverage in an individual class may occur due to the need to keep the topic manageable and the time inevitably spent in students simply moving around. To take an example from one of my own courses, 'Britain and the French Revolution', the recreation of a meeting of members of the London Corresponding Society on the issue of political reform in 1795 does involve a narrowing of focus over what might be covered in a tutor-led discussion. However, through role play students often engage with the fundamental themes of the whole course – the conflict of ideas, the structures of power, the tensions between the forces of continuity and change, and the dilemmas of those seeking change as well as those attempting to preserve the status quo. Indeed, in many student-led seminars the use of sub-groups within the larger class can be used to address a range of issues at least equal to those covered in a more traditional class. Content is not inevitably reduced by the use of active-learning methods. Moreover, to equate coverage with learning is simplistic, for, if this were so, traditional, synoptic lectures would be the best means of promoting high-quality learning, and few believe this. If introduced and implemented carefully, active-learning strategies encourage involvement, intrinsic interest, critical engagement and, not least, fun in learning. They allow students to practise subject and transferable skills in ways that stimulate enthusiasm for the subject and encourage further independent exploration. Above all, they help students to see themselves as historians, engaged in making (more complex) meaning for themselves rather than acting as the passive recipients of the views of others, however well founded.

Connecting to student experience is the key to changing understanding

High-quality teaching requires not only the possession of subject expertise and technical skills, but also awareness of how to deploy these in ways sensitive to student learning in the subject. As Burke (1991: 6) remarks apropos historical writing, 'Our minds do not reflect reality directly. We perceive the world only through a network of conventions, schemata and stereotypes, a network which varies from one culture to another.' So too, when they enter the class, students are not *tabulae rasae*, but bring with them prior conceptions of the subject and knowledge more generally, and perceptions of what makes for effective teaching and learning in history. These perceptions, conditioned and refined through experience, powerfully influence their approach to learning in each class, and how they perceive what teachers are trying to do. Shulman (1989: 10) writes of this: 'we now understand that learning is a dual process in which, initially, the inside

beliefs must come out, and only then can something outside get in
... To prompt learning you've got to begin with the process of going
from inside out. The first influence on new learning is not what
teachers do pedagogically but the learning that's already inside the
learner.' This is echoed in the reflections of Frederick (1999a: 51) on
a career spent teaching history in higher education:

> The longer I teach and experiment with the learning and
> teaching of history, the more I firmly believe that our
> effectiveness depends more than anything else on an
> understanding of who our students are. Not abstractly, but
> who they are specifically, in my classroom tomorrow
> morning: what kinds of diversity exist in that classroom?
> What did we do yesterday and how well did it work? What's
> going on campus? What's the next text or topic we're
> struggling with right now? What mood are they likely to be
> in tomorrow? What's their readiness to learn what I have in
> mind as teaching goals? How much learning can I get away
> with before they shut down?

Whatever teachers try to convey, students' perceptions are the filter
through which that communication passes. This does not mean that
all that students say has to be followed slavishly, for some beliefs will
be unexamined and may be misconceptions based upon past
experience or habit, and helping students to identify and change these
is an important and challenging task. Nonetheless, recognition of
students' interests, prior knowledge and conceptions of learning (and
teaching) in history, and how these can be effectively connected to
course goals, content and methods, is essential in the creation of an
environment for fostering complex learning.

Such an approach does not, of course, imply that traditional
teaching qualities are redundant. Enthusiasm, subject knowledge and
awareness of practical classroom strategies are vital ingredients of
high-quality history teaching. Nonetheless, it is how these are
deployed in the context of each class that makes the difference
between success and failure, and here an understanding of student
perspectives is essential. Ramsden (1992: 8) puts this cogently when
he writes that techniques about how to lecture or run seminars 'are
actually rather easily acquired; it is understanding how to use them
that takes constant practice and reflection. And they are only useful in
so far as they are directed by a clear awareness of educational
principles – in particular, the principle that the content of student

learning is logically prior to the methods of teaching the content.' Thus the principal role of the teacher is not to discover the best methods of transmitting information, but to use information about students' understandings, and misunderstandings in order to create conditions that help them connect their experience, interests and values to key course-learning goals. Such a model of teaching involves a shift in the pedagogic role of the teacher from that of expert, guru or authority-figure to adviser, facilitator and co-learner. This does not downgrade the teaching function, but rather elevates the art of teaching history by emphasizing that, in addition to the possession of subject mastery, teaching demands attentiveness (to students, to context and to one's own assumptions) and the ability to respond flexibly and creatively to classroom situations.

Understanding teaching and learning involves reflective enquiry

If developing understanding requires students to re-evaluate continuously their ideas and experiences, it also demands that teachers connect critically with their own beliefs, values, underlying assumptions and conceptions of the subject, teaching and learning, and how these have shaped their classroom strategies. As Holt (1990: 42) points out, 'the historian's experience profoundly shapes the history he or she writes . . . What is important is that we be self-reflective about that craft, and that we make that reflection part of what students learn and puzzle over.' Becoming more self-reflective by exploring the relationship between personal values, experience and practice, and how these connect with teaching in one's subject and with student learning, need not be a purely individual exercise. Indeed, dialogue with others can be a powerful means of opening up new perspectives on practice. Whatever lens is used, however, reflection and action constitute part of a continuous process of professional development involving careful enquiry and experimentation. If investigation without action in the form of changes to practice is of little practical value, so too experience without disciplined reflection risks the mere repetition of mistakes.

Such disciplined enquiry about classroom practices also recognizes that history teaching is situated in departmental and institutional cultures, disciplinary norms and wider social and political contexts (see Church 1976, 1978; Frank *et al.* 1994; Soffer 1994; Quinlan 1999; Becher and Trowler 2001). All of these influence conceptions of teaching and what is expected of students, and historians are by training well equipped to unravel such forces and how their influence changes over time. Thus, for example, not only does the departmental context powerfully influence whether students adopt a deep or surface approach to their studies, but disciplinary conventions about rules and standards of evidence, and scholarship more generally, have significant repercussions for what are considered appropriate means of delivering the curriculum. More broadly, as indicated at the outset, government emphasis upon efficiency, accountability and economic needs, and wider social forces prioritizing the individual as consumer, have influenced the ways in which the history curriculum is constructed, delivered and received by students. Adopting the same kind of scholarly approach to the practice of history teaching that is routinely employed in research can help history teachers to develop a more complex understanding of these overlapping contexts, and provide the means for devising effective learning strategies and environments.

This book is intended as a resource for all historians wishing to reflect in more depth upon their teaching and upon student learning as a means of enhancing both. It seeks to provide guidance and advice on a range of issues central to the teaching of history, to support those individuals and departments who wish to develop their teaching, and to contribute to a growing body of scholarship on the teaching and learning of history in higher education. It is therefore at once theoretical and applied, research- and classroom-oriented, or, to express it in the language of the scholarship of teaching considered in Chapter 9, it involves the advancement of knowledge, the integration of knowledge and the application of knowledge. Whilst Chapters 5 to 9 provide a range of strategies to address common classroom issues and concerns and to help history teachers explore their pedagogic beliefs, values and experiences, there is throughout a deliberate effort to go beyond a 'tips and techniques' approach. For although tools for teaching are important to hard-pressed university history teachers, as Hutchings (2000: 23) remarks: 'if improvement stops with technique . . . teaching itself is diminished, for if teaching is mostly a matter of technique, it is not, after all, a subject for serious, scholarly attention – the very thing it needs for ongoing, real improvement'. Technique alone is too haphazard in its effects, too easily disconnected from the complex particularities of disciplinary and classroom context, and, particularly, from an understanding of the experiences of history students and teachers, of their conceptions of learning and teaching in their subject. Chapters 2 to 4, therefore, attempt to situate classroom practice within a wider framework of ideas about learning and teaching grounded in the perspectives and experiences of history students and teachers.

Throughout the text I have used the research, reflections and classroom experiences of historians in a range of countries, alongside the findings of those in other disciplines involved in developing and researching teaching and learning. In particular, there is a vast body of educational research on teaching and learning in higher education whose epistemology, methodologies and discourse can at first sight appear alien to the ways in which historians think and talk about their teaching, but whose research-based findings offer much of value to the understanding and promotion of high-quality learning in history. I have been particularly concerned to incorporate these findings whilst remaining true to the language, methods and standards of historical writing. This has been a fine balance to tread, for one person's jargon is another's disciplinary discourse, but I hope that I have succeeded in employing language that is accessible to all historians and in deploying my evidence in a manner that conforms to disciplinary standards of scholarship. I would like to think, however, that this work might convince more historians that the investigation of how history is taught and learned is a matter deserving serious attention, inspire them to research their own pedagogic practices and encourage them to contribute to the development of an exciting, intellectually challenging and potentially transforming field of disciplinary study.

2

LEARNING HISTORY
FOR UNDERSTANDING

> I know I understand a topic when all the arguments become
> clear and everything (well almost) fits into a framework in
> my mind – it sort of makes sense.
>
> (First-year history undergraduate)

Understanding is regarded as a primary goal of learning in history and
an essential objective for history teachers at all levels of education (see
National Curriculum History Working Group 1994; National Center
for History in the Schools 1996; History Benchmarking Group
2000). Thus the benchmark statement for undergraduate programmes
in the United Kingdom begins its discussion of standards with the
following principle: 'We take it as self-evident that knowledge and
understanding of the human past is of incalculable value both to the
individual and society at large, and that the first object of education
in History is to enable this to be acquired' (2000: 1). Even at a basic
level of historical thinking, knowing why an event happened is more
satisfying than simply knowing that it happened, while making a
personal judgement on complex evidence is more rewarding than the
mere collection of information. Indeed, the distinctiveness of the
discipline arguably lies less in its content (for the study of the past is
clearly not exclusively the territory of the historian) than in the
particular blend and interaction of knowledge and skills required for
the attainment of a complex grasp of history. For students, to learn for
understanding is to act more like a professional historian, and the
motivation and confidence that flow from this stimulate further
learning. Understanding also provides a platform for the development
of independence in thought and action through the critical scrutiny
of diverse evidence and the structuring of knowledge into a coherent
personal account. Moreover, as Hvolbek (1993: 7) remarks: 'to be

educated in the humanities (and the sciences) is to be made aware of what one is lacking, it is to be made aware that one must continually generate new questions and do away with the confidence that one's own ideas are absolutely correct'. In seeking understanding, students subject their personal values and beliefs (and those of their teachers, discipline and society) to close scrutiny, and become more self-aware and confident in their ability to act purposefully not only in academic tasks but in situations and contexts beyond the history classroom. A history education centred upon developing understanding therefore provides a powerful means of connecting subject, self and society, and this in turn emphasizes to students the relevance and practical value of studying the subject.

Yet if understanding is a hallmark of high-level learning in history, it is also an elusive notion. When, for example, a student says, 'I don't understand the causes of the First World War', this does not mean the same thing as when the same student says, 'I don't understand how to write a good history essay.' Similarly, when a course handbook declares that 'by the end of this course you will be able to understand the tensions in Weimar society', this does not mean quite the same as when it promises that 'this degree programme will enable you to understand how accounts about the past are constructed'. A student might also 'understand' what the use of evidence in history means, but not be able to deploy historical evidence skilfully to construct a convincing argument. If the language of understanding is context-dependent, the term is most commonly employed by practitioners as a shorthand to denote a 'deep grasp of processes and events in the past' (Jordanova 2000: 95), and this distinguishes it from the simple acquisition of knowledge as information. Whilst there has been increasing discussion of the meaning of both understanding and knowledge in the context of education (see, for example, Nickerson 1985; Eraut 1992; Langer 1992; Entwistle and Marton 1994; Bruner 1996; Gardner 1999; Newton 2000), from the perspective of this book what is most important is how understanding is used in the everyday practice of history teaching and learning. For how students think of understanding in their subject will determine how they attempt to acquire it, just as teachers' conceptions will influence the ways in which they try to improve student learning and what they reward in terms of student behaviour.

Student and teacher representations of understanding in history

In the last three decades researchers have begun to analyse the development of students' historical understanding in increasingly sophisticated ways (see Dickinson and Lee 1978; Partington 1980; Hallden 1986; Ashby and Lee 1987; Shemilt 1987; Lee 1994; Lee, Ashby and Dickinson 1996; Husbands 1996; McAleavy 1998; Williams and Davies 1998; Leinhardt *et al.* 1994; Arthur and Phillips 2000; Stearns *et al.* 2000; Wineburg 1994, 2000, 2001). Although primarily focused upon schools history, this research has provided valuable insights into how history is learned, particularly in relation to how students read historical texts, and recent work in higher education has begun to complement this. Of particular interest here are investigations conducted by Newton and Newton (1998) and Newton *et al.* (1998) into the conceptions of understanding held by university students and teachers, and this work is used as the basis for the following discussion of ways in which understanding is commonly represented.

1 Understanding as the mental representation of events and societies in the past

In interviews with a small sample of history lecturers and recent graduates on what they meant by understanding, Newton *et al.* (1998) discovered an emphasis upon the reconstruction of events – the ability to explain the causes, character, consequences and significance of situations in the past. This involves an awareness of the underlying structures and processes that shape a particular society or historical period, the complex interactions between individuals and social groups and their environment, and fundamental shifts or turning points. Of course, such analysis can operate on many levels of sophistication, but understanding in this sense is generally expressed not as an exhaustive account or narrative but in terms of the structuring of evidence of different kinds into a coherent perspective. One university history teacher in the above study also felt that understanding involved moving beyond the putting together of particular pieces of evidence on a topic to 'maybe something a bit wider, ways of explaining this and, perhaps, relating that to wider aspects of history, setting it into its wider historical context' (52), including different theoretical approaches. This contains echoes of Elton (1967: 149):

the study of history involves the analysis of problems in an extensive setting, both temporal and spatial; the student needs to be capable of close reasoning and the sceptical assessment of evidence, but must perform this common scientific duty in such a manner that the surrounding circumstances of his problem, antecedents and consequences, concomitants and contrasts, affect the solution of the specific details of the problem itself. That is what one means by an understanding of history.

Throughout the student interviews, metaphors such as 'getting a picture', 'fitting the pieces together like a jigsaw' and 'pulling together the different threads' recur as expressions of what understanding a topic in history means, and these correspond closely to research conducted with psychology undergraduates (Entwistle and Entwistle 1997). Here students typically commented that 'understanding is the interconnection of lots of disparate things . . . the feeling that you understand how the whole thing is connected up – you can make sense of it internally . . . If I don't understand, it's just everything floating about and you can't quite get everything into place – like jigsaw pieces, you know, suddenly connect and you can see the whole picture' (148). One of the history graduates interviewed by Newton *et al.* (1998: 53) also felt that understanding related not simply to specific events but to a period as a whole, and conveyed a sense that understanding involves a grasp of a subject beyond the logical reconstruction of events.

> How do I know? It's not a case of being able to quote or just come out with a run of dates and names and places. It's when I think I had a feel for the time . . . It's when I can summon up an image or an atmosphere of the time in my mind (53).

This quasi-sensory insight is similarly remarked upon by Jordanova (2000) and associated with complex learning. In discussing the craft of the historian, she writes that, whilst 'it is hard to generalise about such matters, there is a "feel" that comes from familiarity with a subject, even if it is unwise to romanticise or idealise it' (173). A similar, almost visual, experience was expressed by final-year history undergraduates in a study of revision and essay writing strategies (Entwistle 1995). One noted that in an examination, although only a small proportion of the information learned in revision could be used, 'it was almost as though I could see it all fitting into an overall picture' (50).

2 Understanding as the representation of the nature and significance of people's lives in the past

The desire to explain the complex relationship between individuals and their circumstances is a principal motivation for historians. A. J. P. Taylor remarked that 'history is the one way in which you can experience at second-hand all kinds of varieties of human behaviour, and after all the greatest problem in life is to understand how other people behave, and this is what history enables us to do: to see people in all kinds of situations, in all kinds of walks of life' (Wrigley 1980: 53). More recently, Evans (1997: 189–90) has similarly expressed the view that 'it is precisely the interaction between the individual and his or her circumstances that makes the study of people in the past so fascinating'. For students too, and particularly for first-year undergraduates, interest in history is frequently expressed in terms of a desire to understand people's lives (Booth 1993; Lang 1991; Hallden 1986, 1994). For some this is the prime factor in their interest in social history, often perceived as the history of 'ordinary' people or of everyday life. For others, especially 18–21-year-old entrants and male students, influential personalities capture the imagination, and this is reflected in the popularity of courses on Hitler and Stalin. In the words of one first-year history undergraduate reflecting on the experience of history at school:

> I enjoyed studying individuals rather than themes. By that I mean I prefer a politician's personal ideologies rather than a historical movement's ideas. Individuals and their actions comprise history in my opinion, and that is the most interesting aspect of the past.
>
> (Booth 1997: 211)

For both history undergraduates and their teachers, understanding people in the past is perceived not so much in terms of knowing what they did but explaining their thoughts and actions in specific historical contexts, and, especially, uncovering the causes, consequences and significance of their actions. In practice, this emphasis upon human actions involves the empirical construction of a coherent picture from diverse pieces of evidence relating to, for example, childhood and family experiences, schooling, personal beliefs and values, and ways of acting in the world. This enables a more rounded view to be formed that allows an individual to be placed more fully in the context of their time and place. Comparing and contrasting historical interpretations of an individual's actions is regarded as an important aspect of this, providing an additional perspective that differentiates the exercise from biography.

3 Understanding as facility with disciplinary techniques, procedures and concepts

For most practitioners, understanding represents not only a deep grasp of past events, societies or actions, but also a process of connecting together diverse evidence from primary and secondary sources in ways that are congruent with accepted modes of enquiry within the discipline. This involves knowing the meaning of a particular concept or practice, but more particularly the ability to apply it flexibly and appropriately to address historical problems. For many this grasp of process is an important hallmark of becoming professional in one's approach to the past, and a principal means of enculturation into the discipline. At a basic level, understanding in this sense involves familiarity with the steps required to research information, interrogate and weigh evidence, construct a sound argument and produce a competent history essay. However, at a more sophisticated level it includes awareness of how and why historical accounts are constructed and the influence of the present upon writing about the past. Such competencies are often represented by students in terms of the ability to select and use primary and secondary sources, skills regarded by many first-year undergraduates as defining degree-level study in the subject. More frequently mentioned by final-year undergraduates is the importance of mastering differing interpretations and the historiography of a topic, and through this the attainment of a sense of the dynamic and developmental nature of the discipline as a whole (Booth 2000).

Students also recognize the importance of the use of key historical concepts to make sense of past events. Of course, the nature of the concepts used in historical study varies considerably. Some concepts are very general, for example the key organizing ideas in historical explanation such as continuity and change, causation and consequence, which in the United Kingdom have been at the core of establishing progression in historical thinking in schools in the last two decades (see Counsell 2000). Other concepts are more closely related to a particular period, such as 'orders' and 'estates' in understanding the events of 1789 in France or 'feudalism' in understanding the medieval period. Some – such as revolution, power, slavery, freedom, sovereignty – are not inherently tied to a particular point in time at all, whilst others, such as 'objectivity', are procedural. Understanding in this sense means for students more than simply resorting to a dictionary definition. Rather, it implies using concepts in ways that reflect contemporary usage. For more advanced learners, there is also an awareness of the ways in which particular concepts have been used by historians, and an appreciation that their meaning is context-related.

Progression in understanding

Understanding can, then, be seen as both a state (a deep grasp of events and actions) and a process (the skilful application of knowledge as information, concepts and procedures to historical problems). It is fundamentally integrative, involving connections at many levels of generality and specificity. These include links between new and prior knowledge; between different types of evidence; between rival interpretations of a topic; between the event or situation in question and the wider context (earlier or later periods, inter-disciplinary perspectives etc.); between learners and historical actors; and between all of these and the concepts, theories and techniques employed by historians to create meaning from them. The more numerous, varied and structured the connections, the deeper the understanding and, it can be argued, the greater the likelihood of transference to new contexts. Understanding is therefore always provisional, for new interpretations inevitably arise from the discovery of more evidence, the interrogation of established evidence with new techniques, and from further reflection or theoretically informed investigation of the many possible linkages of ideas.

This raises the complex issue of progression in understanding at undergraduate level. Clearly, understanding is not easily reducible to a set of components the development of which can be plotted in a linear and mechanistic fashion. It is an iterative process that proceeds differentially according to learners' prior knowledge and existing conceptions of the subject, the interplay between the level of historical knowledge and skill in learning, and the context of learning (including the skill of the teacher). For some students understanding occurs as a flash of insight into a historical problem or issue; for many it is a protracted and uncertain endeavour in which there is incremental realization about, for example, what writing an analytical history essay means in practice. It may indeed combine elements of both, with periods of apparent stasis followed by paradigm shifts in which a more integrated sense of meaning emerges. Whether slow or dramatic, however, changing one's understanding involves a qualitative shift in learning rather than a quantitative increase in knowledge. Here the Structure of the Observed Learning Outcome (SOLO) provides a means of exploring and evaluating progress in understanding taxonomy (Biggs and Collis 1982; Boulton-Lewis 1995). It identifies five stages or levels in the increasingly complex way in which students structure material in order to master academic tasks in their discipline, and, although expressed in the language of educational research, these correlate well with classification systems commonly employed in history degree programmes. This organizing framework is described below, accompanied by the reflections of a sample of first-year history students on what understanding means to them.

1   Pre-structural
    'Understanding in history is about learning things about the past.'
    Pre-structural responses operate on a superficial level, missing the point or using tautology to mask a lack of understanding.

2   Unistructural
    'Understanding in history is about getting the facts and putting them down in an orderly fashion.'
    Here the student demonstrates awareness relating to only one aspect or dimension of the issue and a focus on descriptive narrative.

3   Multistructural
    'Understanding in history is about seeing what historians' views there are and how they differ.'
    In this case the student recognizes that there are a number of ways of looking at a topic, that historians have differing views, and that it is important to know the ways in which these are at variance. At the lower end of this broad category the student will merely list the views, while at the higher end their similarities and differences will be indicated in more detail. Essentially, however, students are still working within a descriptive framework. Here there is still relatively little attempt to relate different interpretations firmly to historiographical traditions or to the central question.

4 Relational

'Understanding in history is about comparing and contrasting interpretations on a topic. I can see the ways the different historians' views fit together and come to my own point of view.'

Understanding is seen in a more systemic way as a series of connections, a process as much as a product. The student is involved in the critical comparison and synthesis of material, so that an integrated and coherent view can be constructed.

5 Extended abstract

'Understanding in history is seeing the topic as a whole and from various perspectives, past and present. It involves seeing that everything we judge is formed by our ideas and ideals, yet these change through time. Understanding makes you feel history is alive.'

Here the student additionally connects subject to self and the wider world in a way that indicates some original thinking and awareness at a higher level of abstraction. At this level the student sees the wider issues raised by the question and integrates these, so that self-reflection becomes an integral part of critical reflection on the discipline and vice versa.

In this hierarchical framework there are two principal changes: quantitative increases in the responses, associated with the acquisition of more information; and qualitative shifts in the conception of the subject associated with understanding. At levels two and three, understanding is still seen in terms of increasing the volume of 'facts' (whether perceived as details of the past or of historians' views), moving from a single focus to an awareness of the importance of various factors but in an uncritical fashion. At levels four and five, however, knowledge is seen as relational and is used in increasingly complex and connected ways. To reach the higher levels of learning, students must adopt a 'deep' approach to learning; this, along with other models of learning development, is considered in the following chapter.

Understanding and history skills

In acquiring understanding students become increasingly aware of the constructed nature of historical knowledge and therefore of its 'provisional' status. The student no longer craves certainty and finality, but appreciates and grapples with the malleability of historical evidence. In this process of negotiating complex meaning, we are, as

Toohey (1999: 151) remarks, looking less for mastery than for progress: 'what we are most likely to want from students is evidence that they are becoming more and more experienced in the *processes* which lead to greater depth of understanding and creativity'. This requires not merely gathering information from multiple sources, but analysing, connecting and applying it to specific historical problems. As such, it involves a wide range of skills and abilities which have been at the core of statements of history standards in many countries. A particular focus of these has been the enumeration of the many cognitive skills that together constitute what is often called 'historical thinking' (although whether one considers these skills as inherently 'historical' or generic is a contested issue). Thus the statement of national standards for schools history in the United States reads: 'historical understanding requires students to engage in historical thinking: to raise questions and to marshal solid evidence in support of their answers; to go beyond the facts in their textbooks and examine the historical record for themselves . . . and to do so imaginatively – taking into account the historical context in which these records were created and comparing the multiple points of view of those on the scene at the time' (National Center for History in the Schools 1996). Blackey (1999: xiv) further clarifies this:

> Thinking historically involves developing the ability to articulate problems in need of resolution and to formulate theses based upon what we have discovered; it is learning how to ask the kind of questions for which the answers, once determined, will help solve a historical problem or fill in a gap in our knowledge ... It involves the ability to evaluate sources, to analyze various kinds of data, and to synthesize ideas and both primary and secondary sources. Thinking historically is being able to discern themes and trends, to see patterns, similarities, and differences. It is the core of what historians do, regardless of where we work or what we specialize in. And it certainly should be the one consistent ingredient that is blended into everything we teach.

In the United Kingdom these skills have been articulated most clearly in the Subject Benchmark Statement (History Benchmarking Group 2000) which has outlined the essential qualities to be fostered by a university history education. They are described in Figure 2.1.

Figure 2.1 The historian's skills and qualities of mind

- The ability to read and use texts and other source materials, both critically and empathetically, while addressing questions of genre, content, perspective and purpose.
- The understanding of the problems inherent in the historical record itself: awareness of a range of viewpoints and the way to cope with this; appreciation of the range of problems involved in the interpretation of complex, ambiguous and conflicting and often incomplete material; a feeling for the limitations of knowledge and the dangers of simplistic explanations.
- Basic critical skills: a recognition that statements are not all of equal validity, that there are ways of testing them, and that historians operate by rules of evidence which, though themselves subject to critical evaluation, are also a component of intellectual integrity and maturity.
- Intellectual independence: a history programme is not simply or even primarily a preparation for research in the subject, but it should incorporate the general skills of the researcher, namely the ability to set tasks and solve problems. This involves: bibliographic skills; the ability to gather, sift, select, organize and synthesize large quantities of evidence; the ability to formulate appropriate questions and to provide answers to them using valid and relevant evidence and argument. It should develop reflexivity, i.e. an understanding of the nature of the discipline including what questions are asked by historians, and why.
- Marshalling of argument – in written and oral form drawing on and presenting all the above skills. Such argument should have structure; it should be relevant and concise. In the case of written argument it should be expressed in clear, lucid and coherent prose. Orally it should involve the capacity to sustain a reasoned line of argument in the face of others, to listen, to engage in sustained debate, and amend views as necessary in the light of evidence and argument.

These skills and abilities correspond closely to other efforts by historians to define what constitutes high-quality learning in the subject (see, for example, Stearns 1993; Keirn 1999). Booth and Hyland (2000) identify the abilities outlined in Figure 2.2 as underpinning advanced learning in the subject.

It is clearly invidious to rank these multiple abilities in terms of their contribution to historical understanding, for all are necessary, overlapping and interactive, just as they also depend upon prior knowledge and skills. Nonetheless, I would suggest that three core practices lie at the heart of developing historical understanding. *Critical analysis*, the ability to dissect historical texts and other sources

Figure 2.2   Characteristics of high-level learning in history

- *The ability to seek out knowledge.* This requires the development of a range of research skills that are at the heart of independent and effective learning in any context. They include not only the ability to identify and investigate many different kinds of sources of information, but also the confidence to do so based on a critical awareness of one's own abilities and an appreciation of the range of strategies available.
- *The ability to manage large, disparate and often incomplete bodies of information from a wide range of sources.* This involves building up factual knowledge from primary and secondary sources, sifting and synthesizing it, identifying key elements, considering provenance and purpose, discriminating between the essential and peripheral, and structuring material in a systematic and logical fashion. It also involves the ability to work creatively and flexibly to combine different types of source (e.g. literary, visual, numerical, material or oral), and to assess their values in the context of a particular problem or issue. Evaluative and decision-making skills are therefore fundamental to this attribute.
- *The ability to understand and evaluate the conceptual and methodological frameworks which form the basis of historical knowledge and interpretation.* This requires an awareness of the key concepts and methodologies that have shaped the discipline – particularly of the importance of historiography – and the ability to apply this knowledge in relation to particular topics of study. More broadly it involves a sense of how histories are made, and of the discipline as a whole as a continuously evolving yet contested field of knowledge. This in turn is linked to an awareness of how knowledge may be created and defined, how we come to understand the world.
- *The ability to use historical knowledge and skills to develop one's own insights and interpretations.* This involves being able to see different perspectives on a historical topic, that meanings are usually contested, and that evidence and arguments are often incomplete and ambiguous. It also involves developing the ability to compare and contrast differing points of view, to evaluate their merits, and being able to question received judgements and historical orthodoxy in order to come to one's own judgements. In order to develop their own frame of reference, creating new knowledge from old, students will need to develop considerable self-awareness, particularly the ability to apply past experience and previous learning to that process.
- *The ability to address and resolve problems.* This involves linking new knowledge with existing knowledge, and using the one to inform the other; identifying and clarifying problems, formulating hypotheses and examining alternative methods or solutions, and explaining, testing and evaluating the preferred solution. These activities require high-order

Figure 2.2 continued

> analytical and decision-making skills, and are integral both to the learning of history and to the addressing of practical problems encountered in employment.
> - *The ability to think creatively within and beyond one's historical studies.* This involves students developing a critical imagination that allows them to connect with the past, ask imaginative questions of their material and fashion an interpretation of a topic which can overcome deficiencies in the sources by employing a combination of critical rigour and creativity. It involves the constructive use of analytical thought; the ability not merely to question but also to generate ideas and apply critical thinking in a creative fashion. It also means being receptive to new and challenging interpretations and evidence, and thus requires reflexivity and flexibility.

in a systematic and rigorous manner which opens up meaning and enables the construction of complex ideas and arguments about the past. *Critical reflection,* the careful questioning of the practices, concepts and assumptions of the discipline ('its social rationale, its theoretical underpinnings and its intellectual standing', History Benchmarking Group 2000: 4), and also of the personal beliefs, values and experiences that the historian brings to the study of past events. *Imaginative engagement,* the ability to connect with issues and historical agency in ways that seem to bring the past to life and cast new light upon it. This involves not only using one's own experience to identify with the actions of those in the past, and yet acknowledge their 'ineffable strangeness' (Lowenthal 2000: 74; Andress 1998), but also a recognition that understanding requires knowledge to be reworked to foster new ideas and questions and decide one's preferred interpretations. As Husbands (1996: 62) puts it: 'in the construction of historical understanding, the historian is not a cipher, but an active participant in the dialogue between the present and the past'.

In a history education, subject and self are inextricably linked, and historians have traditionally been keen to emphasize that the benefits of historical understanding are not confined to the subject domain (see Collingwood 1946; Elton 1967; Donovan 1973; Soffer 1994). Of course, this can result in extravagant assertions of the importance of history, as in Collingwood's claim for the subject as integral to the survival of civilized society (Hughes–Warrington 1996). Nonetheless, the core practices of critical analysis, critical reflection and imaginative engagement can facilitate not only subject mastery but also the ability to think more deeply and act more purposefully in contexts beyond the university. A history education might be regarded, therefore, as a means of lifelong personal development and emancipation as well as a fascinating experience in itself. Today issues of self have become increasingly foregrounded in the wake of postmodern challenges to historical epistemology (see Jenkins 1991, 1997, 2003; Appleby *et al.* 1994; Evans 1997; Munslow 1997; Tosh 2000; Thompson 2000; Marwick 2001). Both 'traditional' and 'postmodern' historians have emphasized the liberating power of the study of the subject, not least as a response to those who see history education primarily in terms of the opportunity to develop marketable transferable skills and students primarily as future employees. Thus, in their defence of the truth-telling nature of history, Appleby *et al.* (1994: 306) locate history in 'the human fascination with self-discovery'. Whilst this, they maintain, has often been externalized by a focus on abstractions like the growth of democracy or the emergence of modernity, nonetheless 'the renewable source of energy behind these inquiries comes from an intense craving for information about what it is to be human'. They conclude: 'fundamental to our own engagement with reality has been a conception of women and men as creatures driven to know and to chart their lives by what they believe to be true. History can help here, for it offers a variety of tools for effecting liberation from intrusive authority, outworn creeds, and counsels of despair' (308). Southgate (1996), commenting from a postmodern perspective, similarly makes the point that critical self-reflection can help to emphasize the subject's educational importance, relevance and practicality to students and to a wider public. 'Through an examination of the past', he writes, 'we can be helped to see how we became what we currently are [. . .] Historical study can provide one focus from which we try to make sense of ourselves' (136-7). This self-awareness, he suggests, can help us to interrogate received truths and resist pressures to make us believe in a single truth.

If understanding past events and actions can provide us with the opportunity to hold up a mirror to ourselves and our world, and develop what Barnet (1997: 7) calls 'critical being' (the ability to act autonomously and with purpose in the world), its potential in these emancipatory respects has often not been fully realized in the history curriculum. Self-awareness, self-reflection and self-expression have too often been the victims of an emphasis upon 'objective' and 'scientific' approaches in subject teaching, while the cognitive has been privileged at the expense of affective and imaginative dimensions of learning. Equally, practice in the skills necessary for subject-based assignments has too often ignored how these might relate to performance in contexts outside the academy. Such aspects therefore need to be explicitly integrated in a more balanced learning environment, in which students are encouraged to address their own beliefs, feelings and experiences and practice skills in a wide variety of contexts. In such an integrative education there are no easy distinctions between the domains of subject, self and society, intellect and emotions, but rather all are explicitly acknowledged and enriched. Gutierrez (2000: 370) provides some insights into how this might be achieved from her experiences of teaching history to senior high-school students, and emphasizes that it is a process which must begin with an explicit statement of the connections between subject, self and society:

> In the first week I set out to make it clear that our exploration into the past will help reveal and, in fact, will depend upon the students' knowledge and understanding of themselves. I assure them that understanding what they believe and why they do so, as well as knowing how they think, what they may feel, how they regard themselves, and what motivates them, how and why they act in different situations, and how they perceive the world and their role in it will enable them to make reasonable sense and complex interpretations of the past.

This induction helps students to see the relevance of history to their lives, and appreciate that their historical knowledge and skills can be applied beyond the classroom in ways that lead to personal empowerment and the feeling that one can 'make a difference'.

Conclusion

To think in ways associated with understanding demands not merely the accumulation of knowledge but also its application, in an active, experiential and ongoing process involving multiple skills and abilities. It is therefore not sufficient for teachers to explain or model this, important as such support is. Students also have to be involved actively in the pursuit of it, and use their prior knowledge and their skills in ways which help them to think creatively and make increasingly complex mental connections. To meet this challenge, and create a learning environment that provides students with opportunities to engage with multiple perspectives, involves exploring a variety of sources, historical approaches and interpretations and dimensions of an issue, including social, economic, political and comparative (see Gardner 1999; Voss and Wiley 2000). It also involves scrutiny of personal experience, values and assumptions, and those of fellow students and teachers, as well as attention to the influence of disciplinary norms and wider social forces on historical practice. Such an 'education of multiple frames', as Barnet (1997: 22) calls this complex learning, is a protracted affair, requiring explicit and continuous practice in order for judgement to improve and capability to increase. Developing understanding is an iterative process, and skills need to be applied in a variety of situations if they are to become well developed and transferable to other contexts. Whilst undeniably challenging, a history education that can foster such complex learning enables the study of history to live up to its potential as an intellectually and personally transforming experience. Creating the critical space in which analytical, reflective and imaginative engagement can thrive enables students to reach their full potential, as historians and citizens. Whether this type of learning is described as 'deep', 'active', 'reflective', 'connected' or 'integrative', the first step is to understand how history students go about learning, and what they bring to it in terms of their beliefs, values and experience. This is the focus of the following chapter.

3

HISTORY LEARNING FROM THE STUDENT PERSPECTIVE

> Students want to know why history matters, how it relates
> to their lives, if at all, and how the study of history might
> affect them personally.
>
> (Cruse 1994)

Awareness of student perspectives is essential to promoting high-quality learning. Indeed, as Angelo (1993: 3) emphasizes, 'teaching that ignores this knowledge runs the risk of being inefficient, ineffective, and sometimes even counterproductive'. Understanding how students experience learning in their subject enables teachers to devise the most appropriate strategies to connect student needs and interests to course objectives. Therefore, as Frederick (2001b: 29) puts it, 'the first task with any new class of students is to find out what's inside them, what their stories and issues are, and how their stories might connect to course concepts'. Of course, as all history teachers are aware from student feedback on courses, within any class there are marked variations in conceptions of the subject and in perceptions of the same lectures, seminars and assessment tasks. Students bring to any learning situation a range of experience, interests, values and expectations about the subject and studying it, and these both influence and are influenced by the particular setting in which they find themselves. This diversity ensures that no two teaching sessions are ever the same, and helps to explain why classes in which identical methods and materials are used can be quite different in their dynamics and the depth of student engagement with the subject.

Since the 1970s considerable educational research has been conducted into how university students go about learning (see the useful studies in Richardson *et al.* 1987; Schmeck 1988; Marton *et al.* 1997). Some researchers place particular emphasis upon fundamental differences such as ability and personality traits (Wong *et al.* 1995; Crozier 1997). Others point to the existence of different cognitive or learning styles (Witkin 1976; Kolb 1984; Honey and Mumford 1992; Hartley and Greggs 1997). For many, differences are explicable more in terms of learning preferences or 'orientations' to learning that vary according to task and context (Entwistle and Ramsden 1983; Gibbs 1995; Ramsden 1992; Prosser and Trigwell 1999). Models and theories of student learning and development abound, as reviews of the literature by Pascarella and Terenzini (1991) and Tennant (1997) demonstrate. Most studies, however, as Tennant observes, are grounded in perspectives that take either the person or the environment as their point of departure. In terms of efforts to improve university teaching, the dominant perspective is currently that which emphasizes the impact of the learning environment on student learning and motivation, and thus the importance of the creation of contexts that encourage students to engage deeply with their subject. As Nicol (1997: 2) suggests: 'learning is now understood to be "situated" in academic and disciplinary contexts that influence not only how students construct their subject knowledge, but also how they construct interpretations of how they are supposed to learn, what is worth learning and what it means to be a student'. In history this learning context is still predominantly departmental or subject-based, and includes not merely course content, teaching methods and assessment procedures but the whole culture of a department or subject group.

Many studies of student learning focus upon how learners themselves experience learning. Marton and Saljo (1976a, b), pioneers of student-learning research, used student interviews to identify five main categories of what learning means to adult learners. These are described below, illustrated by quotations from undergraduate history students:

1   Learning as acquiring knowledge – one knows a little or a lot. Understanding means being able to reproduce what one has learned.
    'I know I've understood a topic when I know the main areas very well.'

2   Learning as memorizing. Detail is still important but there is some discrimination between points in terms of importance.
    'I know I understand something when I can remember parts of it without having to consult notes.'

3   Learning as application – being able to apply the knowledge in assignments.
    'I know I've understood a topic when I can write an essay on it and know how to get a good mark.'

4   Learning as understanding – being able to see the author's intention, interpret material in the subject and relate it to previous understanding.
    'I know I understand when something makes sense and I can tie all the different views together and come to my own view.'

5   Learning as an interpretative process aimed at understanding reality.
    'I know I've understood a topic when it all comes together and I can see a period in a different way and trace its significance in the past and for today.'

In 1993 Marton, Dall'Alba and Beaty added a sixth category in which learning is experienced as personal transformation: through studying one's subject one also develops as a person. In this taxonomy, stages four to six clearly represent what university history teachers would consider the most desirable conceptions of learning, while levels one to three encompass conceptions generally associated with lower levels of student attainment. The stage of conceptual development a student reaches will depend upon many factors, both personal and environmental, but will be powerfully influenced by an individual's prior conceptions of knowledge and understanding, approach to learning and perceptions of the educational setting.

Prior conceptions of knowledge and understanding

The previous chapter identified some common ways in which history students represent understanding in their subject. In research on differences between sixth-form history students and history graduates, Newton and Newton (1998) observed that at the beginning of their degree course students often assign more relevance to the accumulation of facts in the creation of meaning. So, too, sixth-form students revealed a greater certainty than history graduates that they could establish the truth of events in the past, and this view of history as retrieving facts to establish truth seems a common conception among students of the subject at school. This suggests that, as one would expect, learners often become more sophisticated in their thinking in the process of studying for a history degree. However, it conceals the fact that there are likely to be significant variations in the level of understanding of students in the same cohort. Figure 3.1 describes a selection of responses to a question on understanding in

Figure 3.1 What does understanding the past mean to you?

> In my opinion, if one understands the past, one should be able to offer a correct description of what life/society was like and why. On an academic level it means studying sources and documents and using brute facts to gain knowledge into events of the past. (Daniel)
>
> Primarily, understanding the past means to collect the facts (i.e. dates, events) of the past. But to truly understand the past, these facts must not only be linked together but explained. Any questions about the past must be solved in order to understand the past. (Sophia)
>
> Understanding the past means I can understand the present and how it came to be so. It can help you get your bearings and orientate yourself in your present circumstances. Understanding the past creates a sense of identity and gives a person something to relate to. Understanding the past for me is not just about learning what happened, but more why it happened and what causes it had. Understanding the past involves having empathy but also being rational and objective. You need to form your own opinion but in an unbiased way. (Louise)
>
> Firstly, learning what happened, then why it happened, and finally learning various historiographical viewpoints in order to find out how established historians have explained why things happened. There are differing explanations for everything, and 'understanding' the past doesn't mean choosing the correct one, but using historians' views as a basis to develop what you believe to be the correct viewpoint. (Katie)
>
> I don't think anybody can ever really understand the past, because our view of the world and therefore our understanding of it is influenced by our own surroundings – which are always changing. We can never, even if we try very hard, succeed to eliminate the influence our own way of life has on our thinking and therefore be objective. But we can try to use the evidence we have and think through how convincing the arguments are. (Katharina)

an undergraduate induction questionnaire administered by one history department to monitor historical thinking skills on entry to university.

Whilst these students possess similar academic qualifications, their conceptions of understanding are manifestly different in relation to purpose (whether history is fundamentally about searching out the truth about events or not), historical method (especially analysing sources) and procedures (whether students should reproduce historical knowledge, put forward a variety of views or a strong personal perspective). Clearly, some conceptions are also more sophisticated than others, and encouraging exploration of these can be an important means of promoting a reflective approach to the subject as well as of learning more about students as individuals and as a group.

There have been many studies of university students' prior conceptions of learning and understanding, most grounded in the pioneering work of Perry with undergraduates at Harvard University (Perry 1970). He identified nine epistemological positions which can be grouped into four stages of intellectual development from *dualism*, representing an absolute view of knowledge in which there is one correct answer, through *multiplicity*, an awareness that there are a lot of interpretations possible and that all have validity so everyone has a right to their own opinion, to *relativism subordinate*, where an analytical approach is adopted to one's work if not related to life, to a full *relativism* where the student appreciates that knowledge is constructed and therefore meaning is contextual, and understands this in relation to both subject and self, yet is capable of taking an informed personal position. Of recent studies building upon Perry's work on intellectual development, one of the most interesting to historians is that of King and Kitchener (1994), founded upon several hundred interviews with university students, including some history undergraduates. They detail a seven-stage developmental model of 'reflective judgement' based upon the epistemic assumptions that lie behind students' reasoning and concepts of justification. In the *pre-reflective* phase (stages one to three) it is assumed that knowledge is gained through an authority or by direct personal observation, and is absolutely correct and certain; that, in historical terms, when all the evidence is collected, the truth will be accepted by everyone. *Quasi-reflective* thinking (stages four and five) recognizes that knowledge claims about some issues are problematic, but finds it difficult to decide how judgements can be made in the light of this uncertainty. Beliefs are justified by giving reasons and using evidence but methods are idiosyncratic, such as fitting the evidence to an established view. Stages six and seven represent truly reflective judgement, and correlate well with what history lecturers would consider the qualities of a student with a complex grasp of past societies.

> These stages reflect the epistemic assumption that one's understanding of the world is not 'given' but must be actively constructed and that knowledge must be understood in relation to the context in which it was generated. An additional assumption is that some interpretations or knowledge claims may be judged as more plausible than others. Thus, while absolute truth will never be ascertained with complete certainty, some views may be evaluated as more reasonable explanations. This view presumes that judgements must not only be grounded in relevant data, but that they must also be evaluated to determine their validity. Criteria that might be used in making such evaluations include conceptual soundness, coherence, degree of fit with the data, meaningfulness, usefulness and parsimony. We refer to this type of reasoning as truly reflective.
>
> (King and Kitchener 1994: 17)

As they record, a large number of studies based upon this work have revealed that traditional-age freshmen at American colleges most often employ stage three conceptions, with only one sample of more academically able students reaching into stage four. Of course, these figures reflect a North American pattern of mass entry to university, and they are not specific to history students, who, given the nature of the discipline, might be expected to appreciate more the uncertain nature of most problems and issues. Nonetheless, the model provides a general framework that can enable understanding to be plotted as it proceeds from views of knowledge founded upon simplistic notions of truth to awareness of the contextual nature of knowledge and how sound historical judgements might be made on complex historical issues.

Approaches to learning and understanding

The approach to learning adopted by a student will depend not only upon prior conceptions of the subject, and of knowledge more generally, but also upon perceptions of the nature of the task and the whole context into which it fits. For example, in essay assignments what is felt to be most rewarded will condition the approach taken, while students may feel that they need to adopt a different approach to essay writing in examinations from that employed in coursework. In a seminal piece of research, Marton and Saljo (1976a, b) gave students a 1,500 word article to read and asked them how they went about the task. They identified two qualitatively different ways in which students tackled this assignment. Some 'skated along the surface of the text' trying to assimilate the facts and details, and this they called a 'surface' approach. Others concentrated on trying to understand the author's intention and interpretation, looking carefully at the evidence and the structure of the argument, and this they designated a 'deep' approach. At around the same time, Pask (1976) identified similarly distinctive learning strategies that he called 'serialist' and 'holist'. Serialists learn step by step, collecting details and making little use of metaphors or analogies. Whilst systematic, they can fail to see the wood for the trees. Holists begin with a broad focus, attempting to see the task as a whole, contextualize new material in relation to previous knowledge, and look for key arguments. Whilst they appreciate complexity, they may be tempted to over-generalize. The serialist/holist and deep/surface distinctions are clearly related, though the latter have become dominant in descriptions of student approaches to learning.

A *surface approach* to studying is characterized by the perception of a task as an external imposition, and thus the intention is to complete it with the minimum of effort consistent with meeting course requirements. Students adopting a surface approach are pragmatically motivated and primarily focused upon gaining a qualification. Characteristics associated with surface learning include:

- routine reliance upon memorization of facts and procedures;
- reproduction of facts, opinions and procedures;
- passive acceptance of ideas;
- fixed ideas about ways to proceed;
- separate treatment of unrelated parts of the task;
- failure to distinguish guiding principles and patterns;
- lack of reflection on purpose or strategy;
- concentration on assessment requirements.

In a study of essay writing on a history course, Hounsell (1997: 114) cites an interview with 'Donna', a second-year undergraduate who seems to embody this surface approach, as indeed does Daniel, the first-year history student quoted earlier. In response to the question 'What's studying history at university about?', she replies:

I'm not quite sure what it is. I don't know. I don't think we get a lot of our own ideas into it. I know we're supposed to but we seem to be reading books, and criticising what people think, more than actually – it's sometimes annoying when you're doing an essay, and you don't really know enough facts, but what you're doing is sorting out other people's interpretations and you feel you can't really criticise them yourself because you don't know the source material. And so, um . . . I don't know. It just seems to me as though you're reading about a period, and trying to fit your reading into an essay. It just seems like a lot of facts more than anything else.

A *deep approach* to learning by contrast is defined by an intention to understand, and, as Entwistle and Entwistle (1997: 145) point out, 'that intention evokes the process of learning which allows deep levels of understanding to be reached'. Characteristics associated with a deep approach to learning include:

- a questioning and critical engagement with content;
- relating ideas together to form a coherent argument;
- looking for connections, patterns and underlying principles;
- formulating hypotheses on the basis of the comparing and contrasting of evidence;
- examining the logic of an argument;
- relating evidence to conclusions;
- relating issues to previous knowledge and adjusting hypotheses in the light of further information;
- reflection on purpose and strategies;
- intrinsic interest in the subject matter.

In an examination of two students' responses to writing an essay on the causes of popular revolt in nineteenth-century Australia, Biggs (1988: 212) quotes from an interview with 'Syd', who, like Katie and Katharina quoted earlier, adopts a discernibly deep approach to studying.

I write to produce something that I like, within the constraints of having to present an acceptable and reasonable essay to the lecturer that set the topic. I want to do well but I am fairly confident of my ability and am not unduly concerned about the particular mark that I get. Basically I like writing and have no difficulty [. . .] Normally I find several reference books which I think have something relevant in them, and read the relevant parts, taking notes of the various points that come up. I like to get a fairly wide coverage. Various points of view all differ to some extent, even if it is only slightly, but sometimes that slight difference can be the interesting twist you can put into the essay. I took notes from all the readings and from them just let things evolve. I correlate them together and they fit a structure, whether it is chronological or something else. Then I give it a twist that has emerged from my reading [...] I really write to suit myself. I try and produce something that *I* would like to read. I can't really write for the lecturer; I can't read his mind.

A deep approach then is about seeking meaning, whereas a surface approach is concerned primarily with knowledge acquisition and reproduction. Whilst the former is an active process, the latter is more instrumental. The distinction between these approaches also possesses an affective dimension, for students adopting a deep approach display an intrinsic interest in the task and an associated curiosity and enjoyment, while those adopting a surface approach are more likely to report feelings of boredom and lack of motivation. Although subsequent research has also identified a 'strategic' approach to learning (characterized by the desire to maximize grades and alertness to assessment requirements and tutors' preferences, allied to consistent effort), the basic distinction between deep and surface approaches has proved valid in a wide variety of disciplinary contexts. It must be emphasized, however, that a student's approach to learning does not constitute a fixed style. Rather, those students already adopting deep strategies to learning may retreat to surface strategies, or fail to transfer previously developed subject skills, in situations that are perceived as threatening or provoke anxiety (such as a heavy workload, unclear expectations or assignments that are too difficult or insufficiently challenging). Of course, some students will remain determined surface learners whatever the context, but, for most, the educational environment established by teachers and the department as a whole will be the major influence upon the approach adopted.

History students' perceptions of the learning situation

Despite variations between students in their approach to studying, there is considerable correspondence in student accounts of the optimal conditions for stimulating deep learning in their subject (see Marsh 1987; Ramsden 1992; Marton *et al.* 1997). What follows is grounded in this research, the experiences of history teachers, and especially the findings of studies of several hundred history undergraduates at two British higher education institutions: one a research-led university attracting traditional students with high entry grades, the other a university college with a more diverse intake in terms of age and qualifications (see Booth 1993, 1997).

Interest, relevance and the rationale for studying history

'From the student perspective', Ylijoki (1994: 3) observes, 'the most prominent element in their experience in university is the rationale of studying, the internal logic of their studying. The answer to this question forms the basis of what they get from university, and what kinds of experiences they will want to have during their study time.' Choosing to study history is commonly expressed in terms of intrinsic interest. Students, as Marty (1994: 1083) remarks, 'want to derive pleasure from intellectual stimulation', and often describe their aims in terms of historical thinking skills: developing critical thinking, acquiring new ideas, sharpening their skills of argument construction and presentation, and gaining expertise in the handling of source material. Personal development is also regarded as important, and whilst career considerations are inevitably less dominant as a factor in choice of course compared to students in more vocational subjects such as Engineering (see Entwistle *et al.* 1989), obtaining a 'good job' is nonetheless an important motivation for many. For most, however, this does not mean becoming a professional historian.

In the study of history, students place a premium upon the personal. Whereas undergraduates in science or professional subjects typically describe learning tasks as demanding logic and the careful application of a hierarchy of clear rules and methods, humanities students tend to see their subjects as requiring personal interpretation, generalization and comparison, and feel less constrained by strict methodological rules. Two second-year history students observe:

> They [science students] go about it more logically . . . scientists deal in fact, while history students and artists deal in theory – we discuss theories and opinion.

History, you can waffle, you can cover up your mistakes . . .
no-one can prove you right or wrong . . . you've got to take
all things into account.

(Ramsden 1997: 209)

For history students, the ability of the subject to accommodate
both academic rigour and personal interpretation is a particular
attraction, and the personal engagement necessary to develop a deeper
sense of understanding is often represented in strongly emotional
terms as a 'love' or 'passion' for the subject. Intrinsic interest is vital, for
as one final-year student comments: 'If you're not really interested in
what you're doing, it's bound to affect your performance. For instance,
if you're put onto a course you don't really want to do, it can be a
tremendous turn-off to putting any real effort in.' What makes history
interesting is its relevance to oneself and the world around. The
following are typical comments on the personal value of studying
history:

I like the fact that history covers almost every aspect of life.
It is interesting to discover our own past. It helps us to
understand why and how life is as it is, and why we are like
we are. It puts life in perspective.

(first-year student)

History defines what we are today. It helps us to understand
what makes people act they way they do, and how their
reactions in the past have created our society today. History's
like a mirror on our own society.

(third-year student)

Older students frequently express an interest in social history and
the history of everyday lives, whilst traditional-age entrants often
incline towards the study of personality and the influence of famous
leaders such as Hitler and Stalin.

I think what interests me is the way you can learn about
people, very much like yourself, who lived and experienced
life years ago. How they coped with life and problems. How
wars affected them and what were their thoughts. It's the
ways in which 'ordinary' people lived their lives that
fascinates me.

(first-year, mature student)

What really gets me motivated is something I can relate to. For example, if we were looking at children in the age of Dickens – I grew up in a children's home.

(first-year, mature student)

Although I did political history at A level, I found that I was less interested in legislation and institutions than in the individuals. Looking at the rise and fall of individuals, seeing why they made decisions and being able to see with the benefit of hindsight where mistakes were made, and why a truly successful ruler could lose everything in a short period of time. If you look back to the source of history and governments that's the individual.

(first-year student)

Studying history is markedly associated with issues of personal identity. As Hvolbek (1993: 9) remarks, 'students want to understand their lives, their history, and their place in the world'. Achieving a stable sense of identity is a particularly important goal in adolescence, but for non-traditional students exploring issues of the self is equally important (Erikson 1965; Head 1997; Tennant 1997; Bromwick and Swallow 1999). History, with its opportunity to study the significance of the decisions and choices of individuals and groups in the past, provides a perfect vehicle for this exploration, and thus connecting the past to the interests of students is a powerful motivating force (Hodgson 1997; Langer 1997). It is clear, however, that the way in which the subject is taught is also vital in sustaining a deep approach to learning. More than any other factor, students explain lack of interest in terms of the way in which the subject is taught. One first-year undergraduate's clipped comment speaks for many: 'Enjoyed least [at school] Tudor history – taught chronologically dictation style, no room for discussion – so little interest developed in the subject.'

The role of teachers

A close engagement with the past is intimately connected to the nature of the relationship that students have with teachers. Good history teachers are most frequently represented as guides and fellow travellers on a journey of discovery. The teacher possesses an up-to-date map of the territory, and can provide the appropriate level of information, encouragement and support to enable students to negotiate the new terrain and gain the confidence to make discoveries for themselves. Among first-year students particularly, there is a tendency to emphasize the possession of subject expertise on the part of teachers (the teacher as a key source of factual information), whilst among final-year undergraduates the emphasis is more often upon teachers using their grasp of the subject to facilitate discussion or provide pointers to further reading. For all students, enthusiasm and commitment are the hallmarks of effective history teachers, often closely associated with a 'passion' for the subject.

> A genuine love and fascination for the subject is important, and in-depth knowledge. A good tutor should also be sympathetic to his or her students and have the patience to explain more complex theories to those less able.
>
> (first-year student)

> I think that a good history teacher has an extensive knowledge, an obvious passion for his or her subject and the ability to communicate this enthusiasm. They must be able to explain things clearly, and be willing to help or reassure students.
>
> (first-year student)

> A good history tutor is someone who is enthusiastic and prepared to discuss the views of students. An enthusiastic teacher can really get you motivated. Then I become interested in the subject concerned and care about what I'm doing.
>
> (third-year student)

In some ways the notion of good practice is most clearly represented by the representation of its opposite. Ineffective history teachers are viewed almost entirely in terms of their inability to relate to students. The following are typical comments:

> A bad history teacher interrogates you, so you dread getting asked a question, or has their own opinions and everything else is wrong, or enjoys showing off their own superior knowledge against the superficiality of their students, so you feel you've got nothing to say. Or just drones on unenthusiastically so you become unenthusiastic yourself and switch off.
>
> (third-year student)

A poor history tutor is someone uninterested in teaching – only there to write books. Or someone who just passes on a great deal of facts for you to remember without any discussion or student participation.

(first–year student)

The principal qualities of effective teachers in the eyes of history under-graduates are listed in Figure 3.2.

Figure 3.2 Characteristics of a good history teacher from the student perspective

- Approachability: accessible and willing to help students.
- Enthusiasm for the subject.
- An obvious commitment to teaching.
- Expertise (most often mentioned by first-year students): possesses sound knowledge of the topic or period.
- Communicates ideas clearly and cogently.
- Brings the subject to life.
- Respects student views and is open to their ideas.
- Encourages student participation.
- Gives clear guidance on reading.
- Provides constructive feedback on assignments.

Teaching methods

The value accorded to the human dimension of teaching in bringing history to life underlines the importance of the social context of learning. Indeed, for many students understanding a topic is only possible when they can explain it to others (whether teachers or peers) with some confidence. Student preference for discussion as a method of learning is therefore overwhelming, and is frequently compared to the experience of schools history, where spoonfeeding is widely perceived to be common. As one student remarks, 'at school discussions were interesting but not held often enough'.

Discussion is definitely the best way of learning history. It makes you really get into the subject. You have to know something about the period in question to be able to speak. It also makes you think and develop your ideas. It also leads you to being open about the ideas of others.

(first–year student)

> I particularly like discussion in seminars. I love the interaction
> between people and the fact you realise all of you know
> enough to be able to talk about it. You really feel part of it.
>
> (third-year student)

Such comments also indicate a change over time in how students
experience seminars. Among first-year undergraduates, recognition of
the value of small group discussion is often mingled with anxiety
about contributing. By their final undergraduate year, greater
confidence and a closer relationship with peers and with teachers
often result in a more relaxed atmosphere and a sense of greater
intellectual satisfaction.

Students recognize that simply assembling a number of people
together for discussion does not constitute a seminar. Rather, teaching
and learning in history are considered a shared enterprise in which
both students and teachers bear responsibility for creating conditions
in which a deep approach to the subject can thrive. There is a strong
belief that whilst students have a responsibility for preparation and
involvement, the teacher's task is to facilitate discussion.
The comments of the following final-year history undergraduates
illustrate this:

> A seminar can only effectively work if at least several
> members of the group have prepared and if those who have
> not done so much are encouraged to make educated
> contributions rather than sitting hopelessly quiet wishing
> they were somewhere else and dreading getting asked a
> question and being forced to answer it. Individuals should
> not be picked on. Seminars are a group activity.

> Students must all have done some reading and be prepared to
> say something. However, most important is the tutor. If he or
> she just rambles on students will not do the reading, then not
> be able to talk. It's self-perpetuating. The tutor must
> encourage involvement.

> A bad seminar is one where few, if any, students do the work,
> or the tutor doesn't direct it in such a way as to inspire even
> the most hard-working to say anything. Hence embarrassed
> silences.

Debate is often mentioned as an effective means of encouraging interest and participation, but for most students variety of methods is the key to success; the use of primary sources, novels, maps, cartoons, films, videos and CD-ROMs are all regarded as valuable aids to bringing the subject to life. The use of diverse methods also, of course, accommodates variations in students' learning styles and prior experiences, as revealed in the following comments by two third-year students.

> I want it [discussion] to be always very focused. I want it. I don't like them to be just [unfocused]. They are a waste of time if you just sit there and everyone just talks about what they feel like talking about.

> I don't like it when tutors focus the whole time because I think that's wrong . . . it is to me very important to understand the relationship between two things which maybe initially you don't think of relating but as you go to discussion you think, 'Oh, maybe they are'; and I think that's very important.
>
> (Anderson, 1997: 190).

The least satisfying experience from the student perspective is to be deluged with information, a dislike often born of school experience. In the words of one first-year: 'the biggest problem is if lots of facts are thrown at you, and then you have to learn them. It's much easier to learn if you are investigating something yourself, and then reporting back and discussing what you think.' Information overload is most often mentioned in relation to lectures. Yet despite criticism of lecturers who present too much information too quickly, new undergraduates are nonetheless far more likely to feel that lectures provide a useful framework for individual study than are final-year students. Among all history students, delivery (enthusiasm, slow pace, pauses, repetition of key points, varied tone, summary of points made), clear structure and the use of interesting and varied examples are considered the hallmarks of a successful lecture. Responsiveness to audience is emphasized by all as the key to bringing the subject alive.

Cultural differences and diverse perspectives on the learning situation

With the growth of a more diverse student population, increasing attention has been directed towards 'cultural' differences in learner perceptions, most notably those associated with gender but also, in North America especially, ethnicity. Whether such factors should be singled out for attention is a contested issue. There is a danger of cultural stereotyping and obscuring the myriad factors (including age, social class, economic status and departmental context) that influence an individual student's approach to learning. Nonetheless, it is important for teachers to try to view learning from the perspective of all students in the history classroom, and evidence suggests that female undergraduates and students from ethnic minorities, for example, can feel alienated from traditional modes of academic discourse (see Border and Chism 1992; Humphreys 2000).

Just as mature students, despite the fact that many display a deep approach to studying, have a tendency to be less confident in their ability to write essays or take examinations than traditional entrants but can feel more confident in interpersonal situations (Richardson 1994; Booth 1997), research indicates that students from some ethnic groups exhibit preferences for particular learning contexts. Thus, in a review of the literature, Anderson and Adams (1992: 21) note that among African American, Hispanic and Native American students, 'the pattern that emerges is that these students demonstrate competence in social interactions and peer co-operation, performance, visual perception, symbolic expression, and narrative and therefore are less comfortable with tasks that require independence, competition or verbal skills'. Some of these tendencies are also apparent among female undergraduates, where many studies have shown a preference for learning methods emphasizing co-operative activity, interpersonal relationships, empathy and attachment over the kind of competitive achievement, individualism and 'objectivity' that constitute the norm in many academic disciplines (Gilligan 1986; Lubelska 1996; Bosworth *et al.* 2000). This view was supported when, in response to what it saw as an alarming imbalance in the number of history 'firsts' in favour of male students, the University of Cambridge's history faculty produced a report suggesting that history tutorials ('supervisions'), in which students present their essays to a tutor, were often perceived by female students as adversarial contests, as stressful occasions rather than situations supportive of learning (Clarke *et al.* 1994). Women were found to experience the practice of academic critique as akin to personal criticism, partly because they identified more personally with their opinion and thus what they wrote in essays and articulated in seminars. They also expressed a greater dislike of arguing strongly unless they really believed what they were saying. Lacking the same degree of self-confidence as men at the traditional age of entry, the female students interviewed felt that classes tended to be dominated by male students (or tutors) who enjoyed the competitive nature of the encounter and relegated women, however unconsciously, to the role of listener and thus spectator. Anecdotal evidence also suggested that some female students resented what they regarded as male speculation on the basis of limited reading, and felt that their own preference for comprehensive synthesis and cautious judgement was not as highly regarded as what they perceived as male students' glib, confrontational style, which, they believed, predominantly male examiners rewarded as demonstrating 'flair' (see Topping 1995; Martin 1997; Francis *et al.* 2001).

In an influential study of the experience of female college students in the United States, Belenky *et al.* (1986) revealed many similar perceptions. Like the female undergraduates cited above, most of the women interviewed felt uncertain about their abilities, and all 'expressed the need to be accepted as a "person" in the learning situation' (196). Many also preferred a structured but supportive framework for learning, emphasizing personal relationship rather than the adversarial clash of ideas. The researchers also noted, however, that whilst many views were held in common, there was also variation in the ways in which women students experienced higher education. Building on the developmental framework provided by Perry (1970), they classified women's 'ways of knowing' into five categories:

1 *Silence*: a state in which women experience themselves as mindless and voiceless and subject to the whims of external authority.
2 *Received knowledge*: a perspective from which women conceive of themselves as capable of receiving, even reproducing, knowledge from the all-knowing external authorities but not capable of creating knowledge on their own.
3 *Subjective knowledge*: a perspective from which truth and knowledge are conceived of as personal, private and subjectively known or intuited.
4 *Procedural knowledge*: a position in which women are invested in learning and applying objective procedures for obtaining and communicating knowledge.

5   *Constructed knowledge*: a state in which women view all knowledge
    as contextual, experience themselves as the creators of
    knowledge, and value both subjective and objective strategies for
    knowing.

Here the principal difference from Perry's categorization of
conceptions of learning outlined earlier is that silence does not appear
at all among his study of predominantly male students. Yet women
respondents reported feeling unable to speak after an academic put-
down, and for them the issue of silence is clearly an important one in
their experience of learning. So, too, there was greater emphasis in
their description of 'constructed knowledge' (which in general
correlates well with Perry's relativism stage of development) upon the
employment of affective as well as cognitive strategies to create
meaning. Here empathy and subjectivity, which they defined as 'the
deliberate imaginative extension of one's understanding into positions
that initially feel wrong or remote' (Belenky *et al.* 1986: 40), are
regarded as equally vital to the process of understanding as the more
'male-oriented' values of 'rationality' and 'objectivity'.

Perceptions of cultural influences on learning can be powerful
means of providing students with opportunities to explore multiple
viewpoints, examine their own values and experiences and see how
these connect them to the past. However, it is important to remember
that all students encounter 'cultural' obstacles, not least traditional
students facing the transition from more dependent modes of learning
at school to an emphasis upon self-reliance and independence in
university study, and that such characteristics as, for example, a
preference for consensus over adversarial debate are distributed among
all students. Whilst such differences require sensitive handling (and, for
some, specific, practical classroom activities – see Davis 1993;
Brookfield 1999; Frederick 2000), a strategy that balances an emphasis
upon the individual, impersonal and critical with the interpersonal,
affective and imaginative dimensions of learning can both
accommodate the diversity of student experience and provide optimal
conditions for promoting understanding among all students. Such a
flexible and varied approach, focused upon discussion, accords with
student needs and expectations and enables exposure to multiple
viewpoints that facilitates understanding. In this sense, as Humphreys
(2000: 20) remarks, the characteristics consistent with high-quality
teaching more generally are those that also facilitate learning in
culturally diverse classes. These features are 'first, a learning-centred
philosophy, in which the faculty member is considered only one of

the classroom participants; second, interactive teaching techniques, such as small group discussions, student presentations, debates, role playing, problem posing, and student paper exchanges; and third, a supportive, inclusive classroom climate'.

Conclusion

A wide range of variables influence student learning. Students enter their degree course, and indeed each class, with prior conceptions of knowledge and understanding, with established preferences and approaches to learning, and with assumptions and beliefs about what constitutes effective learning and teaching in their subject. No student comes to learning as a *tabula rasa*, and there is considerable variation in the ways students go about learning and the sophistication of their conception of learning in their subject. These variations help to explain why one class works well while another, on the same topic and using identical methods, fails to capture student interest. Whatever their prior abilities, perceptions and experiences, however, the learning context in which students find themselves fundamentally influences the strategies they adopt whether they pursue a deep, 'understanding' approach to their studies or a surface approach. Yet, despite variations in learning, history students possess many perceptions in common about what factors in the learning situation motivate them to learn for understanding. Encouraging students to acknowledge the values and experience (and the understanding and expertise, however limited) that they bring to a course, and devising strategies to accommodate diverse learning preferences, are fundamental prerequisites of fostering complex learning. If this demands sensitivity to student perspectives, it also requires the intentions of the teacher to be in view, and this is considered in the following chapter.

4

APPROACHES TO
TEACHING HISTORY

> In reflecting upon my own lecturing, I am troubled to
> recognize how often I wind up telling students what to
> think about the materials we have just covered – providing
> them with conclusions rather than empowering them to
> become their own historians.
>
> (Marchand 1999)

Although what students do is the single most important element in
learning, teachers play an indispensable role: organizing and managing
the curriculum, offering guidance in locating information, modelling
historical thinking and responding flexibly to changing student
needs. Moreover, a teacher's own love of the subject can powerfully
influence student levels of motivation, and, as Frederick (1999a: 52)
reflects, perhaps 'the highest challenge we face as classroom teachers
is to motivate our students to love history as we do'. Good teaching
in history, then, involves far more than the possession of subject
knowledge, important though this is. A first-year lecture on the feudal
system by a specialist on the topic might be erudite and scholarly but
pass over the heads of most of its intended audience, few of whom
might previously have studied medieval history. So, too, in practice,
most historians teach courses where their knowledge of the subject
matter is less than intimate, and oversee undergraduate projects where
familiarity with historical method and modes of discourse, and the
ability to direct students to relevant sources of information, are more
important than detailed knowledge of the topic. Motivating students
to learn deeply in history demands an ability to relate one's
understanding of subject matter to students' current level of
understanding, and connect one's own love of the subject to past
events in ways that are stimulating and challenging. This demands a

variety of skills: a grasp of subject matter and disciplinary rules of evidence and standards of interpretation, of learners and their conceptions and misconceptions, of teaching strategies appropriate to students' level of experience, and, not least, of one's values and practices as a history teacher. Some means of examining teaching practices are considered in Chapter 9; here, however, the focus is upon the educational values and beliefs about their subject, teaching and learning that university history teachers bring to the history classroom.

Teachers' conceptions of history

A great deal of research has demonstrated that the approaches that university teachers take to teaching are intimately related to their conceptions of the subject and of teaching and learning, and that these influence the ways in which students experience learning in their subject (see Dall'Alba 1991; Pratt 1992; Samuelowicz and Bain 1992, 2001; Kember and Gow 1994; Bruce and Gerber 1995; Trigwell and Prosser 1999; Kember 1997; Murray and MacDonald 1997; Willcoxson 1998; Prosser and Trigwell 1997, 1999; Martin *et al.* 2001). Research into schools history teaching has similarly demonstrated the importance of how teachers conceptualize the nature and purposes of history in what is taught and how it is taught (Evans 1988, 1989, 1994; Leinhardt 1994, 2000; Husbands 1996; Wineburg 2001). In the course of recent debate within the discipline over postmodernism, considerable attention has also been paid to historical epistemology. Yet, despite this interest, the conceptions of the subject and teaching held by university history teachers and how these influence the practice of teaching remain relatively unexplored.

Some light on this area was cast by responses to a broad-ranging survey on the practice of American history conducted in 1993. Particularly revealing were replies to a question on the personal value of doing history, of which the following are a representative sample:

> Opening the eyes of children and adults to the interesting people, places and events that have occurred where they live. Helping them to see that history happened *here* too.

> I feel that I am giving a voice to those who have something to say by writing them into history.

I meet people dead and alive. I encounter their ideas. I try to expand my mind, my views, my ideas, as well as my students.

I believe I am part of a necessary function – a storyteller of group memories.

A sense of contributing to a conversation spanning nations and generations.

The 'time-travelling': trying to enter the mindset of individuals in a different time, place and context, discovering in the process much about our own assumptions.

Continual engagement with students and colleagues in ideas and books.

The joy of hearing a student say, 'I never thought of that before'.

Joy in seeing young people come alive to history.

Watching students grow and mature.

(Thelen 1994: 947)

These comments clearly contain much in common. They speak of historians' love of their subject, and their appreciation of its significance in fostering a conversation that is linked to the particularities of place, to trends in the development of societies and, not least, to fundamental human concerns that cut across time. Here the meaning of history is expressed not in relation to research or publication in scholarly journals, but in terms of an ability to connect deeply with others (today and in the past) and with oneself (see Demos 2002). Not only do historians want to see others make the multiple connections that constitute understanding, but, as one respondent remarked, 'my work in history has helped give me a sense of personal identity and it has given me a context for that identity' (Thelen 1994: 944).

The responses to the survey also suggest, however, that practitioners experience history in subtly different ways, and in an intensive study of the connections between disciplinary beliefs and pedagogic practice at a history faculty in one North American university department, Quinlan (1999) observed that differences corresponded broadly with generational factors. Those educated in the late 1960s and 1970s, described as 'humanists' or 'progressives' and influenced by the wider social and political upheavals of those years as well as the expanding boundaries of historical scholarship, adopted a predominantly skills-focused, process-oriented approach to teaching the subject. For them, history constituted a form of 'detective work', a conception of the subject shared by more recently appointed academic staff or 'newcomers'. As one of the latter succinctly put it: 'Ultimately, I don't think the facts they [students] get from my class are as important as the analytical skills, the writing and the talking skills' (457). Newcomers, however, tended to possess a more pronounced espousal of theoretical perspectives on history, evidenced in pedagogic terms by a greater emphasis on epistemology and reflexivity and thus, in classroom practice, on historiography and revisionist perspectives, especially related to race, class and gender. One new assistant professor suggested that 'what would be nice is if they [students] understood . . . that we're always influenced by who we are and what we're taught to believe and taught to think and value. I'd rather the students sort of question how to evaluate what happened in the past' (458). By contrast, those socialized into the profession before the mid-1960s expansion, the 'old guard' (today a small minority of historians), tended to adopt a more content-oriented, narrative-driven conception of teaching, related to their view of 'history as story'. Here, whilst there was recognition of the importance of skills and reflexivity in historical enquiry, these received less attention in teaching the subject than enabling students to gain a sense of narrative sweep, the 'flow of history'. As Quinlan puts it: 'They want students to learn "the story" – or the outcome of historical scholarship. As such they see content as more important than the process of constructing or critiquing the scholarship' (460).

Although restricted in scope to a single department, Quinlan's research casts revealing light upon the relationship between conceptions of history and variations in curriculum goals and delivery. Its findings are supported by earlier work by Evans (1988, 1989, 1994) on the conceptions of history and their relationship to pedagogic practice of a sample of North American school-history teachers. He identified four discernible 'types' of history teacher, each reflecting a particular conception of the meaning of history, which he called relativist/reformer, storyteller, scientific historian and cosmic philosopher. Representing by far the largest category of practitioners, relativist/reformers emphasize the relationship of the past to the present and thus that the teaching of history is important because it helps students to understand current issues. They commonly believe that no historian (and thus no history) can be free from contemporary influences, but that clear patterns can be discerned in past events. These historians tend to be socially or politically reformist, with views ranging from progressive to Marxist that convince them of the need to understand the past in order to create a better future. Issues of social justice are central to their conception of the subject, and an interest in, for example, marginalized groups or the politics of disciplinary discourse leads to efforts to encourage students towards a deeper grasp of historical processes through an emphasis upon problem-solving. They often use present-day analogies, contemporary personal accounts and imaginative connection to past events to foster student learning. Such historians are also strongly represented in the survey of American historians referred to above. As Cassity (1994: 969) remarks, many respondents 'placed a premium on the value of history to us today. The decision to pursue the serious study of history often originated in an assumed and valued connection between the past and the present.' It is also revealing that the three authors whom respondents claimed had most influenced them were Richard Hofstadter, Karl Marx and E. P. Thompson (Thelen 1994: 954). In the following interview extract, one professional historian describes his rationale in recognisably reformist terms, with an emphasis on a sense of moral commitment that has a long tradition in university history teaching (see Novick 1988; Soffer 1994):

> I might characterise parts of the way I was taught as topographical – the Hoskins legacy. I was taught by Joan Thirsk, who comes out of the Hoskins, Tawney (Christian Socialist) tradition. So, I think that I am very moral in my work – I've been criticised for this. Moral indignation is one thing I go by. But the other aspect is the particularity of place. I think that he [Hoskins] influenced me – I recognise the importance of visiting, say, the sites of the Holocaust; it is important to me.
>
> (quoted in Warren 1998: 189)

Scientific historians are those for whom historical interpretation and explanation make history most interesting. They consider that understanding historical processes and developing associated critical skills are the principal reasons for studying the subject, and represent historical study primarily as an intellectual training in critical analysis and interpretation through the systematic and objective use of evidence, the comparing and challenging of ideas and the construction of intellectually justifiable hypotheses. Although they discern some patterns in history, these teachers are more comfortable with critique than generalization and emphasize a mix of the uniqueness and similarities of past peoples, societies and events. Teaching is about encouraging students to compare differing interpretations and sources, and to think independently about the questions raised by historians about the past. Evans (1994: 92) notes that in teaching style these teachers are similar to the relativist/reformers 'in that they pose problems for students while using a variety of methods. However, the key distinction is the source of such problems. For the scientific historian, problems come from the competing interpretations of history, from the structure of the academic discipline. For the relativist/reformer, problems are drawn from present day issues and history made relevant to present concerns. Both are inquiry oriented.' This process-oriented approach to history reflects prevailing disciplinary orthodoxy. A national survey of history departments on the issue of academic standards in British undergraduate history degree programmes found that 'respondents were unanimous in their conviction that one of the central and most important benefits of this process of study is the development of the intellectual or cognitive capabilities of students' (History at the Universities Defence Group 1998a: 6). The goal of teaching, as one put it, 'is to train student minds in methods of critical enquiry' (9), and this constitutes the central thread in the undergraduate benchmark statement for the subject in the UK (History Benchmarking Group 2000). Here history is seen as an intellectual craft to be mastered, and the student as an apprentice historian whose aim is to gain a facility with the analytical, interpretative and research tools of the trade. As Stearns (1993: ix) puts it:

> The central purpose of courses is the inculcation of essential analytical skills that are not easy to define (because they are less precise than their analogues in science) but are vital for a critically informed citizenry. A discussion of humanities goals must include awareness of the need to widen the factual frame of reference, but it should concentrate on identifying and teaching methods by which we gain understanding, interpretative habits that allow us to move from the inevitably bounded examples of any classroom to other instances in which the role of culture demands assessment or the nature of social change must be grasped.

Storytellers 'emphasize fascinating details about people and events, and suggest that knowledge of other times, people, and places is the most important reason for studying history' (Evans 1988: 215). They tend to underline the unique nature of past events and societies and the importance of rich detail in the attempt to capture the complexity of the past. For these teachers, patterns in history are less important than studying the past because it provides clues to our personal and group identities. History from this perspective provides a means of explaining who we are, and is part of becoming a fully educated person. Evans identifies this orientation with a more narrative-focused classroom, and this corresponds to Quinlan's depiction of the historian to whom history 'is about people, their lives, their myths and their stories', and whose principal goal is to ensure 'that students come out with a coherent picture of the historical narrative' (1999: 455). However, the category of storyteller might be extended beyond the rather conservative conception portrayed here to include those employing student-centred approaches to encourage students to identify their personal stories, and to connect these to course content or concepts as part of a holistic or multicultural education. Russell Hvolbek represents this type of storyteller:

> I believe that the primary purpose of teaching history and the humanities is to make students more aware of how their lives connect to past human experience. Teaching is a means to entice students to question actively their own beliefs and certainties, and thus participate in their own education [. . .] When we understand something about the past we have more than information, we have a story about human life, and that story can tell us something about our own lives.
>
> (1993: 6)

Although constituting only a very small minority of history teachers, those described as cosmic philosophers see the uncovering of the patterns and 'laws' that connect events as the most interesting aspect of history. For them, history provides a context for understanding our place in the world and a means of seeking truth – of establishing the underlying patterns in life and events, and of seeing how these might connect into the future. These teachers are often, though not always, inspired by a sense of the religious or spiritual – of the acting out of a higher plan upon human experience. In the words of one historian, this is 'a salvationary view of history, whose ultimate end is concealed in the breast of the Almighty' (see Warren 1998: 184). Understanding the human condition is a particularly important goal, and the task of a history education is to help students develop a sense of the connected nature of mankind and thus greater self-knowledge. The mode of delivery of these teachers tends to be eclectic, and indeed Evans notes that many history teachers possess elements of more than one of these conceptions of their subject. Nonetheless, he maintains that, although some may be genuinely eclectic in their conceptions, most possess a dominant tendency – a primary conception of the subject that powerfully influences their work in both research and what they choose to do in the history classroom.

Drawing upon the results of the survey of American historians mentioned earlier and their own experience of teaching the subject, Shrock and Shrock (1994: 1093–4) capture the spirit of teaching history in a way that embodies the principal conceptions outlined above.

> First, and most obvious, we historians want our students to gain a sense of the past, including their own roots. Although we love the past for its own sake, we embrace it primarily for the context and understanding it provides. As teachers, we probe into the past because of its 'relevance to the present', especially to the lives and futures of our students. We recognize its role in 'broadening' their perceptions, 'perceptions of who they are and how they got that way'. We believe in the value of history to 'open the eyes of students to a new way of thinking about themselves and their community' . . . Second, we teach history to overcome provinciality. We want students to think not only of their own origins and communities but also about other people in other communities . . . We want them to see a connection with all humankind, across barriers of time, geography, and culture . . . Third, we practice history to foster a critical and analytical spirit. By this, we do not mean a mean-spirited questioning of everyone and everything. Instead we mean a spirit that is probing, questioning, seeking what is logical and consistent . . . Fourth, doing history helps us and our students develop skills in reading, research, writing, and discussion. History for us is an 'intellectual conversation' in which good minds become better at 'thinking with care' . . . In the end, we hope all of this contributes to growth – growth that is broad and deep, analytical and imaginative, cross-cultural and historical.

Reflection on what is seen as the meaning and purpose of the study of history can be deeply revealing of how the curriculum is designed and delivered, of what is seen as important for students to learn and how that learning is encouraged.

Theories of teaching and learning

Like students, history teachers enter a classroom with varying conceptions of learning and teaching, and these influence how they perceive the teaching situation and the approach they adopt in a particular class. Whilst in the educational research studies referred to at the outset of this chapter the experiences of academics in scientific and professional subjects have predominated, the findings provide insights that can be usefully employed by historians to investigate how they go about teaching and how this influences students' learning in their own discipline. When they face any new class, history teachers do so with conceptions, whether explicit or implicit, about what learning means, and in Chapter 2 this was examined in relation to conceptions of understanding in history. They also inevitably bring to the classroom beliefs and assumptions about what teaching means in their subject, and about their preferred style of teaching, whether verbal or visual, logical or imaginative, impersonal or personal, and so on.

In an influential article based upon interviews with humanities, social science and science lecturers in Australian universities, Dall'Alba (1991) identified seven different ways in which lecturers represent their teaching:

1 Teaching as presenting information
2 Teaching as transmitting information (from teacher to students)
3 Teaching as illustrating the application of theory to practice
4 Teaching as developing concepts/principles and their relations
5 Teaching as developing the capacity to be expert
6 Teaching as exploring ways of understanding from different perspectives
7 Teaching as bringing about conceptual change.

This taxonomy extends from a simple transmission model of teaching, to more complex conceptions in which the lecturer's focus is increasingly upon how the student relates to content and concepts in the discipline and is encouraged to engage actively with them. Ramsden (1992) draws on this and other work to identify three key ways in which university teachers experience teaching along a continuum from teacher-centred to student-centred, each of which has implications for how students are expected to learn. These theories of teaching he describes as teaching as telling or transmission, teaching as organizing student activity, and teaching as making learning possible. What follows relates these to the experience of teaching in history.

Teaching as transmission

This is characterized by an approach which regards content (whether facts about the past, the interpretations of scholars or key historical concepts and procedures) as a knowledge base that can be transferred to students in a process akin to pouring liquid from one container into another. Of course, no university history teachers would consider themselves the mere purveyors of facts; indeed, instilling students with a thorough knowledge of topics is often regarded by academic historians as a characteristic of schools-history teaching. It is not uncommon in practice, however, for history lecturers to regard themselves as subject specialists, passing on knowledge and expertise to students whose responsibility it is to absorb them and use them to shape their own work. Elton, for example, notably argued that a history education necessarily 'involves some straight infusion of facts and figures', and that in seminars and tutorials 'the superior knowledge and equipment of the teacher calls forth the student's active creation of his own knowledge and equipment' (Elton 1967: 144-5, 161). Exactly how this 'calling forth' occurs is not explained, but it is often assumed to arise naturally as a direct consequence of the expertise of the teacher. Not all of those who employ a transmission theory of teaching do so at all times, or even from a deeply held belief in the need to deliver subject knowledge to students. Rather, some do so from habit, perhaps because they themselves were taught in this way, while others simply lack experience of how to create conditions which enable students to participate more actively in their own learning.

The most obvious manifestation of the transmission model in history teaching is the conventional lecture, in which students take down notes in what is essentially a one-way process. This is not to suggest that all lectures are without value. Indeed, they can perform a variety of useful functions, not least in inspiring enthusiasm for discovering more about a topic (see McKeachie 1994; Blackey 1997; Brown and Race 2002). Nonetheless, all too often the lecturer tends (however reluctantly or unwittingly) to assume the mantle of the authoritative voice of history and the student the role of passive recipient of this specialist knowledge. In this theory of teaching the better the delivery of content, the more skilful the lecturer, and where improvement is considered necessary the focus is upon methods of delivery, whether structuring or pacing or the employment of presentation packages such as Powerpoint. Indeed, some students conspire in this, particularly inexperienced undergraduates who find traditional lectures satisfying because they supply a substantial, structured set of notes for revision (and often comment approvingly on this in course evaluation questionnaires). So, too, lecturers adopting this conception of teaching are generally in favour of a comprehensive lecture programme on the grounds of the importance of 'coverage'. If it is suggested that lectures might be cut from one hour to forty-five minutes, the response will be that too much valuable content will be lost. Teaching content, however, is not the same as teaching students. Whilst the lecture is the most obvious manifestation of transmission theories of teaching in history, it is far from unique in this respect. Thus, for example, such conceptions can also be found in seminars where tutor talk dominates, often in practice as a means of avoiding the awkward silence which tends to descend following the delivery of a student paper or in discussions with poor questioning. It is therefore not surprising that detailed studies of staff–student interaction in history classes in higher education have found that teachers often do most of the talking (see Luker 1987; Quinlan 1999).

The transmission theory of teaching clearly has significant limitations, but a basic weakness is that it cannot adequately explain why students fail to learn or to be motivated. If the material is delivered clearly, students should learn; the relationship between student and teacher is regarded as unproblematic. The teacher's responsibility is to possess subject expertise and convey it in a competent fashion. The student's role is to attend, listen carefully, complete the prescribed preparatory reading and ensure that they possess a 'firm grasp' of the topics. Therefore, if students fail to learn it must be because they are idle or less intelligent (or both), or because they have personal problems or, in the case of new undergraduates, have not been prepared properly for university level study in the subject. Of course, all of these may sometimes be true; students are a diverse constituency. However, lecturers who teach this way fail to see that the challenge then is to reflect upon why students are unmotivated, how they engage with subject content, what they understand already and what else might be done to help them to learn. It is an essentially one-dimensional conception that posits a straightforward relationship between teaching and learning. It is also one that frequently results in a climate of dependency or anxiety in which students fear interrogation by the 'expert' lecturer.

Teaching as organizing and managing student activity

In this 'transitional' conception, teaching is perceived less as a means of instilling knowledge or covering the curriculum, than as a supervision process in which a range of techniques are deployed to ensure that students learn effectively. Whilst the subject expertise and experience of the teacher are seen to generate an authority and responsibility to manage learning in the interests of the learners, the emphasis is more upon the interaction between student and teacher than in the transmission theory. This is a more complex conception which asks questions about how students might learn better and looks to answers which will make the subject more interesting, and thus motivating, for students themselves. 'How can I get my students to participate more actively in classes?' is a question frequently asked by history tutors, and the solution is generally the employment of a variety of methods. The focus here is upon activity, and this might mean the teacher breaking up teaching sessions with debates, sub-groups, brainstorming, mini-projects and so on, whilst remaining in charge of the discussion. This model is also built upon establishing clear procedures to support these activities, as, for example, in guidelines for seminar participation or learning contracts for project work. These teachers ensure that they maintain eye contact in lectures, use visual aids, adopt a clear structure, pace their delivery, indeed all the panoply of teaching methods identified by peer quality assessors (see Higher Education Funding Council for England 1994). They are also keen to discover new, reliable methods of motivating students and so are more interested in pedagogic innovation than teachers adopting a transmission approach.

Here the teacher is analogous to a master craftsman, supervising apprentices who are guided through the acquisition of the skills of the trade by practising upon a variety of products. It is therefore incumbent upon the teacher to set out the knowledge to be learned and frame the issues, whilst building up a repertoire of techniques that help students to engage more actively in the process. In this conception the focus is clearly more upon the student than in the transmission theory, but the issue of how universal teaching techniques connect with student approaches to learning in the particular subject and classroom context remains unaddressed. Failure to learn is seen not simply as the fault of the student but also of a range of contextual factors.

Teaching as facilitating student learning

In this theory, teaching is viewed as inextricably linked to learning through a set of complex interactions between student, lecturer, the learning situation and the subject. The role of the teacher is therefore to work co-operatively with learners to help them engage with their subject in ways that change their understanding. In this conception students are regarded as individuals, and teaching involves finding out about how they learn, their understandings and misunderstandings, and using that knowledge to create conditions that encourage a deep engagement with the subject. Here the teacher recognizes that understanding can only be constructed through an active engagement with the subject matter. This theory is therefore student-focused in a deeper sense. It recognizes that in learning 'it is not what *we* do, it's what *students* do that is the important thing' (Biggs 1999: 24). Teaching and learning are seen to be part of the same whole – teaching history is concerned with making learning possible. This means helping students to become aware of the things that hinder understanding, and encouraging them to think for themselves. As such it becomes an essentially facilitative process, based upon mutual exploration of the subject matter and of what it means to be a historian. In such an endeavour there are seen to be no universally applicable solutions. Rather, teaching activities are related to the particular context and to the varied understandings and conceptions of the diverse students who comprise most history classes. In this theory, improvement is simply an integral facet of teaching, involving the same process of experimentation, constant monitoring and attentiveness to self and students.

The emphasis in this theory is upon creating contexts which encourage students to engage actively with the subject matter in order to make understanding possible, and as such it is far removed from the transmission theory. This approach is illustrated in the following extract from an interview with an experienced university history teacher. In response to a question about the most important ways to enhance student learning, he observes:

> I would say to try to make them think for themselves. I think there's a great danger in the university system that students

will regard you as the fount of knowledge and wisdom, and will have an attitude towards whatever you say which is unduly deferential and uncritical. There's everything to be said for provoking them to disagree with you. I think there's a lot to be said for trying to get them to bring their own thoughts and their own backgrounds, and their prejudices even, to bear on the ways they study a piece of history or on their approach, indeed, to any intellectual problem. So I do think that trying to stimulate independent thought, and even independent emotion, is very important [. . .] One judges oneself as a teacher by the ways in which one can see students' minds and expression and discussion in a certain sense grow during the year. That's a wonderful feeling.

(Dunkin 1991: 42)

The most skilful teachers are those capable of deciding upon strategies that provide students with the best opportunity to learn, on the basis of an appreciation of the interactions of the many contextual factors in any particular learning situation and consideration of well-established educational principles. They appreciate that content and skills are both necessary in order to develop historical understanding, and are able to integrate these into a flexible programme that gradually increases students' responsibility for their own learning in ways sensitive to their particular needs. This might involve sometimes adopting a more interventionist approach (for example to explain goals or to help clarify complex concepts), and at others an almost invisible role. Its central thread, however, is the effort to uncover students' existing knowledge, skills and understanding, and use that knowledge to create conditions in which all students can engage actively with historical issues and evidence.

The theories of teaching outlined above are distinct but inevitably overlap. Thus the final conception assumes the importance of sufficient coverage and varied techniques, but connects more closely with student needs and the ways students go about learning in their subject. Of course, all such models are constructs, a conflation of views, and thus cannot fully reflect the views of any individual lecturer. Rather they represent key points on a long continuum extending from teacher-centred to student-centred approaches, and from content delivery to the facilitation of understanding. Some research suggests, however, that those who express their view of teaching in such metaphors as 'presenting', 'giving', 'conveying', 'delivering' or 'feeding', or who talk of learning in terms of 'getting knowledge' or 'answering questions' or 'working through material', are more likely to adopt an approach to teaching towards the transmission end of the spectrum. Similarly, those who represent teaching as 'guiding', 'challenging', 'empowering', and learning as 'understanding', 'challenging one's own ideas', 'analysing', 'engaging', 'exciting', are more likely to adopt an approach to teaching towards the student-centred end of the spectrum (Martin *et al.* 2001). This mirrors the pioneering study of Fox (1983), who used the metaphors employed by lecturers to construct a classification of teachers' conceptions ranging from simple transfer theories based upon notions of delivery, through 'shaping' theories (in which teachers 'develop' key skills or 'train' students in key techniques) and 'building' theories (often associated with the word 'concept', in which the lecturer provides the materials and plan for the complete structure to be erected), to more developed theories in which the student is regarded as a partner in learning with attitudes, experiences, abilities, interests and goals which need to be listened to. These more developed theories he called the 'travelling' theory and the 'growing' theory – from the metaphors used by lecturers to describe them. In the former the lecturer is the 'guide' who has been to the 'frontiers of knowledge' in at least some areas and can use this experience to support the travellers, among whom there are diverse types with differing reasons for the journey, to find their own ways of crossing increasingly difficult terrain and making discoveries for themselves. The travelling theory places the emphasis upon the subject, although, as the research of Quinlan (1999) in one history department suggests, the use of 'guiding' metaphors to describe pedagogic goals does not preclude an essentially didactic approach to teaching. The focus of the 'growing' theory is more upon the student as a person, and changing their ways of responding to the world, with the teacher's role as finding ways to prepare the ground so that effective learning can ensue. Here the teacher is likened to a gardener who has a general plan of what he or she wants but is conscious that this is likely to change. Thus attentiveness and flexibility are required but most important is the preparation of the ground, and this is at the heart of student-centred approaches to teaching.

Conclusion

Like students, history teachers bring to any teaching situation diverse prior experiences of teaching and varied conceptions of their subject and of teaching and learning in it. These experiences, and the conceptions, assumptions and habits that arise from them, influence curricular decisions and classroom practices, and thus student learning. Although conceptions of teaching vary, whether they are located more towards the teacher-centred or student-centred end of the pedagogic spectrum is an important distinction. What characterizes history teachers at both school and university who are rated highly by students and colleagues (whether they regard themselves as 'innovative' or 'traditional') is their adoption of flexible strategies founded upon the ability to engage with students personally and on a level commensurate with existing knowledge, skills and understanding. They understand how knowledge is structured in their subject and which aspects are straightforward and which difficult for students at particular levels of experience, and are thus alert to misconceptions as well as adept at creating flexible strategies and student assignments on the basis of this knowledge. In the complex interactions between student, lecturer, subject and environment that condition learning there is always the potential for misunderstanding. Frustration can occur if, for example, a lecturer holds a more facilitative conception of teaching whilst a student holds a transmissive theory, or vice versa. Becoming a skilled teacher, Ramsden (1992: 110-11) suggests, 'requires developing the ability to deploy a complex theory of teaching in the different contexts relevant to the teaching and learning of that subject'. It also requires that personal conceptions and theories of history and how these relate to history teaching are clearly articulated by tutors to students. This helps to minimize the confusion that is often felt by students as they go from class to class encountering different educational beliefs and practices, and underlines the need for them to review their own beliefs and perspectives on history and learning in the subject.

Of course, history teachers do not teach in a vacuum, and, alongside conceptions of the subject and learning, perceptions of contextual factors also influence the approach taken to teaching. The level of support offered by departmental, institutional and disciplinary cultures, and trends within higher education more generally, inevitably have a powerful impact upon how teaching is viewed and valued, and thus upon student learning. History teachers who display sensitivity to student perspectives, are aware of their own conceptions of the subject and of teaching, and understand the contexts in which they operate are most likely to be able to create strategies that inspire students to learn deeply. Reflective, learner-oriented practices are not without challenges, and practical strategies designed to support them are the focus of the remainder of this book. Such approaches, however, provide a powerful means of motivating history students, communicating the love teachers have for their subject and fostering the search for deeper levels of understanding. Here learning and teaching are not viewed in dualistic terms but rather as a single interactive process and a shared responsibility. They are, in the words of Eble (1988: 9), 'constantly interchanging activities. One learns by teaching; one cannot teach except by constantly learning.'

5

CREATING A CONTEXT
FOR LEARNING

Perhaps the most significant feature of the Oxford history
course was that few undergraduates had any clear idea of
what it was trying to achieve ... Nor did we know why the
content of the syllabus was as it was. In practical terms, if the
course had a coherent rationale, it was not displayed to
undergraduates. In such circumstances it was difficult to
evaluate one's progress: one tended to set oneself short-term
goals which avoided the fundamental issue, and reduced the
syllabus to a series of fragments.

(Lee 1970: 327)

Creating the conditions in which high-quality learning can flourish
is the first priority of teaching in any subject. As Biggs (1999: 25)
remarks, 'the context that we set up is at the core of teaching'. Whilst
encouraging student activity is important, careful arrangement of the
whole learning environment is necessary to establish a setting
conducive to the development of complex historical thinking. The
climate created at the level of both the individual classroom and the
department as a whole powerfully influences students' motivation and
level of engagement with the subject matter (see Parlett 1977;
Ramsden 1988, 1997). In the mid-1980s a detailed investigation of
the curriculum in nine British history departments revealed some
deeply entrenched disciplinary values and beliefs (Boys *et al.* 1988).
Prominent was a reluctance to articulate explicitly the goals of history
teaching, which many believed 'spoke for themselves'. In this 'cult of
the implicit' (Church 1978: 135), history was self-evidently worth
studying for its own sake, and whilst it developed a wide range of life
skills, these were felt to arise as a natural by-product of close
engagement with the subject matter, and so required neither explicit
expression nor specific attention. Traditional assumptions also

dominated curricular decision-making, an area regarded as the exclusive preserve of disciplinary practitioners. Thus curriculum change was regarded as a product of the internal dynamics of the discipline, evolving in line with new topics and approaches arising from ongoing disciplinary research, and any external attempt to influence the history curriculum was perceived as a fundamental threat to the 'integrity' of the discipline.

Whilst only a rough snapshot of curricular thinking in the discipline two decades ago, this supply-side, content-driven curriculum model will be recognizable to many historians currently teaching in higher education. Today, however, those designing history courses, whether at the level of the individual module or the degree programme, cannot so easily escape a more direct engagement with stakeholders, whether employers, government or students. As Cowan (1996: 22) remarks: 'We live in a world in which the importance of the study of history is no longer self-evident, and the provision of history courses has to be seen as an area of educational activity in competition with others whose coherence and justification are more easily perceived.' Historians designing courses must respond to external pressures to articulate overtly intended aims and outcomes, and provide an education that explicitly addresses the employment needs of graduates (see Porter 1999). Above all, in the context of a more diverse student population in terms of background, interests, prior knowledge and skills, they must consider students more carefully. As Calder *et al.* (2002: 49) point out: 'Who are my students and what are they *really* learning? is a question an increasing number of teachers are asking.' To think in terms of course design for learning that is subject-based yet transferable to other contexts, intellectual and practical, critical and imaginative, flexible yet carefully structured, and framed in terms of student needs, is undoubtedly a challenging task. Yet if course planning is a more complex exercise than it once was, there are some well-established educational principles that can provide guidance.

Principles of effective learning environments

Research on teaching in higher education emphasizes the importance of viewing the learning environment as a system, each element of which influences student learning in a dynamic and interactive fashion (Entwistle 1992; Entwistle *et al.* 1992; Ramsden 1992; Biggs 1999). Learning is always situated in a particular curricular context, comprising not only syllabus, teaching methods, assessment practices and resources but also departmental climate, institutional requirements and disciplinary norms and expectations. So, too, history courses as described in university prospectuses and course documents represent only the official course of study. Alongside this paper curriculum runs the curriculum actually delivered by teachers, and what Snyder (1971) calls the 'hidden curriculum' of what students actually learn and experience based upon their perceptions of what is required. Graff (1991) further reminds us of the influence of the 'co-curriculum', the non-formal learning occurring outside official study time, which in North America in particular has been the locus of efforts to make student experiences in campus activities, halls of residence and part-time work a more integral part of the learning experience (see Kuh 1994, 1995; Schroeder and Mable 1994; Eraut 2000).

In planning a history course it is therefore important to be responsive to a wide variety of factors in the overall learning environment. The following list suggests some of the principal elements to be considered.

- Students' existing knowledge, conceptions of the subject, conceptions of learning and teaching in it, expectations and needs, goals, skills, motivation, time available, habitual ways of thinking and working, and self-confidence.
- Teachers' conceptions of the subject, of learning and teaching, extent of teaching experience, subject expertise, research interests, goals, degree of enthusiasm, expectations of students and of self, acquired habits of teaching, and emotional responses to teaching situations.
- Course organization in terms of coverage, structure and sequencing, timing of sessions, and the relation of these to the aims and objectives of the course.
- Teaching and assessment methods used, how they are introduced and organized, the relationship between them, and the ways in which they are aligned with course aims, content and structure.
- Costs and resources, including staffing levels and their relation to student numbers, staff time available for teaching, marking and student support, the quality of library and ICT provision, teaching accommodation and equipment, timetabling provision, and (in resource-based courses) copyright issues.
- Climate, including departmental modes of working, faculty and institutional rules and regulations, departmental and wider disciplinary expectations and standards (including the value

accorded to teaching), co-curricular activities and quality-assurance requirements.

Clearly some of these are more directly under the control of the individual teacher than others, though it is worth remembering that even with limited resources and room for manoeuvre a teacher can make a significant difference to the quality of students' learning. The prime concern is to attempt to bring as many variables as possible into a positive alignment that fosters an understanding approach to the subject, and minimizes the distance between official and hidden dimensions of the curriculum.

Investigation of student learning across many disciplines has generated a number of guiding principles for the design of learning environments, whether classroom-based or online (see Chickering and Gamson 1987; Chickering and Reisser 1993; Gibbs 1992d; Ramsden 1992; Harris 1999; Paloff and Pratt 1999). Research on history students' perspectives similarly suggests the need to pay attention to some key balances in the design of history courses and curricula.

Students and teachers

Today's student population is more diverse than ever before. As Cowan (1996: 23) observes: 'Instead of relying on the comforting assumption that students came from similar backgrounds and shared similar interests to those of their teachers, anyone who begins to consider how to design a history curriculum is obliged to take several steps back from questions about content and even from modes of delivery to consider the contrasting experiences of potential students of history.' Connecting to student experiences and involving them in discussion about course requirements enables the creation of a course setting that is clear and transparent, and a climate of openness and trust. Such constructive dialogue increases teachers' understanding of student perspectives, facilitates the development of critical reflection and is conducive to student self-expression, confidence and ability to adapt more easily to course demands. More particularly, it encourages a view of learning as what Bruce and Gerber (1995) call a 'participative pedagogic experience', in which teachers and students are active partners in the shared exploration of the subject.

Challenge and support

Students often expect that an undergraduate history education will help them to think more critically and independently, and in fostering these qualities (and the self-confidence intimately related to them) existing conceptions of the subject need to be challenged. As Chickering and Gamson (1987: 1) point out: 'High expectations are important for everyone – for the poorly prepared, for those unwilling to exert themselves, and for the bright and well-motivated.' Tasks that test students' intellectual and personal capacities are closely linked to motivation; equally, however, challenge inappropriate to existing levels of knowledge, skills and understanding erodes interest as well as confidence. Tasks that are too easy quickly become boring; those that are too difficult create frustration. High expectations must be matched by encouragement and constructive feedback, and (particularly important from the student perspective) a sense of personal connection to teachers and course. Where face-to-face contact is not possible, as in some online courses, finding ways to support this sense of personal connection is particularly important, whether through formative tests, bulletin boards or the many conferencing facilities now available in virtual learning environments. However, even in online courses many students feel the need for the support provided by actually meeting with tutors and peers. As history students studying on one online course commented, 'online learning makes face-to-face contact even more important' (Hall *et al.* 2001: 93). In conditions which complement challenge with safety, old ideas can be reconsidered and new ones tested and refined without undue anxiety. Support, however, is not merely a function of individual teachers and the immediate peer group but of the department as a whole, and the climate created at this level has a considerable influence not only on learning but also on the retention of students (McGivney 1996; Moxley *et al.* 2001). Many students who drop out of university are influenced by a perceived lack of personal and academic support, often compared unfavourably with their school experience. Whilst in a system of expanding student numbers supporting individual students is appreciably more difficult, it is nonetheless a priority for departments, whether through online means, more targeted tutor contact or peer-support schemes.

Structure and freedom

If most new history undergraduates anticipate greater freedom in learning than they have previously experienced, there is also often considerable anxiety about the degree of independence required and competence in the skills required. Courses therefore need to be structured in ways that help students to progress towards more complex forms of understanding. Thus, for example, lectures may be more appropriate on first-year courses than on final-year undergraduate courses, while more advanced students can be encouraged to take greater responsibility for their own learning. So, too, whilst modular structures allow greater student choice, and resource-based and online courses permit more flexible routes through material, clear structuring and sequencing of material in terms of learning are essential in order to ensure coherence and progression in learning. Deciding upon the appropriate balance between structure and freedom is one of the most challenging aspects of course design. It is certainly important for students to have a sense of control over activities, and of ownership of the course as a whole. From the student perspective, the ability to choose one's courses, discussion topics and essay assignments is particularly important, with a large majority of history students believing that without it motivation is severely curtailed.

Independence and interdependence

Whilst enabling students to become more independent as learners is a key objective of all history programmes, independence is not synonymous with individualism. Individualism, often in a competitive sense, is regarded by many students, rightly or wrongly, as a key characteristic of studying history in school, and has to be balanced by the recognition that co-operative activity is an integral part of developing understanding. Educational research has clearly demonstrated the importance of collaborative learning in developing critical thinking, interpersonal skills and self-awareness. As Chickering and Gamson (1987: 1) observe: 'Learning is enhanced when it is more like a team effort than a solo race. Good learning, like good work, is collaborative and social, not competitive and isolated. Working with others often increases involvement in learning. Sharing one's own ideas and responding to others' reactions improves thinking and deepens understanding.' Creating contexts in which discussion can flourish is essential to high-quality learning, whatever the mode of delivery. In practice, many history students recognize that interaction with others is a vital means of helping them to make connections between ideas, refine interpretations, and develop subject and transferable skills. However, as they also attest, the shared nature of the experience often amounts to little more than the reading out of a paper (even if today this has been reclassified as an oral presentation), followed by a dialogue between one or two of those present or a monologue by the teacher.

Activity and reflection

Creating a framework in which students feel able to participate fully, and engage critically and imaginatively with the subject matter, is a *sine qua non* of effective teaching. However, while 'learning by doing' is important, activity is not by itself sufficient. Reflection is required to turn experience into understanding, yet all too frequently a heavy workload, often related to a large number of assessed assignments, leads students to adopt a surface approach to learning. This was remarked upon by several of the history students interviewed by Hounsell (1997: 110) in a study of essay writing. One noted: 'I mean basically I'm a full-time essay writer', while another commented, 'I've got so many other things to do (laughs), essays to do, I just sort of churn them out . . . You know, think of something else, get on with something else.' Likewise the models of essay writing that dominate schools history at senior levels are all too often formulaic and emphasize thoroughness of knowledge, and in higher education students are not infrequently given assignments seemingly designed to encourage descriptive narrative. Building time for reflection (on subject matter, what has been learned and the experience of learning) into course design is therefore essential.

How these educational balances can be negotiated in the practice of course design in history is examined in relation to the development of a level one skills development course by Booth (2001). This emphasizes that enabling students to become more confident and sophisticated learners is as much about removing barriers to learning as it is about adding to their repertoire of abilities. Through a learning environment built around their experience and needs, students are encouraged to confront their assumptions about history and practice a variety of subject-specific and transferable skills. Similar experiments in online course design are described in history case studies presented in Hall and Harding (2001), where attention is drawn particularly to the importance of clarity of structure, accessibility and flexibility, and the provision of opportunities for ongoing dialogue and interaction, as a means of supporting learners through a progressively challenging problem-solving process. In online courses user-friendly presentation is also an important factor in engaging interest. As one history teacher remarks, 'those designing IT components should remember that onscreen prose must attempt to engage the reader . . . [Our] workshops included onscreen cartoons and some joke-related websites, as well as graphic images, all of which were designed to engage the user' (94).

Above all, effective curriculum design commences with the design of aims and intended learning outcomes, which is considered in the following section. Before addressing this, however, it may be useful to review proposed or current courses in the light of the educational balances discussed above and the following questions:

- Why does this course need to be taught?
- Who are the students and what knowledge, understanding, skills and attitudes do they have?
- What are the four or five essential things I want them to learn?
- How are these best expressed to students?
- How is content best structured to achieve the learning goals of the course?
- How will assignments connect the material with students' prior knowledge, experience and beliefs?
- How do I know that students have progressed?
- What resources are available to support the course?
- How does this course fit into the wider curriculum?
- How do my own experiences, values and beliefs influence course design?
- How will departmental, institutional and disciplinary contexts influence the course decisions?
- How can I involve students in the planning process?

Gould (1973: 253) suggests a simple exercise, conceived in the context of geography, to aid reflection on and the planning of an entire degree course. This involves imagining that one has been asked to form a new department and given free rein to design a curriculum that will promote high-quality learning in the subject. Given the chance to begin *ab initio*, what would this curriculum look like? How far would it resemble what already exists?

Aims, objectives and outcomes

The aims of a course represent general statements of overall purpose, and in history are often employed to refer to the acquisition of knowledge and understanding of past societies and cultures. Objectives refer to the specific things that students need to learn in order to attain the overall aims, and are often expressed in terms of the acquisition of subject-specific skills (for example critical reading of historical sources or use of evidence) and transferable skills such as the ability to communicate fluently in writing and verbally and work in groups. Learning outcomes have also become a common means of explaining to students what they will be expected to know and be able to do at the end of their course (Otter 1992; Moon 1995; Melton 1997). In a concise review of the benefits and problems of learning outcomes approaches, Atkins *et al.* (1993) note particularly their value in sharpening statements of aims, clarifying the relationship between goals and assessment, focusing students' attention upon the full range of skills developed on a course, and helping them to see the practical utility of their subject. Specifying learning outcomes can also help students to identify more clearly what is important (and thus what they need to do to demonstrate their achievement), and enable them to make more informed course choices. There are, however, challenges, not least in maintaining a balance between expressing outcomes in such general terms that they are difficult to evaluate and producing too specific a statement that trivializes complex goals. An outcomes approach may also encourage a focus on easily measurable indicators of achievement, at the expense of more advanced attainments associated with complex concepts such as understanding. An inflexible departmental approach to learning outcomes can result in conformity, with teachers adhering to a common template with little evidence of reflection. Finally, the expression of learning outcomes may prevent students from defining their own outcomes or valuing course outcomes not specified by the teacher, and thus hinder the development of independent thinking.

Learning outcomes therefore require careful attention in order to ensure that they:

- reflect real goals of historical understanding, and not trivial attainments which can be memorized and will fail to challenge and motivate students;
- focus upon essential knowledge and skills. Too long a list is difficult for both teachers and students to be mindful of.

- are realistic: manageable for students at a particular level of study and within the timespan of the course;
- are explicit (for example 'able to compare historians' interpretations of the causes of the First World War' and not 'explain the causes of the First World War');
- unpack the meaning of key concepts, such as historical analysis or use of evidence, by attempting to break them down into their component skills;
- are clearly communicated to students, and expressed in language that they can understand. In course material for students they need to address the individual – 'you' rather than 'students'.
- are carefully aligned with the aims, teaching methods and assessment practices on a course. It is particularly important to include (either as part of the outcome or separately) a description of what would constitute the type of performance by which attainment will be judged.

The experience of one historian in redesigning a world history course to encourage students to think more analytically reflects this advice (Stearns 2000). Having not previously addressed explicitly what students should take away from the course, there was a particular need to decide on the essential skills that students would have learned by the end of the course, and to break down the general abilities students were expected to develop (notably skills of comparative analysis) into their key elements.

> Clearly, I did not venture a full list of the goals I would seek in history learning more generally . . . I made the choice to emphasize certain analytical skills in this particular course, a choice that can be criticized but has the merit of being both definite and finite. Historical habits of mind are wide-ranging, and the whole edifice cannot be built in a semester. The priority is to get at least some sense of where one particular course fits within a larger analytical edifice, to be explicit, and to have real goals beyond coverage, while at the same time not pursuing too long a list of goals.
>
> (Stearns 2000: 426)

In writing learning outcomes, it is helpful to consider what a student would need to do to convince you that they are where you want them to be in terms of knowledge, skills and understanding at the end of the course. This exercise, suggested by Diamond (1989), helps to ensure that planning is grounded in practical realities, and encourages reflection in terms of concrete high-level attainments. Involving others, whether colleagues or students, can also be productive. Students in a new class, for example, might be given the opportunity to refine specified objectives or outcomes as part of induction on to a course, both as a means of enhancing knowledge and developing critical reflection. Such involvement can provide a counterweight to the rigidity sometimes evident in learning outcomes approaches, and create space for students to become more active participants in their own learning.

If outcomes are considered in terms of the goal of deepening students' understanding, it can be useful to distinguish between three key dimensions of learning which can be related to the framework outlining progression in understanding described in Chapter 2. The examples describe learning outcomes drawn from a variety of history courses.

Learning outcomes for factual and technical knowledge

In history this might include not merely the acquisition of factual knowledge about a topic or period, but also the meaning of key concepts and the application of basic procedures.

You will be able to:

- describe the principal characteristics of popular rebellions in early modern Europe;
- identify key historiographical developments in writing on the standard of living question in the Industrial Revolution;
- trace the principal causes and effects of the American Civil War;
- state Elton's views on the nature and purpose of history;
- list some of the problems of working with historical statistics;
- describe the meaning of patriotism in the context of eighteenth-century England;
- use the online library catalogue to locate and retrieve historical information.

Learning outcomes for historical insight

Insight is clearly closely associated with understanding as represented by historians. Outcomes at this level are not so easy to test in the same way as factual knowledge or a practical skill. If we want students to understand the causes of the First World War, we are expecting them to examine existing interpretations in a critical fashion and use established disciplinary procedures of evidence to arrive at an interpretation. Possession of knowledge of key events, dates and personalities is axiomatic. However, as there is no single, 'correct' answer, the level of understanding has to be assessed in relation to the quality of students' research and the way they go about arguing their case, for example, in an essay assignment, in relation to the sophistication of the analysis and use of evidence, structuring of argument and consistency of conclusions with the ideas presented throughout. At this level of outcomes students are expected to learn a way of thinking and arguing that can be evaluated by identifying the procedures they need to be able to use and the kinds of evidence that would convince tutors that they had done so.

You will be able to:

- compare and contrast Marxist, revisionist and post-revisionist interpretations of the French Revolution;
- analyse critically the work of E. P. Thompson on the making of class in nineteenth-century England;
- evaluate the contribution of the Annales school to the growth of twentieth-century social history;
- compare the value of some key primary sources on popular culture in the Second World War, including written, oral and visual testimonies;
- apply the concepts of 'estates' and 'orders' in interpreting eighteenth-century French society;
- formulate historical arguments in a variety of written forms, including essays, reports and gobbets.

Learning outcomes for self-awareness and personal development

In history the achievement of personal growth is an important objective, and complex understanding demands attentiveness to one's own beliefs and their relationship to wider socio-cultural forces. Yet, although essential, it is more difficult still to generate measurable learning outcomes and specify exact levels of performance in this area. Complicating this further is the fact that whilst the creation of personal meaning from the fragmented evidence of past events is regarded as integral to the attainment of understanding, the expression of this in written work by the use of the personal pronoun 'I' is still often discouraged.

Self-reflection is most easily integrated into courses with a particular emphasis upon process, such as history study or learning-skills programmes. However, it is possible to include it as part of an ascending hierarchy of goals on any history course. This might begin with the acquisition of factual knowledge of the topic, followed by the ability to compare and contrast historical interpretations and apply key concepts, to relate the topic to wider trends in historiography, come to a coherent and independent viewpoint, and, finally, evaluate one's views of what it means to study history on the basis of experience on the course. As Toohey (1999: 148) points out, 'goals for self-reflective learning will usually require students to articulate a personal position on some aspect of their course, be able to identify the views and experiences which shaped their current thinking and show that they understand the impact that their beliefs will have on their own practice'. The use of reflective essays, autobiographical writing and course portfolios provide some means of generating evidence that progress has been made towards this learning outcome. Whilst such pieces of work are more difficult to grade, there is also more chance of reading an individual, imaginative and unplagiarized piece of work.

You will be able to:

- reflect critically upon why you decided to write your essay on your chosen issue or period;
- explain to others through an oral presentation the influences that shaped your decision to study history;
- evaluate your contribution to the seminars as a whole on the course, including a critical assessment of your strengths and weaknesses;
- write a report of what you learnt as a result of leading your seminar or giving an oral presentation;
- identify your own views on history and explain how these have shaped your learning on this course.

Whatever aims, objectives and learning outcomes are chosen, it is essential that students know what they are and understand them. An explanatory statement of goals and outcomes, key themes, teaching and assessment tasks, assignment deadlines and contact information is therefore vital. To this can be added a statement of the teaching philosophy underpinning the course, and how feedback from previous cohorts of students has helped the course to develop. These provide a focus for discussion of demands and expectations at the first meeting on a course. For online courses clear participation guidelines are particularly important, especially an explanation of how often students need to log on, how much they should contribute to discussion, and how participation will be evaluated. Rowntree (1981) suggests asking a new group of students to write down two or three questions that they expect the course will deal with, and using discussion to modify existing goals and suggest one or two new ones. Put starkly, the clearer students are about the expectations on a course, the more likely they are to meet them.

Content, structure and coherence

In practice, new history courses are often planned in the following fashion. First, teachers arrive at an idea about the subject area they would like to teach, based upon their own research interests or recent trends in scholarship. They proceed to sketch out a possible syllabus, then teaching and assessment methods, and only at the point at which the course submission document has to be written are learning outcomes considered in any detail. Whilst this model of course planning is driven by the logic of the subject matter and, particularly, staff research interests, in a learner-focused curriculum decisions about course content and delivery are more closely linked to the needs and interests of students at a particular level of study. Thus the issue of what the course intends to achieve in terms of student learning is a consideration from the outset and leads naturally to issues of content, structuring and sequencing of material related to both students' likely level of understanding and the logic of the subject matter. In this model, content and aims are interlocking elements in a dynamic and iterative process of design, in which objectives suggest content to be covered but thinking about content also suggests refinements to objectives.

In a subject encompassing so diverse a range of subject matter, and in which history teachers differ in their conceptions of the subject, there is little likelihood of consensus about which periods, themes or types of history are essential in an undergraduate history programme. However, historians are generally agreed (albeit for different reasons) upon the need for students to explore societies beyond their own, and there has been notable growth since the 1960s in courses extending beyond Western Europe and North America, to include the study of the history of sub-groups and of interdisciplinary approaches (see Harrison 1968; Frank *et al.* 1994). The principle of breadth is enshrined in the benchmark statement for the study of the subject in

UK higher education, which requires students to study history 'over an extended period of past time' and in 'more than one society or culture' (History Benchmarking Group 2000: 4). How 'extended' this period should be, however, is a matter of less agreement, particularly as student interest is at present heavily concentrated in the twentieth century and modular programmes are founded upon the principle of student choice.

The issue of coverage is closely connected with that of coherence. In 1997 this was highlighted in press coverage of the 'revelation' that history undergraduates at Oxford University no longer had to cover the whole range of English history from medieval to modern, but rather could choose which periods to study. Whilst this may have been no surprise to the majority of history departments, which had long abandoned any pretence to such comprehensive coverage, it generated considerable breast-beating in the press over the possible 'ignorance' of history graduates about key events in their country's history. This, of course, reflects a popular notion of the historian as expert on the past – the whole of the past. What particularly concerned historians, however, was that, in the words of one Fellow in Modern History at Oxford, the history curriculum had become 'a kind of self-service restaurant [. . .] the result is incoherence and confusion'. As another put it, 'any history syllabus is a matter of choices. The point is it has to be coherent' (Clare 1998). The issue of coherence is particularly pressing in modular degree schemes and is most commonly resolved by the insertion of compulsory elements to ensure breadth of chronological and geographical coverage and the study of core concepts. However, if unrestricted choice is permitted, students need more than ever to understand the key principles and outcomes of each course and how these fit into the overall degree programme, so that they can create a coherent pathway in terms of the essential skills and qualities to be developed. This, in turn, requires greater support and guidance from teachers in relation to course choices. Whilst this can be time-consuming (although advice can be made available online and through peer support groups), dialogue about coverage and coherence can create a strong sense of ownership of a course, stimulate interest and motivation, and enhance critical reflection.

If the issue of essential content is contentious, so too is that of the relationship between knowledge acquisition and skills, which on individual courses within a degree programme arises perhaps most prominently in relation to large survey courses (see Kornblith and Lasser 2001). Whilst for some teachers a course context that emphasizes the acquisition of a substantial amount of knowledge about past societies and peoples is a priority, for others more importance is accorded to the development of transferable skills (see Brecher and Hickey 1990). In practice, of course, skills and content are intimately related: skills are required to acquire knowledge and translate information into understanding, and are always applied in relation to content. Jordanova (2000) expresses this well in a discussion of historians' skills. She notes that whilst it is important to be clear about the types of skills that the study of history develops,

> it is unhelpful to draw too firm a distinction between skills and the matter to which they are applied. Historians' skills are refined through use, that is, through their application to concrete historical problems. In this way a fund of knowledge is built up, and it is meaningless to divide it into techniques and substance, since the two are blended through constant interaction [...] I am arguing against a polarity between skills and substance because I see these two aspects of the historian's craft developing together in mutual dependency. Skills need applying to something, and that something, which has a number of facets, helps in refining skills.
>
> (Jordanova 2000: 173)

Structuring courses in ways that allow skills to be learned explicitly through application to a variety of historical issues and situations, is an integral part of developing complex learning in the subject.

In relation to the contentious issues of content, coherence and skills in course design, three key points need to be made. First, there is no universal template that can be applied to every situation. Rather, decisions made will ultimately be determined by the particular characteristics of the students, teachers' conceptions of the aims and purposes of a history education and the available resources (including staff availability). Second, however great the amount of material covered in the syllabus, experience suggests that most students will not attempt to learn more than the small percentage of it necessary to fulfil the assessment requirements. An insistence on coverage of every aspect of a particular period is therefore not the most productive use of time. What is required is clarity about the knowledge and skills that are regarded as essential for students to learn (and are thus worth ensuring that they concentrate on in the time available), and awareness of how they acquire content knowledge. Students can be referred to where to find additional material or given handouts outlining knowledge in less central aspects of a course. Third, it is the quality of student engagement with the material, and not coverage per se, that makes for greater sophistication of learning. Indeed, an emphasis upon coverage often leads students to skate across the surface of the material in their efforts to keep up or acquire 'the knowledge'. This is a particular danger for first-year survey courses that attempt to cover many centuries and countries and mistake coverage for learning. As Calder (2002: 43–4) remarks, 'when history is covered, something important gets covered up', and his model of 'uncoverage' offers 'a deliberate attempt to lay bare for students the central assumptions, forms of enquiry, and cognitive habits that transform data into knowledge for practitioners of our discipline'. Thus whilst Jordanova (2000: 195) correctly points to the considerable advantages of exposing students to 'a variety of historical fare', including world history and different periods and types of history, it is nonetheless possible to achieve high-quality learning in a syllabus focused upon a single century. This does, however, demand the creation of a learning environment that supports an approach enabling students to investigate topics in depth within a comparative and longer chronological perspective.

In any history course a clear and transparent structure is vital if students are to negotiate their course in a coherent fashion, not least because course structures tend to be inherently more open and loose than in the sciences, with students 'returning with increasing levels of subtlety and insight to already familiar areas of content' (Neumann *et al.* (2002: 407)). There are many ways of achieving this clarity, and some examples of these are outlined for history in Hitchcock *et al.* (2000), and more generically in Rowntree (1981), Baume and Baume (1992) and Toohey (1999). History courses, however, commonly conform to three basic types of structure based upon:

The logic of the subject matter Traditionally in history degree programmes this has been chronological. In programme terms, this is often characterized by a progression from a broad sweep of European or world history in year one to the in-depth study of a short period in the Special Subject in the final year. This is only one type of arrangement and chronology is often interwoven with geographical and thematic elements, for example from nation-based study in year one to comparative history in the final year. It is also extremely common to cover a period in a chronological fashion. Thus, for example, European twentieth-century history courses routinely proceed in sections: from 1870 to World War One, the interwar period, and post-World War Two to the present.

Cognitive structures Here the central organizing concept is the development of key disciplinary concepts and intellectual abilities; for example, critical reading, historical analysis, interpretation of primary sources and reflexivity. Students might encounter increasingly sophisticated cognitive tasks, for example progressing from an initial emphasis upon the acquisition of knowledge in year one, to the ability to grasp existing historiography, to the development of independent interpretation, or, more generally, from critical reading of secondary sources to the ability to use primary sources critically and imaginatively. On individual courses, it is similarly common to see progression from ensuring a grasp of fundamental concepts to their application on specific topics and from simple to more complex concepts.

Generic skills and abilities   This is becoming a more common means of structuring in modularized, multi-pathway degree programmes as a means of providing a coherent pedagogic rationale. Progression here might be in terms of the types of skills developed and the ways these are evaluated. Thus a programme might progress from developing basic study skills in the first year to enhancing more sophisticated self-reflective skills, or from emphasizing ability in written presentation to oral modes of communication, or from individual to group-based tasks and assignments, or, in many history programmes, from tutor-led activity to more independent modes of learning, such as a dissertation, at advanced levels of study.

Each approach has advantages and disadvantages. Subject-based structures encourage immersion in the discipline, and are in alignment with many history students' rationale for studying the subject. They can, however, appear too inward looking given that most history graduates will not become professional historians. Cognitive-based structures encourage rigour in thinking, emphasize the intellectual nature of a history education, and can provide a clear conceptual or theoretical framework on which to hang key information. However, in history, the paucity of systematic research on the meaning of such core concepts as critical thinking or analysis as they relate to pedagogy impairs their translation into practice. The skills or competency model casts light upon areas which tended to be overlooked in the traditional history curriculum, emphasizes the relevance of a history degree to students' future lives, and makes it easier to articulate progression in terms of learning in modular programmes involving several disciplines. It can, however, erode the disciplinary base to a point where concern might be raised about whether students are really studying history or something quite different. Typically, most history programmes today therefore contain elements of all three approaches, as Cowan (1996) demonstrates in an account of the design of a history degree. Here broad chronological coverage was planned alongside an explicit skills strand, which focused upon historical and intellectual skills (notably historiography and interpretation using secondary and primary sources) but also the development of generic skills such as IT literacy. This can work effectively because, as is suggested in Chapter 7, skills are best developed through subject-focused study and developing understanding involves the necessary interaction of subject knowledge and intellectual and practical skills. What must be ensured, however, is the clear articulation of how the course is organized to deliver each of these elements, and how progress in understanding is demonstrated.

Conclusion

How the elements comprising a history course or curriculum are configured will in practice depend upon a range of factors, not least student characteristics, departmental size and traditions, resources and institutional regulations. However, allowing sufficient time to create a course context in which deep, active learning can flourish is vital to both departments and individual teachers. This demands attentiveness to a wide range of variables in the learning environment, and their alignment in ways that ensure that the curriculum experienced by students accurately reflects that described in course documents. The clear expression of expectations and requirements is a particular necessity, as is open and constructive dialogue with students. By these means a climate can be created in which students feel safe to explore complex ideas critically and imaginatively, and practice skills without undue anxiety. Dialogue with students is valuable not only at the beginning or end of a course, but also as part of an iterative process in which planning and operation interact dynamically throughout its life as experience results in fine tuning of content or restructuring of material. Creating a context for high-quality learning is an ongoing process, and whilst teachers have ultimate responsibility for the manner in which they run a course, a learner-centred focus lies at the heart of the design process.

There is no universal template that can be applied to ensure progress in students' understanding, but there is much evidence that students learn best in environments containing the characteristics represented in the acronym 'responsive'. Such learning contexts are *relevant* (aligned with students' experiences and interests); *enjoyable* (recognize the importance of an engaging and positive atmosphere); *safe* (support the open dialogue and trust necessary for the testing and sharing of ideas); *participatory* (encourage all students to be actively engaged); *outcome-oriented* (clearly specify objectives in terms of intended learning outcomes); *needs-focused* (work from students' existing knowledge and prior experiences); *structured* (with goals, teaching methods and assignments carefully sequenced and aligned); display *interest* (in students' learning and progression to complex forms of understanding); *varied* (offer a variety of tasks and assignments); and have high *expectations* of students. Equally importantly, there are some things to avoid. As Gibbs (1992d: 154) observes, 'the features of courses which are most likely to be found where students tend to take a surface approach [to learning] are a heavy workload, relatively high class-contact hours, an excessive amount of course material, a lack of opportunity to pursue subjects in depth, a lack of choice over subjects and a lack of choice over the method of study, and a threatening and anxiety provoking assessment system'. This reminds us that coverage, however important, is not synonymous with understanding. It also underlines the importance of the classroom context in the overall learning environment, and this is addressed in the following three chapters.

6

STRATEGIES FOR ACTIVE LEARNING IN THE HISTORY CLASSROOM

Good practice encourages active learning. Students do not learn just by sitting in classes listening to teachers, memorizing pre-packaged assignments and spitting out answers. They must talk about what they are learning, write about it, relate it to past experiences, apply it to their daily lives. They must make what they learn part of themselves.

(Chickering and Reisser 1993)

What happens in class provides students with their most direct insight into what is really valued as opposed to what is declared to be important. Classroom climate and assignments are key components in the complex of factors that make up motivation (Brown *et al.* 1998); and enthusing students to engage deeply with historical sources, questions and problems is a priority. This has been at the core of educational initiatives to promote active learning (Bonwell and Eison 1991; Denicolo *et al.* 1992; Meyers and Jones 1993). Active learning emphasizes the importance of academic and personal engagement with the subject, of 'doing' history and applying the wide range of skills involved to address historical problems rather than receiving information and ideas from the teacher and attempting to reproduce it. Students are therefore encouraged to adopt a proactive approach to their studies in which participation, critical reflection (on subject matter and the process of learning) and progressively greater responsibility constitute balanced elements in an integrated learning and teaching strategy. In the practice of classroom teaching, particular attention is directed to collaborative activities. This is not to deny the importance of the relationship between student and text, but to underline that dialogue (with peers and teachers) helps to break down isolation in learning and permits multiple voices and perspectives to be heard and compared.

Active learning facilitates both academic understanding and personal growth. It provides a means by which teachers can foster a wide range of life-skills among increasingly diverse students, whilst maintaining a focus upon historical thinking and understanding. It reflects historians' traditional justifications of the value of seminar teaching and project work. Unfortunately, discussion about active learning has become entangled in sterile arguments over the value of 'traditional' and 'innovative' methods of history teaching (see Gillespie 1999). Concerns have been expressed that such methods require historians to teach things, such as collaborative skills, for which they are unqualified, promote a focus upon process at the expense of content, dilute the important role of the teacher, and erode the status of lectures. However, as was pointed out in Chapter 1, active learning is not inherently inimical to coverage, though the emphasis is certainly more upon depth of learning. Moreover, whilst the teacher's role is viewed in terms of facilitating learning rather than delivering knowledge, this does not mean that no support is offered to students in developing their conceptions of the subject. Rather, the focus upon learning requires teachers to think carefully through what kind of intervention is required as students progress in conceptual understanding and skills. Nor do history teachers need to teach group skills, so much as be aware of what is required to foster them and create conditions in which they can flourish. Finally, active learning methods are not incompatible with traditional forms of instruction such as lectures. As Frederick (1999a, 2001a) and Blackey (1997) demonstrate, opportunities for interaction and close engagement with historical themes and issues can be created in the most unpromising tiered lecture rooms. What is questioned is the conception of the lecture as a one-way transmission of information, which many studies have shown to be an ineffective means of developing the skills associated with complex learning (for reviews, see Brown and Atkins 1990; Bligh 1998).

Whilst all modes of teaching, whether traditional or innovative, can benefit from active learning strategies, the success of such methods depends upon the way in which they are introduced and implemented in particular contexts with specific groups of students. Effective learning is no more an automatic consequence of using an 'interactive' CD-ROM, or participating in small group discussion, than is the development of listening skills from simply attending a traditional lecture. Student perspectives on which factors promote participation, and which prevent it, provide a good starting point for reflection. Whilst the former were considered in Chapter 3, here it may be helpful to list some of the reasons most frequently mentioned by history undergraduates for adopting a passive role in class.

Figure 6.1 Factors in non-participation: student perspectives

- Lack of interest or enthusiasm on the part of the teacher.
- Teacher domination: talks too much, fails to listen to student views or only accepts views that confirm his or her own interpretation.
- A climate of interrogation: the teacher picks on individuals or demands instant solutions to complex questions.
- Lack of clarity: questions asked are too numerous, vague or confusing, or it is not made clear what is expected or what sort of contributions are valued.
- Lack of focus: the class wanders off the question or the teacher fails to build on student contributions.
- Tasks that discourage class participation; for example, the reading of class papers.
- Student inexperience and lack of confidence in academic modes of discourse; for example, not knowing how and when to contribute to discussion.
- Fear of embarrassment: anxieties about appearing unintelligent in front of the teacher or other students.
- Fear of not knowing enough or that one's ideas are not well-enough formulated, whether a reality or due to a lack of clarity about the preparation required.
- Lack of value placed upon group discussion in formal assessment procedures.
- Group size: the larger the group, the less safe it may feel to contribute and the easier it becomes to adopt a passive role.
- Use of physical space: the teacher takes up position at one end of a table as the authoritative figure and becomes the focal point of class responses.
- Cultural factors: age, class, gender or ethnicity make students feel they do not belong.

The consequent perception of the history classroom as a dangerous and hostile environment leads to a pedagogic culture of silence or non-co-operation. As one history teacher reflects about her first experiences teaching history seminars: 'In general I found a real problem in ensuring that everyone contributed and there were no awkward silences ... I couldn't help comparing the stilted and stunted progress of a seminar with the type of debate and conversation one has in everyday life. It was such an artificial atmosphere – with heavy overtones of the schoolroom – that I wasn't all that surprised that people had so little to say' (Games 1996: 53). What then can be done to ensure that students participate actively? How can the subject be brought to life, and students encouraged to imagine it beyond a set of facts or memorized views to be learned for an examination? What follows are some practical strategies. Whilst they are not always specific to history, for history possesses no monopoly on good ideas, to be successful they must form part of a systematic approach to teaching in which course goals, content, teaching and assessment practices are carefully aligned, and be used flexibly in accordance with the student experience and disciplinary practices described in earlier chapters. They must also reflect a teacher's personality and love of the subject, for, as Palmer (1998: 10) astutely remarks, ultimately 'good teaching cannot be reduced to technique; good teaching comes from the identity and integrity of the teacher'.

The first class

The first class on any course sets the tone for the whole programme. It conveys to students messages, both implicit and explicit, about what teaching and learning in this subject will be like and what are their own and tutors' roles and responsibilities. How this session is conducted will influence whether students decide to stay or withdraw from the course, and, more particularly, condition the degree of cohesion and motivation of the whole class. Some students may be anxious about how they will cope; others will be more relaxed, perhaps being familiar with the teacher or more confident about their prior knowledge. Some will be looking for confirmation that they have made the correct choice of course, while those for whom this is a compulsory class or second-choice option may be feeling resentful. The creation of a safe climate for discussion and a collective sense of ownership is therefore vital. Indeed as Gonzalez (2001: 176) notes in an account of a second-year history project class, 'without a sense of ownership there can be no critical understanding; it comes only with a perception of the learner as a subject, not an object of learning. These are small beginnings – but in that first hour [of the introductory class], the initiative for learning, the impetus, had to come from the students. The moment that they inaugurate the process, they become its subjects not its objects.'

Clarifying expectations and requirements

It is important to explain clearly why the goals and tasks decided upon are important and what is expected of students, for at this stage students are often anxious about the demands of the course and what they will have to do to succeed. Beginning with basics (what one means by lectures and seminars) and key concepts (what historical analysis means on this course), and inviting students' views and experiences, involves them from the outset and minimises misconceptions. Hill (1996: 49–50), recounting her initial experiences of history seminar teaching, comments:

> telling the [students] clearly what you need them to do, and why, is important. A seminar is supposed to be a collaborative exercise. When starting with a new first-year group for the second time . . . I asked them what they thought a seminar was, what it was for, and how they could contribute to and gain from it. Their ideas were very similar to mine – that they could learn from each other, express their own ideas, and so forth. And I think that this, for a while at any rate, effectively implicated them directly in responsibility for their own seminars.

Such dialogue can also be an effective means of introducing the notion of active learning as well as key historical concepts to students in the context of their own discipline.

Arranging classroom space to encourage participation

How teaching rooms are arranged says a great deal to students about the sort of interaction expected. As Meyers and Jones (1993: 50) remark: 'When all students see of their classmates is the back of their heads, and all eyes are directed to the teacher at the front of the room, a not-too-subtle message is delivered as to what is really important. No matter what we *say* about wanting students to be more responsible for their learning, the physical and psychological environment of a classroom speaks with more authority.' Creating conditions for interaction is imperative. In large, fixed-seat lecture theatres students can be grouped at the front or in a part of the room if numbers are small. However, in a large lecture class it is most effective for students to work in pairs along the row, or with another pair in the row behind, to discuss issues and report back to the whole class. In seminar rooms, if furniture is movable, a U-shaped arrangement of chairs works well for classes of up to thirty students (and for student presentations), leaving room at the front for a flip chart, overhead projector or other facilities and allowing students to move their seats to discuss particular issues. A circle of chairs is also inclusive, providing the opportunity for a balanced exchange of views between members of a seminar class, and allowing the focus to shift with the discussion rather than being permanently upon the teacher. The circle can also be broken into smaller circles for sub-group discussion.

Making introductions and learning names

Students beginning a course are often unacquainted, and in modular degree programmes teachers may be unfamiliar with more than a few individuals. It is therefore useful to ask students individually to say a few things about themselves to the class. This can include what they hope to get out of the course, or one thing that looks interesting and they are looking forward to finding out more about. In culturally diverse classes they can be asked to describe how they would define themselves, with the teacher modelling this process. Introductions can also be effected by online posting, where simple questions such as 'Who are you?' and 'Why are you on the course?' can enable students to connect with each other and provide feedback on students' backgrounds, level of experience and expectations. In a seminar group, members can 'interview' the person sitting next to them for a couple of minutes and introduce them to the group. Or, still less threatening, each person can introduce themselves to two or three others (Preston 1996). A variant on this is to provide a list of statements that might apply to anyone in the group, for example all those who prefer modern, early modern or medieval history, or political, social or economic aspects of history. Members of the group circulate, find those who fit the description and introduce themselves. My own preference is for simple, short icebreakers related directly to the course and to historical study but there are many more adventurous possibilities (Malseed 1992; Jones 1994).

Treating students as individuals makes for a sense of belonging on a course, but remembering names is a problem routinely expressed by university history teachers. Learning a few names per week is a good discipline. Drawing a plan of where students are sitting for the first few classes (and putting this on a flip chart for all to see) can help, as can place cards (which are more visible at a distance than name labels or badges). Repeating students' names at the end of the first couple of seminars is also helpful, though best attempted in a light-hearted manner, as mistakes will inevitably be made. Asking students to do this saves embarrassment, or they can be asked to state their name whenever they make a contribution in the first few seminars. Departmental passport photographs of each cohort of students can also provide an aide memoire, and a copy can be posted on a student notice board for more general use. Finally, it is important that teachers introduce themselves, which is a good opportunity to convey one's research and teaching interests, philosophy of teaching and enthusiasm for the subject to be taught.

Negotiating ground rules

This is a simple but powerful means of clarifying expectations, establishing mutual responsibilities and emphasizing student ownership of class activity. Ground rules also allow students to become acquainted with each other, and help to identify needs, expectations and conceptions of learning. Frederick (2000: 6–7) describes the guidelines for students on his African-American history course as follows: 'Although we will not all agree about our interpretations of the African-American experience, we agree that the only "political correctness" appropriate to this course is the search for truth and the commitment to encounter and engage the course goals, the texts, and each other with openness, honesty and mutual respect.' He notes that simply holding this up and pointing at it can bring order to overheated discussion of a contentious issue. A well-tested exercise for establishing ground rules is to ask students to think about the principles for an effective history class. In groups of five they spend ten minutes generating lists, using their experience of the best history class they have had or the worst (more fun). Discussion as a whole group results in a composite list (six or seven ground rules are sufficient, any more can be difficult to remember and enforce), which can be e-mailed to all group members or posted on the course website. Ground rules devised by history students invariably include most of the following: everybody does some preparation; everyone participates; discussion is to the point; nobody dominates (including the tutor); a variety of views are aired; all views are listened to and respected; a relaxed atmosphere is maintained. In online classes a ground rule pointing to the need for early posting of questions or replies is important. The exercise can be taken further by asking students to think of three things that will ensure that rules are adhered to. It can also be helpful to agree one's own commitments (availability, role as tutor etc.) to reinforce the fact that this is a two-way contract. Ground rules can be revisited and renegotiated mid-semester, and this also provides an opportunity for reflection on the progress of the course.

Letters to successors

Information provided by a previous cohort of students can help a new class to focus upon key themes and issues. At the end of a course, students are asked to compose a letter that will be sent to subsequent students encapsulating insights and experiences. This addresses such issues as the most important things one can do to be successful in this class, things I wish I'd known at the start of the course, the most common mistakes I/we made in this class, or whatever seems important for a student to know. These can be posted on a course website and/or extracts produced for incoming students to work on in small groups and look for common themes. This can lead into a ground rules task or whole-class discussion on course requirements. A shortened version of this exercise is Brookfield's (1995) 'survival keynote'. Students completing a course are asked to compose a five-minute introductory talk by a previous student on how to survive the course. They work in small groups without the teacher present to identify recurrent themes, and report back to a plenary session. The insights generated are then used with new students to explore feelings about the course and the topic as a whole.

Brainstorming

Brainstorming can be employed at any point in a course to stimulate creative thinking, but it is has a particular role to play at the beginning of a course or topic (De Bono 1986). It can reassure students that they bring more to a course than they think and raise to the surface attitudes and feelings about a period or historical event as well as factual knowledge, enabling the teacher to identify misconceptions early. In brainstorming sessions students are asked to call out everything they know about the course, for example 'Europe 1750–1850' or 'World War One', and each contribution is recorded on a board, flip chart or overhead. The only rules of brainstorming are that all ideas and views are welcomed and recorded without critical comment, and that contributors try to build on each other's ideas. If time is available, students can then be asked to link the words into themes or patterns. The procedure works well when used with a spider diagram or topic web, with the general theme or period written in a circle in the middle and ideas from the group radiating from it. If time is short the teacher can group the words as students call them out, or ask where each word should be placed on the growing diagram. Mind maps are a similar, if slightly more elaborate, aid to creative thinking in brainstorming sessions (see Buzan 1995). Walk-around brainstorming is also a common technique for generating ideas and allowing students to get to know each other, as well as introducing some physical movement into a class. Key questions/issues are posted on walls, and students have five to ten minutes to walk round and jot their ideas down on each topic. They then form small groups and each group is given one of the items to discuss. The groups then report back the two or three best ideas.

The first encounter with a new class provides the best opportunity for persuading students that this course is going to be an interesting and worthwhile experience. Employing such strategies can begin to create the positive sense of ownership and community, and thus safety, necessary for critical discussion. As one of my own students commented during a ground rules exercise: 'In a good history seminar you feel part of the group and are more likely to talk. If you feel threatened you just keep quiet, and after a while you get bored.'

Promoting active learning

A wealth of generic techniques can be employed to facilitate active learning (see, for example, Bligh 1986; Brown and Atkins 1990; Gibbs and Habeshaw 1990; Gibbs 1992c; McKeachie 1994; Jaques 1991; Race and Brown 1993; Davis 1993; Brookfield 1999). In a number of articles Frederick (1981, 1986, 1995, 1999a, b, 2000, 2001a, b) has described a range of practical strategies for developing active learning in history classes. What follows draws upon these and the efforts of historians in several countries to help students to connect critically and imaginatively with historical themes and issues, and make their thinking visible in ways that encourage discussion and reflection.

Prepared questions

Students can be provided with guidelines about what to look for in their reading (for example, key points made by the author, authorial position, strengths and weaknesses), and this can be used to structure an agenda at the beginning of a discussion class. Wilson (1980) describes how he combined prior reading with topic mapping in an economic and social history class, asking students to read something relevant and be prepared to say a few words about it. This was used to construct a topic web on the overhead or board with the discussion at the centre. Around this topic headings were written in, and discussion followed on whether an item constituted a new topic or a sub-heading of an existing one. This established an agenda for the session, and the process can be refined further to decide the order in which issues are discussed and the time to be allocated to each. During discussion it is possible to add other issues to the topic web and, if time runs out, provide supplementary reading. Davis (1993) similarly suggests asking students to bring one key question to class and explain why it should be discussed, followed by choosing one of these to begin discussion. This can be achieved by online posting by students, or alternatively questions can be posted by the teacher and students asked to submit responses which provide the jumping off point for class discussion. Questions can also be used at the start of interactive lectures. Students write a sentence or two in quick response, followed by work in pairs then groups of four, and record their views, including disagreements, on posters or Post-its put up on the wall. These form the basis for whole-class discussion and summary by the lecturer. They might then be asked to read a handout of the argument from a key text on the subject. Linking these questions to the essay list can help to ensure maximum involvement.

Truth statements

One way to introduce a topic or obtain feedback on student understanding of an issue is to ask students to generate statements (alone or collaboratively) that they believe to be true about an issue. 'It is true about the Vietnam War that . . .'; 'It is true about the role of women in twentieth-century century Britain that . . .'; 'We know it to be true about the early Middle Ages that . . .', and so on. These can be listed on the board and discussed by the whole class, with some students presenting them and the rest raising questions. Frederick (1999a) notes that this technique is particularly effective for exploring historical issues with a strong ethical and emotional dimension, such as class, race and gender. Alternatively, truth statements can be employed to encourage students to state their position on a topic via a 'line-up' (see Gibbs 1992c). Here students are asked to stand at a position in the line that represents their view on a particular statement, for example 'Postmodernism has greatly enhanced the practice of history' – 'Postmodernism has been a pernicious influence on historical practice'. Students talk to each other about their view and identify whether they are in the right place, and this frequently leads to lively discussion. The exercise can be further refined by introducing more subtle variables or used to decide team membership for a subsequent debate.

Debates

Many undergraduates enjoy debating historical issues. Debate can energize students and enable them to think more critically and reflectively about evidence. Whilst sensitivity to those students who dislike confrontational modes of learning needs to be maintained, and there are particular issues related to gender and ethnic background, debate is a powerful means of enhancing understanding and self-confidence. Students are asked to prepare in teams for a seminar debate and told that each side will have to explain their five key points, followed by questioning from the other side. A jury is composed of those students who do not wish, for whatever reason, to be on either side. Debates can be conducted in large lectures as well as seminars, and many historical topics ('Was Burke more accurate than Paine in his analysis of the French Revolution?', 'Was Chartism doomed to fail?', and so on) lend themselves naturally to a debate format. By using the central aisle in a lecture theatre to divide the sides, students can be allocated to opposing camps, each of which is asked to make three or more key points. If space is available, those who refuse to take a position can be placed in the centre and all three groups asked to make their case. As Frederick puts it: 'Students in the middle . . . might learn how difficult it is to try to remain neutral on heated emotional issues; those on the fringes might learn how complex truth is' (1999a: 58). If time is short, a hands–up vote allows everyone to contribute and provides a convenient means of bringing discussion to an end. A debriefing session allows students to reflect on where they felt they were on strong, and weak, ground, and provides an opportunity for teachers to contribute their understanding in a way that offers some confirmation of the complexities of the topic without imposing a 'correct' answer.

Sub-groups

Most students feel more secure sharing their knowledge and ideas in small peer groups. As one student on an oral history course comments: 'One very strange thing which I hope will change is that a few class-mates hardly say anything publicly, and yet when we work in small groups they're full of ideas, imaginative and articulate' (Thomson 1998: 80). Groups of three to five students can be profitably employed at the beginning of a class to create an agenda, generate new ideas or simply add variety to proceedings. It is particularly important that tasks are achievable in the time available, and that students are instructed to feed back their ideas concisely (their two or three key points) to the whole class. Other techniques using sub-groups include 'pyramids' and 'crossovers'. In pyramiding, students work alone on an issue for five minutes to collect their thoughts together. They then work in pairs for five to ten minutes to share ideas. Two pairs share findings for about ten minutes, and finally report to a plenary session. It is important that there is progression in tasks so that momentum and interest are maintained. Crossover groups allow students to discuss in small groups, then transfer between groups so that they can work with different people on the various tasks. The key to all forms of sub-group activity is clarity of tasks. Specific questions tend to work best, for example: 'What are the strengths and weaknesses of Thompson's interpretation of eighteenth-century Methodism?', 'What were the most important factors preventing women from obtaining the vote in the nineteenth century?' Experience suggests that ten to fifteen minutes is sufficient as a single activity in a one-hour seminar, though additional time needs to be allocated for feedback and discussion.

Case studies, simulations and role play

Case studies and simulations offer in-depth study of a particular situation, real or imaginary, and are often combined with role play, which contributes a kinaesthetic dimension to learning (Van Mentz 1983, 1992; Ellington *et al.* 1982). They add colour, encourage the development of oral and interpersonal skills, and foster appreciation of the complex nature of situations and human experiences in the past. Role play in particular gives students the opportunity to feel what it is like to have to make real decisions in a specific historical context, and it can be easier for students to play with ideas whilst acting out a role than to put forward their 'own' view. Role reversal, encouraging students to confront an issue from a different perspective from the one they normally adopt, is also effective in this respect. Computer simulations can be a stimulating interactive means of enabling students to use their historical knowledge to address problems, and there are now many available.

Such activities are often accompanied by detailed instructions and briefings, and if sufficient time is available students can undoubtedly analyse a topic in great depth. Role play can also be sequenced over a whole course to introduce students gradually to what can feel to some a risky venture (see Dawson 1990). My own preference is for simple exercises that can be used as one of several strategies in a single class. A short lecture can be used to set the scene, followed by dividing the class into several interest groups, each with a clear task. Many scenarios are possible. Frederick (1999a: 59) gives as an example a New England town in 1779 'in which a variety of groups (landed elite, yeoman farmers, Tory loyalists, militiamen and Continental Army soldiers, riff–raff, lawyers, ministers and tradesmen) are charged with drafting instructions for delegates to a state constitutional convention'. McKeachie (1994: 171) reports a simulation in a survey course on Russian history around elections in 1917. Students acted as parties and constituency groups, forming alliances, sending delegates and so on, and an election was held. Kornfeld (1993) based a combined role play and debate on a discussion of the proposed United States Constitution in a Philadelphia tavern in 1787. He explicitly located it towards the end of a course, in the belief that at this point students would have a good degree of knowledge and would be able to evaluate the different positions more skilfully. Royal commissions, advisers to a leader, rival groups in a movement or competing interest groups are all common scenarios, or students might be asked to adopt the persona of historians of different schools at a conference on a contentious topic, which places additional emphasis upon historiography. History affords almost limitless possibilities. In such activities the process needs to be monitored carefully, for conflicting groups can sometimes become over-heated in debate and digress from the issue (though this does offer practical insights into the decision-making process faced by individuals and groups in the past).

Visuals

Many of today's history students have a visual orientation to learning. Cartoons, posters, photographs, paintings and video clips engage students quickly and directly and work on several levels of meaning. Whilst there are issues in using visual evidence to teach history (see Ramsden 1996; Mattheisen 1993; Burke 2001), studying prints such as Hogarth's 'Marriage à la Mode' and 'Gin Lane' can provide an excellent means of exploring key themes in a particular society. Frederick (1999a) suggests a simple process for teaching students to 'read' visual sources. He first asks students to describe what they see, and only then to analyse what it means. This gradual approach allows students to begin with facts and then proceed to feelings and interpretation. Discussion can be moved on to consider alternative sources of information on the topic, and the issue of how historians can interpret visual sources and how this differs from analysing written evidence. Students can also work in groups to create their own visual metaphors (for example, an image or logo to represent the ideas of Carr or Elton on the nature of history, the appeal of the Nazis to a particular social group or a key concept such as democracy), and report back to the whole class (see Davies 2000). Any topic can be expressed visually, and such images often evoke emotional as well as intellectual responses, especially when used in conjunction with music. Frederick (1999a: 61) observes: 'Imagine, for example, viewing brutal images of slavery while listening to the uplifting hope and thanksgiving of spirituals and gospel, which creates a dissonance between models of victimization and cultural affirmation in understanding black history.' Students can be asked to write down images and feelings invoked by a speech or piece of music and share these in pairs or small groups, finally reporting to the whole class on findings and questions raised and relating these to issues of objectivity and interpretation (Davison 1993). Roach and Gunn (2002) also note the value of combining visual and kinaesthetic aspects of learning to help the understanding of concepts in a seminar exercise in which groups of students built a representation of a medieval town, following instruction on key factors in town formation.

Stories and autobiographies

Stories enable students to connect themselves to their subject in affective, imaginative and reflective ways (McDrury and Alterio 2001). They enable the teaching process, in the words of Palmer (1998: 74), to 'honour the "little" stories of the students and the "big" stories of the disciplines and tradition', and link the two together. This is a particular feature of Frederick's approach to active learning in history (1999a, b, 2001a, b). 'Critical incidents' in students' own lives are used as a place to begin a course or topic. For example, students on a course on African–American history are asked to tell a story about a recent event in their lives where race mattered. All will have an experience of this, and they write first, then exchange stories in groups of three or four, and finally share 'themes, issues and patterns' with the whole group. These are discussed, and lead to work on a primary source which links their themes directly to the past. In effect, students' critical incidents act as a case study for further discussion. So, too, on topics such as the American Revolution, radical politics, social protest and female emancipation students can begin by describing a struggle with an authority figure in their own lives, and proceed in the same way to primary sources and subsequently secondary accounts. This use of personal critical incidents can also be employed in developing thinking in oral history or indeed historical skills generally (see Thompson 2000; Thomson 1998). Here, autobiographical exercises (alone or in pairs) are frequently used devices to encourage students to reflect on self as a means of connecting to history and how it is made. Sharing with others what they decided to include and exclude, and why, leads to discussion of the relationship between history, memory and identity and the nature of historical analysis. The power of stories can also be used in lecture narratives. Students are given a break and asked at a key point: 'What do you think happens next?' This can lead to brainstorming, followed by discussion or another period of lecturing. It works best when an unfinished human story is the focus, such as that of a poor, female migrant to an early modern town ('What will happen to her next?'), or a wealthy businessman attempting to buy his way into the nineteenth-century elite by purchasing a landed estate. This might be linked to personal accounts or, later, the use of autobiographies (Hoberman 1999), or students can write each other's 'biography' (Frederick 1999a).

Counterfactuals

Counterfactuals provide a means of developing understanding through analogical thinking. Questions such as 'What if Charles I had avoided the English Civil War?', 'What if Germany had invaded Britain in May 1940?' and 'What if there had been no Gorbachev?', all plausible scenarios, have received increasingly serious attention from academic historians (Ferguson 1998). Whilst counterfactual exercises have to be handled carefully if they are to avoid becoming little more than uninformed speculation, they offer the opportunity to think imaginatively about the past, consider how situations might have appeared to contemporaries and review a topic from a different perspective. They also connect students more forcefully to the essential uncertainty of events in the past, alert them to the ways in which history is constructed by historians, and encourage consideration of the multiple connections between causal factors that are integral to historical understanding. As Ferguson points out, we ask 'what if' questions routinely in our lives, and by encouraging us to weigh up possibilities such questions help to sharpen both critical and creative skills.

Storyboards

Storyboards help students to generate ideas on a topic and plan responses. Six boxes are drawn on a flip chart and students are asked in groups to work out their approach to the topic, sequencing the aspects to be covered in order in the boxes. These can be used to create an overall agenda for the class. Alternatively, Davis (1993) suggests dividing a topic into three to five sub-topics or questions written on flip-chart sheets distributed around the room. Students are allocated to each issue or question, write ideas and solutions on Post-its, one idea per note, and attach these to the chart. After ten minutes the groups move on to the next chart and post notes there, until all groups have visited all the charts. The Post-its on each of the charts (or one or two depending on the time available) are then discussed and refined. This works well on many historical topics, including historiography, where students can be asked to list the strengths and weaknesses of authors' arguments, outline key themes and record their feelings about each view, and how far it corresponds with their own experience of studying history.

Games, puzzles and competitions

Whilst these have mostly been the preserve of schools history, they can assist the development of a wide range of analytical, personal and interpersonal skills, and build confidence on topics that are regarded as difficult and therefore intimidating. Davies (2000) records a technique for teaching numerical data to history undergraduates. After an introduction by the teacher on party electorates in the twentieth century, students in small groups are given an incomplete table of numerical data related to the 1992 British general election. Each group has to identify the missing figures and blanked out axes, and some 'bogus' figures, and feeds back to the whole class. The teacher reveals the answers and there is further large group discussion about the process. In this example, the competition between groups increased motivation, and although some students disliked the competitive element, it does usefully underline that collaborative learning and competition are not mutually exclusive. Students also noted that discussion and collaboration helped them to overcome their fear of statistics. There are many possible games (see Ellington *et al*. 1982), and adapting those found on television or video can work well with students. One history teacher, for example, devised a historical *Blind Date* in order to illuminate issues of choice of partner, love, sex and death in seventeenth-century England. Another used a version of 'Trivial Pursuit' to help students of twentieth-century Japan to become familiar with the background history and the geography of a country unfamiliar to most. Online quizzes have also become increasingly popular as a means of reinforcing factual knowledge, and, more traditionally, map quizzes are an established means of discovering what students know about a country and focusing attention on the culture-bound nature of perception.

Critical reading of primary and secondary sources

Helping students to develop well-founded interpretations, and a sense of history as an ongoing conversation with the available sources, is a core task in history education (Berkhofer 1999). Frederick (1999a: 60) advocates modelling the process oneself with students using handouts or overheads of a piece of text. He then invites students, 'either ahead of time (preferably) or at the start of class, to "find one or two passages from the text you found particularly significant and be prepared to justify your choice." Or "find one quotation you especially liked and one you disliked." Or, "identify a passage which you think best illustrates the major thesis of the chapter [article or book], and why".' Students are likely to identify different passages or interpret them in different ways, which leads to lively discussion. This can be done in lectures or seminars with primary or secondary sources, proceeding from the simple and descriptive 'What does it say?' to the more complex interpretative issue 'What does it tell us?' to 'What are its implications for understanding the topic?' Davies (2000) suggests asking students to work in small groups to simplify or paraphrase a text, such as the Declaration of the Rights of Man of 1789 or the terms of a treaty. Ideas are written on to a poster, with each clause or point to be represented in no more than three words. Key words in a text can also be written on to Post-its and stuck on the wall, with students justifying their choice. Stovel (1999) describes similar activities, including the paraphrasing of a document by pairs of students. King and Kitchener (1994) similarly recount one teacher's attempt to encourage critical reading and reflexivity by asking students to read two reports of a battle in the Vietnam War, and then posing questions such as 'When two accounts differ can you believe one more than the other?' Using this exercise in association with reflective journals brought to the surface not only issues of historiography and interpretation but also emotional responses affecting historical judgement. Calder (2002) employed the same technique on an American history survey course, providing students with two divergent secondary texts and focusing discussion throughout the course around these and associated primary sources. Collections of documents are now widely available, whether as printed documentary collections or on CD-ROM or the Internet, and can help students to connect personally as well as critically to the sources, whilst providing the intellectual scaffolding to lead them to more nuanced conceptions of the topic (see Frederick and Jeffrey 2002; Bain 2000; McAleavy 1998).

Encouraging observation and active listening

Observation and listening are integral parts of reflective learning, and involve attention to what is said and by whom, how it is said, when it is said, and the context of the communication. Whilst many of the strategies outlined above involve such skills, the following explicitly focus upon encouraging students to gain confidence and experience in these areas as part of deepening their understanding of subject and self.

Fishbowl or inner circle

Sometimes employed as a technique for breaking down large groups without everyone having to perform an activity, this is a productive listening exercise. Here a number of students form an inner circle to discuss a topic, with the rest sitting in an outer circle as non-participant observers. The latter are asked to listen carefully to the discussion, note key points and feed these back to the whole group. It often surprises students how different the accounts of what is said and what happened can be, and this can be used to lead into general discussion of the topic and the problems of evidence and interpretation. If students are also asked to observe the pattern of interaction, this can be used to introduce discussion of disciplinary modes of learning and the practicalities and importance of listening more generally, including 'listening' to historical evidence.

Dyads and triads

Working in pairs, students take turns to think out loud about a topic with one person having five minutes to talk and the other listening. Potts (1986, 1995) records his use of this method in a course on Mexican history, the aims of which were to help students become more aware of content ('What is the Mexican Revolution?') and key historical concepts such as democracy and revolution, and gain self-confidence and self-knowledge.

> Students would pair up, to take turns as talker and listener. The listener was not to interrupt at all, however silent, incoherent, irrelevant or whatever the talker might be, and was to give obvious attention. A standard pattern on a set question came to be something like this, for students A and B: A four minutes, B four minutes; A four minutes, B four minutes, A and B open discussion for four minutes . . . Then we might change partners and repeat the process. Next we might form a group to share conclusions quickly before going on to other questions and exercises.
>
> (Potts 1986: 68)

Clearly this is a demanding task and requires detailed explanation of aims and expectations along with ground rules emphasizing the importance of non-interruption by the listener and of timekeeping. Brockbank and McGill (1998) describe a similar technique using groups of three students. This involves a presenter on an issue, an 'enabler' who can ask the presenter to clarify points via open questions, and a reporter who listens actively to what is being said, when and how (using only non-verbal signals to demonstrate that he or she is listening), and generally observes the interaction. At the conclusion of the session between presenter and enabler (about twenty minutes), both reflect back their views of what was being said, and the reporter feeds back to each what was heard (about ten minutes). The triads can be moved around so that students have experience of each role, and the experience fed into general discussion of the topic and the skills involved.

Hearing the subject

Palmer (1998) reminds us that active listening concerns not just attentiveness to others but to the subject. Brookfield (1999) suggests an exercise in which students 'listen' to a piece of text or visual and try to experience it emotionally as well as cognitively, jotting down some parts verbatim, paraphrasing others, recounting images and feelings and so on. The point at this stage is not to interpret but to experience the material. This experience is then shared with the larger group. Frederick (1999a) combines this with a further stage of interpretation when asking students to analyse the cartoon 'Westward-Ho', an 1872 representation of 'American Progress'. After giving a description of the cartoon, the students move on to how they interpret it, and the inevitable differences here lead to a fuller discussion of male and female imagery and of the issues of historical interpretation.

Reflective journals

Informal writing enables students to speculate, explore their personal ideas and reactions, and capture the process of thinking about history as well as connect together ideas, and provides a potentially powerful means of encouraging observation, personal expression, reflective thinking and self-awareness (see Moon 1999; Creme 2000). Entries can be written in or out of class, and students asked to write what they think and feel about issues, concepts or what happens in class. Journals allow the expression of feelings (which may not be possible elsewhere in written work in history), and provide students and teachers with valuable insights into levels of understanding and the whole process of learning in the subject. Stefani (1997) argues that journals are particularly appropriate for mature learners, as they tend to have a clearer sense of their own goals. However, they can be equally successful with traditional-age undergraduates if their purpose and relevance to history is clearly articulated, there is a focus on specific tasks, and students are given freedom to decide on their own means of proceeding within a guiding framework of questions provided by the teacher. Moon (1999) suggests that students can be requested to write an explanation of a key concept for a lay person or an imaginary dialogue with an expert on an area of their subject, or to reflect on seminars they have experienced. Bain (2000) provides several strategies for use with history students, including freewriting (initial thoughts on a topic), story writing (creating a connected narrative on a topic from reading), reading through writing (capturing thoughts on texts), self-reflection (by considering the same question at regular intervals), and public reading (sharing of extracts with others in class, with teachers sharing their own journal entries). Whilst students often complain about the work involved in journal writing, Reber (1993: 124) notes that although initially sceptical, students using journal work on her first-year world history course gradually began to appreciate its value. As one put it: 'I thought having the journal was a good idea. In the beginning of the course I didn't think I was going to like the idea, but as the semester went on I began to realize how helpful the journal really was. It allowed us to learn to read something and then have to sit down and write the ideas you got from the reading material. I also think it possibly helped improve some writing skills.'

Taking a break and creative silence

It is often stated that history lectures 'should enable the students to develop their skills in listening, selective note-taking, and reflection' (History Benchmarking Group 2000: 5). In practice, however, note taking is often random and listening superficial. As an exercise in listening, students can be asked to refrain from taking lecture notes for a short period of five minutes, then write down what they consider to have been the key points made and discuss these with one or two other students. A period of creative silence in the middle of a lecture also helps students to digest information, concepts and arguments. In it students can be requested to note the key things they have learned so far. Some history teachers find it helpful to use the opening minutes of a lecture, when some are inevitably still arriving, to get the students to sit quietly and ask them to reflect on one question that they have from the previous session or one key thing they learnt. In seminars, too, a short break is productive, and a ground rule invariably insisted upon by students in seminars scheduled for more than an hour. However, even waiting a few seconds for students to reply to a question can allow them to organize their thoughts (if silence is recognized as a normal part of discussion and not perceived as intimidating).

Online discussion and listening

As Sicilia (1998: 78) points out in a discussion of technology in the history classroom, electronic discussion groups can easily lose direction and provide 'yet another opportunity to sound off with a string of declarations and unsupported assumptions', or to make inappropriate remarks that deter some from participating. Like face-to-face seminars, one or two individuals can dominate discussion, while others find it easier to become 'lurkers', simply using the information provided by others without contributing themselves. Nonetheless, with clear guidelines about conduct and posting and active moderation by the teacher (see Salmon 2000), online discussion does allow students more time to produce considered responses to the sort of complex issues raised in history, and can be less intimidating than face-to-face discussion for more introverted or anxious students. In an online seminar the absence of non-verbal gestures is an added incentive to listen more closely to words, and how loud someone shouts makes no difference, and nor is their class or ethnic or gender background so apparent. Whilst it cannot replace the spontaneity of a good traditional seminar, online learning offers particular opportunities for developing close listening skills in an environment less encumbered by the background noise of accents, emphases and emotions. Moreover, as Hunter (1998: 112) observes, 'the capability of composing their answers, pondering about what they are saying, and then editing their answers before posting seem to make some usually reticent students more willing to contribute'.

Conclusion

The strategies outlined represent only a small sample of those employed to promote active learning in history classes. Here student activity, however varied, is regarded as merely one aspect of high-quality learning founded upon interaction, ownership and critical reflection. To change student understanding also requires such activities to be congruent with the values and purposes of the course, integrated carefully with content and with assessment procedures, and sensitive to the factors influencing student engagement, different needs and the levels of prior knowledge and understanding. Active learning is challenging for students, and teachers also need to become comfortable in a role demanding not only knowledge of subject content and procedures but also skills of facilitation and intellectual and personal support. Ultimately, of course, history teachers have to make pedagogical choices according to their goals, the composition of students and the subject being covered. However, those employing active-learning strategies in a reflective and flexible manner consistently report high levels of student motivation and engagement with the subject, and, in the best cases, a satisfaction born of teacher and students working together as historians and co-practitioners. Many university history teachers begin their careers wishing to avoid repeating the passive experiences they themselves experienced as undergraduates. As one put it: 'I wanted as complete a contrast as possible with the excruciating ninety-minute torture sessions I remembered sitting through as an undergraduate' (Hill 1996: 49). Active learning provides a means of achieving this and bringing history alive to the diverse students who populate today's history classroom.

7

PROMOTING INDEPENDENCE IN LEARNING

Where they have been carefully planned and properly implemented, attempts at encouraging active learning have been uniformly rated favourably by teachers and students. There is also evidence that freedom in learning or student autonomy together with good teaching which encourages students to form their own conceptions, will lead to deep approaches to learning which enhance personal conceptual understanding.

(Entwistle 1992)

Developing student autonomy is a key feature of degree programmes in the humanities. The notion, as Boud (1995a) points out, encompasses three groups of related ideas. First, autonomy is a fundamental goal that teachers and students can aspire to, a characteristic of the educated person. The confidence to think and act independently, working with others yet with a well-founded sense of one's ability to manage large bodies of information and handle complex issues, is regarded as a yardstick of high-quality learning in history. As one historian remarks: 'I want students to become self-aware and honest, able to confront the world adequately, to make their own judgements, and to recognize and respect their own considered (not manipulated) needs. And yet again, I do not want that autonomy to lead to arrogance or rampant individualism. I want it to be wed to sensitivity to others and willingness to co-operate and assist' (Potts 1995: 149). Second, autonomy is an integral part of the process of becoming a capable learner. The ability to motivate oneself, take the initiative, manage time effectively and monitor one's own learning are recognized by history students and teachers as essential skills in developing subject mastery. Third, autonomy describes an approach to educational practice that emphasizes student control over learning. Whether such learning is described as 'flexible', 'open', 'self-directed', 'capability', 'experiential', 'problem-based', 'reflective' or 'lifelong', student control of the learning process is fundamental and in history is traditionally most evident in project and dissertation work.

The conditions required for the development of autonomy are described by Chickering and Reisser (1993: 273–4):

> When teaching completely specifies what will be studied, when learning involves memorizing information and developing only the content and skills deemed important by the teacher, and when grades depend upon absolute conformity to these requirements, emotional and instrumental independence do not flourish. These qualities are fostered when students can help define key areas of content and competence can be pursued and when objectives for learning are established collaboratively, taking account of individual interests and motives within general parameters set by the curriculum and course. Such development is strengthened when students must cope with diverse tasks that have consequences for themselves and when they must identify, find, and get to whatever resources are needed to achieve the objectives. It is also strengthened when they are asked to participate in defining the products or behaviours that will be evaluated, the methods to be used, and the criteria to be applied in making judgements about whether the desired learning has occurred.

One might therefore plot the degree to which independence is promoted on a continuum that encompasses the degree of student control over what is studied, how it is studied (including when and where), and the extent to which students are actively involved in the assessment process.

As this makes clear, autonomy does not arise automatically from learning independently. Rather, as Kolb (1984) emphasizes, experience has to be reflected upon in order to transform existing knowledge. His model of experiential learning integrates reflection into a four-stage cycle, beginning with having an experience, followed by observation and reflection on that experience, leading to analysing, theorizing and drawing conclusions which are then used to plan and test hypotheses in new situations.

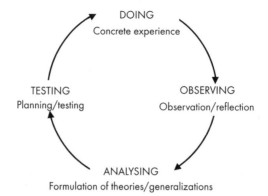

Figure 7.1 Kolb's experiential learning cycle

This model emphasizes learning as an integrated process, with each stage supporting and feeding into the next. The learner can enter at any point but must then complete the stages in sequence, with each cycle leading into another in a self-reinforcing spiral. In a summary of strategies for fostering such a deep approach to learning, Gibbs (1992b) identifies individual and group project work, peer tutoring, self-study materials, reflective journals and study skills training, and Kolb's model clearly fits neatly with such activities. Entwistle (1992) provides a similar list of teaching methods associated with learning that promotes initiative and enterprise. These include resource-based methods; open and distance learning; instructional technology and computer-based learning; project work; simulations; collaborative group work; negotiated learning, including learning contracts; supervised work experience, work-based learning and placements; peer teaching and self-assessment; profiling and records of achievement; and learning-to-learn workshops to encourage autonomous reflective learning. What follows is a discussion of these strategies in the context of historical study.

Learning through peer tutoring

Goldshmid and Goldshmid (1976) identify five principal ways in which students learn by teaching and advising others: discussion led by students, proctoring (individual supervision by a senior student), tutorless student groups, pair learning, and parrainage (older undergraduates counselling new students). Of these, student-led discussion is the most common in history, and can be as simple as student direction of a debate or role-play or as complex as students managing the whole of seminar activity. The greater the degree of student control, the more the need to include student-led activity as part of formal assessment on a course, and this is discussed in the following chapter. In one student-led seminar course in modern British history, students choose topics to be discussed from a list reflecting course content and decide which they will lead the group on. Three or four students lead each fortnightly seminar and are responsible for deciding on the exact focus of the topic, their respective roles (for example, giving an introductory presentation, summarizing, concluding and chairing elements of the discussion), and the approach they will take to the issue. They construct an agenda comprising aims and objectives, key issues for discussion and the teaching methods they will use, and allocate specific reading for group members using the course bibliography. This agenda is circulated to all members of the group who use it to structure their own preparation. At the seminar the group leaders are responsible for giving short introductions to the topic and summaries of points made as the seminar proceeds, and for guiding discussion. They receive feedback from the group at the end of the seminar and, using this, write a short report on their view of the topic, the process of working together and the strengths and weaknesses of the seminar, upon which they are assessed (Booth, 1996b).

Accounts of peer tutoring emphasize the need for clear and explicit guidance to students on rationale and requirements and negotiated ground rules. They also underline the importance of teachers in creating an effective learning environment and as a key resource for advice and support. Without these, anxiety will result and students will resent the greater effort required in this form of learning (see Goodlad and Hirst 1989; Goodlad 1995; Jaques 1991). In the move towards autonomy student self-help groups or study teams can also be valuable, enabling students to provide each other with advice, encouragement and assistance in completing course assignments.

Undergraduate research projects

Discovery learning through research projects or dissertations is often viewed by history undergraduates as the 'highlight' of their higher education experience (History at the Universities Defence Group 1998b: 4). Projects require students to apply knowledge and procedures they have acquired, and to demonstrate a range of planning, research, analytical, bibliographic and presentation skills.

They also not infrequently result in work of considerable sophistication and creativity. As Light and Cox (2001: 134) suggest, of all courses 'the aspect of study with perhaps the most potential to change people is the project'. Project work offers the opportunity to investigate a subject of one's own choosing in some depth and at one's own pace, and encourages critical reflection and intellectual risk taking. The attraction of this is captured in the comments of the following two second-year students on their experience of history project work.

> You've chosen to come to university to do a certain subject because that's what you're interested in but then you sort of get various aspects of it but it's what other people think is going to be interesting for you, not what you yourself would find interesting . . . This was something you really worked hard for and you had an end product you could be proud of.

> You could go off on a tangent and if it didn't work out there wasn't any pressure on you. You don't have to conform to it, you just go back to where you were and try something else and in that way it was good. You do have moments when you're saying, 'Where is this going, I don't know what I'm doing and I don't know what anybody else is thinking'. But because you've got this deadline a long way away you've got enough time to research things, to try things out, and that was the best thing about it for me.
>
> (Gonzalez 2001:185)

Supervision is a key issue. Too much direction destroys the sense of independence in learning but, equally, it is important to recognize students' need for support, particularly if things go wrong. There is now an abundance of practical advice available on the supervision process, and clarity of expectations and of assessment criteria are obvious starting points (see Brown and Atkins 1990; Henry 1994; Fry *et al.* 1999; Light and Cox 2001). One means of reconciling the tensions between student self-direction and supervision is through the sharing of project drafts. Steffens (1989) records how students in his class on seventeenth-century intellectual history met together in peer groups of three to discuss drafts and suggest improvements. They were asked to comment on points that interested them and issues upon which they would like more information or clarification, and to offer constructive comments to the writer. At a later stage, each student was asked to prepare a ten-minute summary of a colleague's paper and present this to class, and the writer was given five minutes to respond and elaborate. This peer-review process was well regarded by students, one of whom commented that it 'helped a great deal in the clarification of my thesis as well as the general direction of the paper. Interestingly, there can be many good ideas that exist in one's mind that do not automatically make it to the typing paper. Often it requires an open exchange of criticism and advice to facilitate that connection' (133). Students in another history department shared drafts in various stages of completion with a departmental research group, including postgraduates and staff who also discussed progress on their own work. This not only facilitated the process of writing-up by convincing students that their ideas made sense, but also increased their awareness of the department as a place of research as well as teaching and as a supportive community. As one student remarked, 'the group gives us a lot of support – you really feel that you are not working on your own. You also get the chance to develop a close relationship with the staff, which might not happen otherwise' (Currie 2000: 40).

Research logs encourage students 'to be more aware of themselves as researchers, to be more conscious of themselves as historians' (Steffens 1989: 131). He records how these were employed as a running record of what students observed themselves doing as they worked on their project on seventeenth-century history: how they chose their topic, how they decided what information to include and what to disregard, and how they decided to structure the report and to write it. They were combined with seminars in which students wrote in their log ideas they had on possible areas for research, how their topic might develop and where they were now, and shared these with peers. In a final session, students were asked to review their research logs and write a two-page synopsis of their research and writing activities. They were encouraged to think about how they got started, how the reading and writing affected each other, how the first draft was produced, and what was most helpful in the revision process. Hodges (1998) additionally used a research journal as a means of encouraging students to record thoughts on the craft of history in preparation for dissertation work. Whilst the use of logs or journals is not unproblematic (see Chapter 6), in Steffens' case they proved successful because the rationale was clearly explained, non-directive suggestions were made about what they might contain, and they fed directly into a reflective essay as well as the research project. The logs therefore constituted an integral part of the course, were controlled by students and had an obvious practical value.

History group projects

Collaborative project work helps to cultivate interpersonal skills in addition to the research and written communication skills engendered by individual projects, and enables students to tackle larger and more complex topics. Key issues in history group-project work are group formation, individual accountability and the assessment of individual contributions. Random allocation of students to groups is time-efficient, but encouraging students to allocate themselves to groups by ranking their preferences according to interest in a particular topic creates more involvement whilst allowing the teacher the possibility of avoiding obvious groupings of close friends. Nicholls (1994: 164) notes the many unfamiliar skills demanded of students in group projects and the difficult issue of individual accountability:

> The shift from structured forms of teaching to the participative learning entailed by group-work brings with it many challenges for students and demands from them new types of competence, such as setting their own targets, negotiating between themselves and others, coping with the advantages and disadvantages of sharing tasks, understanding the dynamics of shared activities (leadership roles, co-operation, interpersonal relationships and so on). The tutor's dilemma comes from determining precisely how far to intervene to manage this activity in such a way as to maximise its advantages while protecting individual members of the group from the shortcomings of one or more of their colleagues.

Whilst the issue of the 'freeloading' student is addressed in the following chapter, one simple means of ensuring transparency is to request that a project group minutes its meetings and submits them for discussion at regular supervision sessions with the tutor. These can be used as evidence in individual reflective accounts of the process of undertaking the project (and thus enable the production of individual marks if required), or submitted by the group as part of a final assessment portfolio.

There are many types of group project, varying in complexity and in the level of commitment demanded of students. They range from simple activities completed in an individual class, to those like syndicate work running across a whole semester in which teams of students work on different assignments on a related theme and report back to the whole group in a final presentation and plenary discussion (Collier 1983). Clark and de Groot (1992) describe group research projects on two second-year history courses on the American Revolution and Nineteenth-century Iran. Broad topics were identified, within which students decided on more specific topics to research for completion within a ten-week period. The tutor acted as guide, adviser and point of information, and commonly attended the start of meetings of the group but soon withdrew to allow students to discuss issues among themselves. 'Work on this kind of project', they comment, 'aims to develop the skills students need to act effectively as a group: to listen as well as to argue, to communicate their ideas in what often become heated debates, to negotiate outcomes and to accommodate conflicting views . . . to learn to take decisions.' They also noted gains in student motivation and understanding, and that group project work 'gave greater maturity to those who were already confident and new confidence to those who had formerly lacked it' (2–3). Bruley (1996: 119) similarly comments that, in a twentieth-century women's oral history project, students gradually became more confident and thus required less supervision as the project progressed: 'In the last couple of weeks, when the group came to analyse its findings, it had virtually become autonomous. It was clear that I was no longer required to direct the group. Henceforth I did not sit in on all sessions (some of which became very extended) and reverted more to the role of external adviser and technical facilitator.' Although challenging for students, group project work enhances the academic and personal confidence, flexibility and the decision-making skills that underlie independence, whether in high-level history learning or in everyday life.

History fieldwork: site visits and work-based learning

Formal learning beyond the classroom offers a powerful means of linking subject knowledge and personal experience, as well as allowing students opportunities to demonstrate commitment and initiative (Gallman 1998; Koman 1999). Visits to historical sites to study the physical, non-written, evidence of the past vary from day-trips incorporated into existing class time to field courses lasting from a weekend to a week or longer. They help students to acquire contextual information, and enhance their awareness of the range of sources available to historians and their ability to interpret them (Hallas 1996; Dawson and de Pennington 2000). Work-based learning generally involves students working for a period in a commercial or public organization, or undertaking commissioned projects for external clients or public service of direct benefit to others in the community (see Nicholls 1992; Winstanley 1992; Donovan 1998; Bailey *et al.* 2000). It encourages students to consider the purposes of studying their subject, and by enhancing self-reliance, self-confidence and maturity opens up further developments in intellectual understanding, as well as in understanding of the world around.

Whilst the nature of fieldwork in history varies considerably, the key to its success is partly logistical. This includes factors such as the arrangement and costing of activities, timing, travel and accommodation, negotiation of roles and responsibilities and record keeping. Keeping such schemes as simple as possible is advised (see Goodlad and Hirst 1989; Roberts and Mycock 1991; Roberts 1992). More fundamentally, however, it is vital that the principal focus is upon learning and reflection, and that activities connect with issues, problems or underlying concepts of direct relevance to the academic discipline and are meaningful to students. In some cases, of course, this is relatively straightforward. Students visiting a local museum or battlefield can easily make links between academic and popular uses of history. So, too, those working for external clients on archiving company records or compiling a bibliography of items on local history for a public library can see an immediate connection between the task and the subject they are studying. However, as Donovan (1998) demonstrates, even student placements less obviously related to 'historical content' can be connected to the subject through linkages to fundamental historical concepts such as continuity and change. Thus first-year students working on community projects with the homeless linked their experience to a survey course through class comparison of past and present social conditions, examining to what extent the 'good' poor still exist and comparing historical and contemporary notions of personal and social responsibility. They then wrote a two-page reflective essay discussing their service in the light of course lectures and readings, for, as Donovan points out, 'when well done, reflection synthesizes the experience outside the classroom with the intellectual activity inside it' (155).

There are numerous methods of facilitating reflection, and some of these were discussed in the previous chapter. Project work is common, and group projects are particularly well-suited to this type of learning for, as Johnson *et al.* (1994: 7) point out, 'the use of collaborative learning groups approximates more closely the world of real-world employment and problem-solving'. Learning contracts can be used to emphasize student (and tutor) responsibilities, including the need for reflection on experience, and also enable students to negotiate their own pattern of study with their tutor and with an employer (Knowles 1986; Stephenson and Laycock 1993). Nor, as Nicholls (1993) demonstrates, do these need to be complex and bureaucratic documents. A single sheet providing an outline of the agreed project, methods of assessment, possible costs, dates of progress meetings, the name of the external client and date and signatures of student, client and tutor can be sufficient. Questionnaires can offer a preparatory means of helping students to identify the skills they bring to fieldwork or work placements, and those they need to work on, while worksheets and site questionnaires encourage reflection on experience. On field visits these can be structured for intellectual progression, for example: Why is this site where it is? What does it tell us about the community? How does it connect into wider trends or ideas in society and culture? (Dawson and de Pennington 2000). Sharing thoughts and feelings on experience and problems in 'action learning sets' of half a dozen students can also stimulate reflection and self-awareness (see McGill and Beaty 1995).

Whilst fieldwork activities clearly have financial and time implications for both students and staff, the benefits in terms of intellectual and personal development are often considerable. If connected to activities which encourage students to learn actively in ways that retain a close connection to the central issues and concepts of the discipline, they provide a means for both promoting independence in learning and relating history to everyday life.

New technology and resource-based learning

Whilst the term resource-based learning is difficult to define precisely, in history it is commonly used to refer to learning through self-instructional materials. Methods employed to engage the student in self-study vary greatly in sophistication, from simple collections of printed sources to the design of virtual learning environments. At their core, however, is the goal of helping students to become more autonomous learners. Resource-based learning, above all, provides opportunities for flexible, self-paced study adapted to the needs of the individual learner.

Traditionally, printed course readers containing primary and secondary sources have been the staple form of resource-based learning in history, with some, like those produced by the Open University in the United Kingdom, including self-assessment exercises and model answers (Marwick 1996; Peters 1998). Encouraging students to generate their own questions from the sources can also facilitate deeper reflection (see Graham 1999). History readers are also combined with course guides, including synopses of lecture material, bibliographies and other support documents, to provide a total course package (see Cowan 1994; Hyland 1994), and with study guides including advice and examples on common tasks such as researching a topic, taking notes and writing essays. Commercial textbook study guides now routinely provide a range of supplementary resources. Thus, for example, Nash *et al.* (1994), *The American People: Creating a Nation and a Society*, comes with a variety of supplementary resources, including a primary source book, a video laser disc of photos, film clips and animated map segments, and a guide for instructors containing key themes and chapter outlines, learning goals, enrichment ideas and a list of further resources. The developments with most promise, however, have been those associated with new technology, as this provides access to study materials outside formal hours and off as well as on campus. Moreover, as Spaeth and Cameron (2000) point out, whilst early software necessitated intensive instruction of students in the use of the technology (a time-consuming labour about which few historians felt confident), today's technology is simpler to use. This enables a greater focus upon what has always been a principal objective of history teaching, that of 'facilitating student investigation of primary source material rather than relying simply upon lectures and secondary reading' (329). In the last decade, the most innovative areas of history resource-based learning have been the CD-ROM and the Internet. Both provide access to multiple sources and perspectives (including text, statistical data, pictures, moving images, sound, maps, archival materials, biographies, chronologies and bibliographies), and thus make it possible for students to construct sophisticated historical accounts.

In a review of history-related CD-ROMs, Rosenzweig (1995) notes four principal categories: databases of information, documentaries (narratives of events), games (especially simulations) and books (including textbooks). Increasingly, these are integrated, whether on more interactive CD-ROMs or on the Web, as in the twelve 'electronic tutorials' developed in Britain in the 1990s as part of a government-funded Teaching and Learning Technology Programme (TLTP). These covered a range of periods from medieval to modern, including such topics as urban and gender history, and allowed users to navigate the material in many ways and not exclusively in linear fashion (see Spaeth 1996; Wissenberg 1996). Such resources can also be customized, and some teachers have further encouraged students to create their own history CD-ROMs containing resources and commentary (see Evans and Brown 1998). The success of a CD-ROM clearly depends upon the extent to which it is focused upon learners and learning rather than upon delivering content, however many bells and whistles have been added to make it attractive. As Sicilia (1998) points out, the most effective history CD-ROMs focus upon providing primary sources that can be used for projects, and enable students to work the material in a variety of ways prompted by questions that promote progression in understanding. A CD-ROM is most effective when it emulates the ways in which a historian works: 'the history student begins by learning the general scope of the information available. She or he then poses historical questions, looks for patterns in the results, poses new questions, and so on, and begins to fashion an argument from the patterns. Using this tool can be an exciting, iterative process of historical investigation and problem-solving, made possible through historians' close interaction with the evidence' (Sicilia 1998: 80). There are now many case studies modelling computer-based approaches to learning in history (see, for example, Trinkle 1998; Spaeth and Cameron 2000; Hall and Harding 2001). Winslow *et al.* (1998) offer an insightful account from the perspective of a history teacher, with little experience of teaching with technology, teaching a first-year course (using the CD-ROM 'Who Built America?') to students who were not history majors and few of whom possessed computer experience. Here students' unexpected lack of confidence in using technology in educational contexts is noted, as are the frustrations of inadequate computer access and the unreliability of institutional networks, all common complaints of historians working with technology in teaching. However, they also point out the considerable benefits in terms of the breadth of resources available, students' closer engagement with the material than on a traditional survey course, the greater originality evident in written work, and improved computer literacy.

The Internet provides an inexpensive gateway to enormous and wide-ranging resources, and has become a vast historical archive and research tool that can be accessed at any time and in many ways (see O'Malley and Rosenzweig 1997; Glasfurd and Winstanley 2000). Its resources offer almost limitless scope for undergraduate history research projects. Assignments requiring students to search for web-based materials to support seminar discussion have also become widespread (see McMichael 1998), as have those which ask students (individually or as groups) to assess the value of individual websites or compare several sites. Here 'bad' sites (those containing factual inaccuracies or little of value for academic research) can be as useful as good ones. For as Cameron (2002: 3) remarks, 'the flawed site can be taken apart in a seminar session, and generally the worse the site, the more productive the discussion arising from it can be, both with regard to critical skills and with regard to promoting discussion on the topic'. A project involving the creation of a website by students further encourages critical and imaginative thinking. Such a site might be primarily bibliographic, containing a shared library of information on a topic and links to all the sources a student has found on a particular theme as part of a project, or cover an aspect of history (Seed 1998; Glasfurd and Winstanley 2000).

Integrated course websites or virtual learning environments (VLEs) also offer great potential for promoting independent learning, and make it easy to administer online courses by merging technologies. They include learning resources (such as workbooks including tasks, primary and secondary sources, self-testing questions with built-in feedback) and support materials (for example, timetables, study guides and communication tools such as bulletin boards and chat rooms) within a structured online environment. This allows students to pursue individual pathways of study at a time and place of their own choosing, within a coherent learning framework that supports synchronous or asynchronous discussion between members of the course and with teachers (see Brown *et al.* 2001). Online work can also be combined with face-to-face sessions to discuss student progress and can be monitored for assessment purposes. The development of historical thinking skills, reflexivity and collaborative and research skills is at the heart of the online level-two course on eighteenth-century enclosure and the local community described in Hall *et al.* (2001). Here resources include a guide to study and studying online, a module workbook (providing links to materials at the points in the tasks when students need them), and a list of the resources organized so that students can recognize them by type (core texts, reading, document sources, maps, database of land ownership patterns, etc.) and pursue their own independent enquiries. Students are guided through a carefully structured problem-focused investigation, using self-contained but linked tasks that build understanding progressively. At each stage they are required to post questions, comments and findings on the bulletin/discussion board and invite responses, and this contribution is assessed along with a coursework essay drawing upon reading, online resources and discussion.

Whether print-based or computer-mediated, resource-based learning provides a powerful complement to more traditional modes of delivery. The extent to which it succeeds in building learner autonomy, however, is dependent upon how far materials are considered in terms of supporting student learning rather than simply delivering information. Learning history online can be just as passive as in a traditional history class, with students saying little, waiting for others to contribute, addressing the tutor rather than peers in discussion forums, or attempting to prove to the tutor the quantity of work done rather than critically engaging with material. If preparation time and training (for staff and students) and adequate technical support are necessary, the essential requirement is careful attention to the principles of effective learning environments outlined in Chapter 5. Computer-mediated learning, however, demands a clear understanding of the software and particular attention to the structuring of material, for, as Holden (2001: 2) points out, 'poor design, navigation and the sheer volume of online material can be off-putting to students who can easily feel overwhelmed'. Features need to be built in which motivate, support and encourage students to engage critically and imaginatively with the material (see Paloff and Pratt 1999; French et al. 1999). This, in turn, emphasizes the importance of the teacher in providing clear guidelines, encouraging and directing student contributions, providing feedback and setting tasks clearly and at the right level for students. Paloff and Pratt (1999: 20) note that 'the keys to the creation of a learning community and successful facilitation online are simple. They are as follows: *honesty, responsiveness, relevance, respect, openness,* and *empowerment.*' In online learning, as in traditional classes, the quality of interaction between students, teachers and the learning context is the key measure of, and route to, effectiveness.

Developing the skills for independent learning

Even the most academically qualified entrants often lack confidence in core history skills and awareness of their approach to the subject. In a study of teaching in one North American history department, Quinlan and Akerlind (2000: 30) noted that 'faculty perceptions of students were quite consistent. The average student is seen as ill-prepared − lacking in "cultural literacy", deficient in their basic reading and writing skills and expecting too much "spoon-feeding and "hand-holding".' It is a view routinely expressed by tutors and commentators throughout Western higher education (see, for example, Sheppard 1993; Stearns 1993; Booth 1997; Pearce 2000; Tillbrook 2002). There are clearly many skills necessary to developing independence. These include study skills (such as library and research skills, critical reading strategies, note-taking, and essay-writing); intellectual skills (such as ability to adopt a critical approach to evidence, compare and contrast diverse views and arrive at a personal judgement); communication skills (written and oral); personal skills (such as self-reliance, self-management, self-awareness and self-confidence); and interpersonal skills (such as teamwork, active listening and responding). Traditionally, history departments have produced guidance sheets, now increasingly Web-based and interactive. A range of subject-specific texts to support student skills development is also available (see, for example, Abbott 1996; Black and MacRaild 1997; Pleuger 1997). These are often used in association with skills workshops, some conducted online and many involving students taking the initiative: exchanging experiences of learning in the subject, critiquing draft assignments and undertaking project work (see Hunter 1998; Graham 1999).

Skills development, however, is not highly regarded by most history students, for whom motivation is more closely linked to studying issues and problems in the past. Moreover, as Gibbs (1992b: 15) observes:

> The development of study skills alone is unlikely to be effective, as most skills can be used to implement either a surface or deep approach [to learning]. However, it is possible to develop learning skills in the context of developing a sense of purpose, an awareness of task demands and flexibility in adapting to different demands. Skilled learners are more in control of their learning, experience greater ownership of it, and hence motivation.

Skill in learning particularly involves becoming attentive to the whole process of what is being learned, and how, in order to become aware of where one is and how to move on. The value of this approach was demonstrated in a comparison of two programmes to improve students' learning in two history departments (Martin and Ramsden 1987). In one, a standard study-skills programme, students received lectures on key study skills (note-taking, writing, examinations, etc.) and were provided with handouts and follow-up tasks such as comparing two articles. The other was a 'learning-to-learn' programme in which the skills were integrated into the subject matter of history itself via workshops, and students asked to reflect upon the purposes of what they were required to do in relation to subject-specific tasks. Whilst this latter approach was initially less popular with students, they became far more positive as the course went on, the reverse of the study skills students' experience. The learning-to-learn students also more frequently advanced their skill in learning, though the researchers were quick to admit that differing departmental contexts may also have played a part in this. Booth (2001) similarly describes the development of a programme aimed at assisting first-year students to become more skilled and reflective history learners. Here learning-to-learn workshops and a group project were integrated with positive results into a course exploring issues of historical meaning and interpretation in the light of postmodernism.

The conclusions of these investigations of history undergraduates is in alignment with generic research on skills development (see, for example, Gibbs 1981; Zuber-Skerritt 1987; Gibbs *et al.* 1994; Norton and Crowley 1995; Kaldeway and Korthaven 1995; Bloxham 1997), and provides some well-founded advice for helping students to become more skilful, independent learners. To be fully successful, such initiatives must be:

- embedded in the subject. History students come to university to study their subject, and integration of subject and skills is essential, whether this involves reflection on the philosophy and practice of history or on specific topics in history.
- tailored to students' existing conceptions of subject learning (for example, of what constitutes a history essay). Approaches which fail to take this into account are of value only at a basic level.
- focused upon reflection, so that students can identify accurately their individual needs, strengths and weaknesses, monitor progress, and establish accurately what works for them as individuals;
- varied in content and methods used in order to motivate and sustain interest;
- structured to facilitate progression in tasks, in alignment with developing conceptions of subject learning;
- assessed by continuous methods which allow sufficient time to practise skills and encourage reflection on subject and process;
- essentially formative and supportive, or students will be afraid to challenge existing habits;

- part of a departmental skills strategy that enables students to encounter the skills addressed by skills courses in mainstream history courses.

Developing the skills for independent learning is a challenging process. It requires students to negotiate several phases of development, from disorientation and expression of dissatisfaction to exploration and equilibrium, and points between (Taylor 1986; Chickering and Reisser 1993). However, the ultimate benefits lie not merely in the practical skills developed but in growing insight into disciplinary practice – a reflexive sense of subject and self. 'It helped me', observed one student, 'to realise why I liked history in the first place' (Booth 2001: 21), while another reflects that, despite initial scepticism, 'I'm beginning to get something out of it . . . perhaps a better understanding of me as a student' (Martin and Ramsden 1987: 161).

Conclusion

Student autonomy is widely regarded as a key competence in history programmes, reflecting an ideal of intellectual attainment (the ability to come to a considered, independent judgement) and action (the ability to work resourcefully on one's own). It is also used to describe an approach to pedagogic practice that encourages students to take responsibility for their own learning. There are many means by which independent learning can be facilitated. These include individual and collaborative research projects, student-led seminar work, resource-based materials, activities beyond the classroom (such as site visits and work-based learning), and a range of associated methods through which students can negotiate their own learning or reflect on it, for example learning contracts and research logs. All acknowledge that for high-quality learning to occur students must learn experientially, working out their ideas and abilities for themselves in a process which includes a cycle of activity, reflection, the formulation of new concepts, and the testing of these in action. A considerable literature also emphasizes, however, that whilst the benefits of this type of learning are significant, they do not arise automatically. As Wisdom and Gibbs (1994: 10) point out in the context of resource-based learning: 'whether the potential benefits are reaped or quality collapses depends on careful and thoughtful course design, sufficient planning and preparation time, adequate resourcing, thorough implementation and a continuing cycle of evaluation and development'. Managing independent learning therefore demands the same systematic planning and reflection as traditionally delivered courses. First, it requires student needs to be identified, based upon an assessment of their experience and abilities as independent learners. This may involve questionnaires to uncover the skills students feel confident in and discussion of their perceptions. Second, the rationale and meaning of independent learning (and especially what in practical terms it means for students) must be explicitly stated and discussed. Third, the required learning skills must be taught in ways that are embedded in disciplinary content and concepts.

Promoting autonomy in learning is therefore a complex and long-term process. A major obstacle is the strength of existing habits of studying. Increasing levels of autonomy can result in anxiety, and in some instances student resistance. In new undergraduates this is further bound up with the multiple transitions of becoming a university student. Whilst some disorientation is inevitable, it is important to help students to negotiate this, recognize the experience for what it is (a challenge to their habitual ways of thinking), and eventually reach a position where they can reflect on their experience as a basis for further exploration. Once this stage is reached, students routinely report that they become more motivated, more confident and more deeply connected to their subject. The role of the teacher is therefore vital. Essential tasks include assisting students to develop strong learning skills in their subject (not least critical analysis); supporting them by acknowledging the frustrations and difficulties they encounter; advising them on ways forward; providing specialist knowledge, especially on where to look for information; and acting as a 'critical friend' able to cast a rigorous eye over work and encourage self-criticism. This reminds us that developing autonomy involves not only independence but awareness of interdependence. As Boud (1995a: 58–9) suggests, 'with teachers and learners working effectively together, the results of autonomous learning will hopefully go beyond task accomplishment to include development of the student as a learner and a person. In this way autonomous learning becomes a liberating experience for the learner.'

8

ASSESSING FOR
UNDERSTANDING

'I'm a history major', he said, 'and each time I use "I" in a
paper, they knock half a grade off.'

(Palmer 1998)

Assessment is perhaps the single most important influence upon
student learning. As Brown and Knight (1994:12) remark, 'assessment
defines what students regard as important, how they spend their time,
and how they come to see themselves as students and then as
graduates'. Whilst for teachers assessment is often regarded as a duty
to be despatched as swiftly as possible at the end of an assignment or
course, for most students it is the starting point of learning and a
constant preoccupation (see Ramsden 1979, 1997; Entwistle and
Ramsden 1983). In students' eyes, the assessment on a course
represents its true purposes far more accurately than what teachers say
is important. Even a cursory glance at assessment requirements in
course documentation sends out signals about what is valued, how
much effort is required, and when and where this needs to be
directed. Students also recognize from experience that official
statements of intent do not always correspond to the operation of
assessment in practice, that stated learning outcomes do not invariably
reflect what is measured in the grading process, and that grading
criteria do not prevent marking disparities between teachers. Such
perceptions can lead to an approach to learning in which survival and
success are felt to hinge upon cue-seeking, and understanding is
sacrificed to what are seen as the requirements of the assessment
system (see Entwistle 1995; Entwistle and Entwistle 1992, 1997). This
is reflected in the comments of one final-year history undergraduate:
'Tutors' methods and approaches are extremely diverse. I found that
to obtain good marks from various tutors I had to "play the system",

i.e. learn what they wanted; this greatly disrupted my development'
(Booth 1996a: 263). Of course, seeking clues about where to focus
effort is ubiquitous even, as Baldwin (1992) demonstrates, among
those who obtain first-class history degrees, and is not necessarily
disadvantageous to learning. However, the more instrumental the
learning strategy, the greater is the likelihood of students adopting a
surface approach to subject matter.

Assessment can be used for many purposes, and these have been
well documented in the educational literature (see Rowntree 1979;
Crooks 1988; Atkins et al. 1993; Brown and Knight 1994; Brown et al.
1997). Thus assessment in history programmes is commonly employed
to:

- grade students;
- predict future performance;
- act as a vehicle for selection (for example, to further degrees);
- facilitate students' choice of future options on a course;
- demonstrate that standards are being maintained;
- provide employers with evidence of what students are able to do;
- motivate students;
- increase students' responsibility for their own learning;
- enrich the student learning experience;
- facilitate the development of understanding;
- provide students with feedback on their progress;
- inform teachers of students' progress in learning.

These purposes overlap (and may conflict), and which are considered
most important and the balance between them will differ according
to the stage of a course as well as to teachers' perceptions of the
requirements of the system in which they operate. For practical
purposes, however, the functions of assessment can be divided into
three: *diagnostic* (to identify strengths, weaknesses and barriers to
learning), *formative* (to provide feedback to students on their progress
and how they might improve their performance), and *summative* (to
measure what a student has achieved). In practice, of course, these are
not as distinct. In grading a coursework essay, for example, written
comments are intended to identify students' strengths and weaknesses
and help them to improve their performance, but the mark allocated
also generally constitutes part of the student's final grade on a course.
Equally, comments indicating where a student needs to improve may
appear formative in teachers' eyes but judgmental from the student
perspective. If this underlines the fact that the perception of

assessment held by students is ultimately what counts in terms of learning, it also reminds teachers that their own conceptions of teaching and learning will condition the whole approach taken to assessment, from what are considered its key purposes to the particular practices favoured and the marking criteria regarded as most important.

Assessing to promote deeper understanding involves particular attention to formative aspects of assessment. Measurement of student performance is viewed not merely as grading but as a human interaction, the aim of which is to understand students' grasp of the subject and their abilities and attitudes in order to help them make sense of the past and, through it, of themselves and their world. Assessment is therefore fundamentally, as Ramsden (1992: 186) observes, 'about understanding the processes and outcomes of student learning, and understanding the students who have done the learning. In the application of these understandings, we aim to make both student learning and our teaching better.' Here assessment is regarded as an integral part of the whole process of teaching and learning and not as a separate element confined to a specific part of a course. It constitutes a key component of course design and of every teaching session, for each seminar or lecture provides opportunities for feedback to both student and tutor, and many teaching methods such as projects, oral presentations and seminar debates are also assessed tasks. If designing an assessment strategy to promote understanding therefore involves attentiveness to the whole learning environment, it demands particular attention to ensuring that expectations are clearly understood by students; that assignments reflect and measure the range of student achievements; that students are involved as active participants; and that feedback on learning is used to best effect. These are considered below.

Clarifying expectations

As Newton (2000: 172) observes, 'an understanding is not directly accessible to others, and we cannot rely completely upon someone's opinions about it. Instead we have to rely on what can be inferred from various behaviours.' This is a skilled task, for the abilities that comprise historical understanding are themselves complex. It involves considerable personal judgement, not only in relation to each of the behaviours to be evaluated but also in how they combine to demonstrate understanding. Thus, for example, whilst one might evaluate the quality of an essay in terms of level of analysis, structure, use of evidence and presentation, these are not usually each given separate marks which are then added up and divided by four to measure students' level of understanding. Rather, a judgement is made about how, together, they create an overall impact; that is, one infers from particular applications of knowledge an overall level of understanding. This process is difficult to express precisely to students, and it is unsurprising that they sometimes express uncertainty about what is being valued, just as it is that teachers are reluctant to simplify complex goals in order to make them easily measurable.

In order to improve, students need to know what is expected of them (what they have to do to get a good mark and when they have to do it) and what their performance means in terms of their level of understanding. Ensuring that the whole process of assessment is as transparent as possible is therefore essential, and criteria checklists and grade descriptors have become ubiquitous in history assessment as a means of achieving this. An example of an assignment checklist provided by Hounsell (2000: 188) in relation to coursework essays is typical. Its key elements comprise knowledge (extent of reading, concentration on significant and relevant points), analysis (answers the question directly, grasps key issues, ability to differentiate and evaluate different historians' viewpoints, ability to handle concepts); structure (ordering of ideas, balance between analysis and narrative, avoidance of repetition, arguments supported by use of evidence); and presentation (clarity and economy of style, spelling, grammar and punctuation, effective introduction and conclusion, use of references and footnotes, length). Similar criteria are common for grading history dissertations, usually with greater emphasis on research and use of primary sources (see, for example, Heywood 1989: 272). Criteria checklists employed in the assessment of oral presentations and seminar work are not markedly different (see Brown *et al.* 1994; Allen and Lloyd-Jones 1998; Doran *et al.* 2000). These routinely focus upon content and analysis (amount, quality and level), structure (introduction and conclusion, logical progression, summarizing), and delivery (pace, tone, eye contact with audience, fluency, timing, appropriateness of language, use of audio-visual aids, teamwork, answering questions). Typical student-led seminar assessment criteria specify the importance of research (breadth and depth of reading), analysis (including focus, awareness of historiography, explanation of issues and concepts), and management of the seminar (for example, planning, use of handouts, acting as chair, group interaction, summing up, and quality of teamwork).

Whilst a list of criteria appropriate to the intended learning outcomes is essential, it is insufficient to improve learning. Students also need to grasp clearly the meaning of the terms used in history assessment and develop a shared understanding of these with tutors. Discussion of expectations and assessment criteria is best attempted in the first class on a course. However, if insufficient time is available a specific session can be devoted to introducing students to disciplinary discourse on assessment alongside other key concepts in the discipline, perhaps involving them in a marking exercise using departmental criteria (Price *et al.* 2001). Examples of essays from previous years, with marking checklists attached, can also be placed in the library so that students can see what is required and better understand departmental marking conventions. Involving students in the process of formulating criteria particularly aids awareness of what is needed to succeed. Heron (1995) suggests asking each member of class to generate three key criteria towards a collective list. More experienced students might also be given the opportunity to devise criteria or decide the weighting to be allocated to key criteria. Graham (1999: 208) reflects on the power of such participation on a course on the history of childhood, commenting that, although this 'was the first occasion on which they [students] had been involved in devising assessment criteria . . . the end of course review indicated that it had been a valuable demystifying experience, though several were initially of the opinion that it was solely the instructor's responsibility to devise the criteria'.

Diversifying assessment

Coursework and examination essays remain the foundation stone of history assessment, though the merit of unseen essay-based examinations in fostering or measuring historical understanding is a contested issue. Apologists particularly invoke the safeguards against plagiarism inherent in the unseen examination, and argue that writing essays under examination conditions 'gives students the opportunity to develop relevant life-skills such as the ability to produce coherent, reasoned and supported arguments under pressure' (History Benchmarking Group 2000: 6). Critics counter that a test of nerve should not be confused with a test of understanding, and that anxiety leads students to resort to memorization and the reproduction of information. As one final-year history undergraduate puts it: 'What is the function of exams? I study a topic for hours, involve myself in research and then have to answer a question on it in forty-five minutes or an hour. I feel I am not allowed to show what I have learnt; exams place a student under great pressure that for historical study I do not think is appropriate' (Booth 1996a: 263). Such debate is not new, indeed the issue of whether examinations promote memorization more than understanding or reflection was the subject of intense debate among historians in universities in the United Kingdom during the second half of the nineteenth century (Soffer 1994). There is insufficient space here to rehearse this issue fully, and open-book examinations or prior-notice questions certainly provide a means of reducing the pressure upon students and encouraging more insightful answers. Nonetheless, there is often a gap between theory and practice in history examinations. The demonstration of complex and independent thinking is all too often sacrificed to a perceived need to memorize notes, and key life-skills such as oral communication, group work and self-awareness are not evaluated. Moreover, examinations all too often provide little feedback to students about how to improve.

In recent years the range of history assessment has grown markedly. The benchmark statement for undergraduate history programmes in the United Kingdom (History Benchmarking Group 2000: 6) states that 'diversity of assessment is vital for two main reasons. First, the full range of a student's abilities is most unlikely to be revealed through any single mode. Second, the increasingly diverse educational background and formal qualifications presented on entry suggest that the degree programmes should afford all students the opportunity to show what they know, understand and can do.' There has been a recognition that whilst the traditional history essay can foster the integration of knowledge, skills and understanding, students are often critical of the effect of a relentless diet of history essays on motivation and intellectual risk-taking (see Hounsell 1997, 2000; Bartul 1999). This has resulted in efforts to extend the range of writing tasks to include, for example, book and film reviews, comparison of journal articles, assessed bibliographies and book proposals, as well as longer projects. Assignments requiring students to write a briefing paper for a government minister, analyse an event through the eyes of a contemporary or write an article or editorial for a serious or popular newspaper have also become increasingly common as a means of introducing more personal and imaginative forms of writing (see Meyers 1986; Hannam and Swain 1990; Fitzgerald and Hodgkinson 1994). Such tasks encourage students to connect self to past, as does autobiographical writing in diaries, logs and portfolios of evidence. Assessment has also been extended to include oral as well as written skills, reflection on process as well as product, and skills and competencies more generally, often allied to self and peer evaluation methods. Many of these reflect the focus upon collaborative tasks in active learning, and the need to reward skills traditionally under-represented in history assessment yet valuable in employment. Group-work assessment can relate both to activities *in* groups (such as oral presentations, poster sessions, chairing or facilitating discussion, and general contribution to the whole seminar programme) and activities *by* groups of students (most notably group projects, but also collaborative presentations and peer management of seminar activities). Whilst such assessment is challenging, there is agreement among tutors and students experienced in it that it improves the quality of contributions and ensures that activities such as oral presentations and class discussion are taken more seriously (see Doran *et al.* 2000; Allen and Lloyd-Jones 1998; Booth 1996b; Hyland 1996a).

If diversifying assessment allows students to demonstrate their achievement more fully, when not implemented with care it can lead to assessment overload, constraining students' ability to pursue areas of their own interest and encouraging them to adopt a surface approach to their studies. In this respect we might heed the note of caution sounded by Toohey (1999: 168): 'sometimes, in order to preserve everyone's time and sanity, one assessment task or technique has to serve conflicting purposes even though theoretically two different assessment tasks might do a better job'. Here it is important to return to one's key goals and purposes in terms of student learning. What is it essential for students to learn in terms of knowledge, skills and understanding? What is peripheral? Or perhaps most tellingly, what is of enduring value to students beyond their academic studies?

Involving students

If assessment is fundamentally concerned with improving learning, involvement in the process motivates students, enhances their sense of ownership of a course and increases their responsibility for their own learning. There are many possible levels of student participation. Brown *et al.* (1994) note that students can be involved in both setting tasks and evaluating performance. In relation to the former this might include:

- *choosing the tasks they will complete*: for example, which topic they will write an essay or project on, or which elements of a mixed-mode assessment procedure they will complete, or the assignment tasks that will count towards their final mark;

- *setting the assessment tasks*: for example, creating their own essays or alternatives to an essay, or negotiating an individual pattern of assessment through a learning contract;
- *discussing assessment criteria* provided by the teacher as part of a class exercise in order to clarify issues and make assessment processes more transparent;
- *negotiating their own criteria* as individuals or a group, either *ab initio* or using an extended list or exemplar provided by the tutor or generated by previous students.

Students can also be required to make judgements about how far intended learning outcomes have been met. This might involve:

- *selecting the evidence* to submit in order to meet assessment criteria, for example through the use of portfolios of work;
- *making formative comments on their own or others' work* to help with the subsequent writing of an essay or report on an oral presentation;
- *suggesting self-assessed marks or grades* on essays, oral presentations, contribution to the seminar programme and so on, to be taken into consideration by the tutor when marking;
- *assigning marks or grades to self or peers* to count as the final decision on a piece of work.

Student involvement in assessment is an integral part of encouraging active and independent learning. Thus on one third-year American history course students develop their abilities to evaluate their own work by submitting with their essay outline comments on what they consider to be its strengths and weaknesses. These comments provide material for discussion in an essay tutorial, as well as providing the tutor with greater insight into the way the student perceives essay construction (Hounsell *et al.* 1996). A European history course at the same university encourages similar self-reflection. Students are asked to use tutor feedback on an essay to think through their performance, using a self-assessment form which invites them 'to comment on how they have sought to address, within the essay submitted, shortcomings identified in previously marked essays' (90). Students can also be asked to specify at the end of an essay the particular aspects of their performance that they would like advice upon, and this can be revealing of anxieties and self-image as well as time-saving in terms of marking. In a student-led seminar course in modern British history, students are asked to evaluate the performance of the student seminar leaders using a simple form requesting comments on 'the best things about the seminar' and 'ways it might be improved'. This peer feedback is used by the seminar leaders to write short individual reports which contribute to their final course grade. The triangulation of peer, self- and, finally, tutor assessment that decides the allocated mark constitutes a practical means of encouraging reflection on subject and learning (Booth 1996b). Peer feedback can also be useful on project drafts, and students can be asked to discuss a first draft of their essays in pairs or online, with the feedback being used to complete the final draft.

The challenge of non-traditional assessment

Whilst the benefits of extending the range of history assessment have been noted, new forms of assessment are not without their challenges. What follows draws upon studies of innovative modes of history assessment (Booth, 1996b; Allen and Lloyd-Jones 1998; Doran *et al.* 2000; Nicholson and Ellis 2000), as well as work by colleagues on related disciplines, notably Wisker (1997) and Bradford and O'Connell (1998). As many such assessment practices relate to collaborative learning activities, such as student-led seminars, group projects and oral presentations, discussion focuses particularly upon the concerns most frequently raised by history tutors in this area of teaching and learning, though the issues considered are also relevant to other types of assessed work.

Who should assess?

Tasks involving the collaborative activity that characterizes much active learning in the history classroom are particularly suited to self- and peer assessment, though such methods can be used to foster reflection, self-awareness and autonomy on any assignment. Boud (1990: 109) suggests that 'learning is an active endeavour and thus it is only the learner who can learn and implement decisions about his or her own learning: all other forms of assessment are therefore subordinate to it'. Self- and peer assessment can certainly make students think more carefully about aims and criteria, and generate valuable feedback to students in a context of rising numbers and time constraints on teachers. For many history teachers, however, these methods are problematic. There is particular concern that students' views on the performance of peers will be swayed more by confident presentation than by depth of research and historical understanding, and that there may be collusion in awarding high marks. Some students also feel that their subject knowledge and experience are inadequate to ensure accuracy of marking. Peer grading, especially, creates fears of a conflict of loyalty, though Hyland (1996a) notes that in an initiative in one history department two-thirds of students felt that the peer assessment of oral presentations had helped to make them more reflective about their own work, and this mirrors findings in other disciplines (Boud 1995b).

In reviews of the literature on self-assessment, Brew (1995) and Boud and Falchikov (1989, 1995) note that case studies in many disciplines suggest that the majority of students' marks agree broadly with those provided by teachers. Over- or under-rating seem more likely to arise from students' lack of understanding of assessment criteria, or the kind of rating instrument used, than from any particular student characteristics such as learning orientation, gender and so on. The research also suggests that high achievers are more likely to underestimate their performance than low achieving students, and that senior students tend to make better judgements than those at the beginning of their degree. Reviews of peer assessment suggest that whilst over-marking may occur, this can be offset by training and by allowing teachers to act as moderators of the mark allocated (see Heywood 2000); this might be an acceptable compromise for those wishing to introduce peer assessment but who are concerned about the accuracy of student marking. In history, there is little systematic research evidence on the reliability of either self- or peer grading, but a great deal of support for employing such methods formatively as a means of improving student reflection. Advocates emphasize, however, that if student self- or peer assessment is to be introduced, it is essential to ensure that students understand clearly what is expected. Restricting assessment criteria to a few of the most important learning outcomes can also help students to feel more confident in applying them. Toohey (1999) further suggests allowing students to distinguish among a limited range of performances, such as 'excellent', 'competent' and 'acceptable', rather than awarding marks, and this can encourage acceptance by more reluctant students. Beginning with self- and peer assessment in an advisory capacity (list three strengths and three weaknesses) rather than grading can also generate confidence in the process. With senior students, self- and peer marking might first be used to complement tutor marking rather than replace it. Experience suggests that if such practices are embedded into a course from the start and progressed gradually, and if training is provided and a climate of trust established, new methods of assessment are less likely to meet resistance from students.

Weighting and balance of assessment

Deciding how to weight different criteria is a common problem for those involved in non-traditional assessment. It arises most starkly in relation to the balance to be allocated to content/analysis and delivery elements in assessing oral presentations or student-led seminars. Some tutors resolve this by simply according equal importance to both. It is, however, also common practice to allocate proportionately more of the mark (say 60 per cent) to the former, to reflect the aspect of performance given priority in traditional assessment, with the remainder given to presentational aspects. The balance of weighting ultimately depends upon the primary purpose. Is it more important to test and develop students' presentational skills or their understanding of the material, or are both equally important? How important is the development of analytical skills, or personal transferable skills? Whatever the answers, purposes need to be clearly explained to students and reflected in the marking criteria. Most important, however, is that the balance of weighting decided upon reflects the primary learning objectives of the course and student levels of confidence and experience.

A related issue is the weighting of non-traditional forms of assessment in the marking scheme on a module as a whole. Doran *et al.* (2000) noted that the weighting given to oral assessment in the United Kingdom varies greatly between history departments, from 5 per cent of the overall total to 40 per cent, with the average being 10–15 per cent of marks available. Clearly, what is appropriate will differ according to aims and student experience. However, it is important that weighting is sufficient to motivate and reflects accurately the workload required, and 15–25 per cent of final course mark tends to ensure that students take the exercise seriously without creating undue anxiety among conscientious students. It also underlines the variety of learning outcomes students are expected to achieve in a history education, without unbalancing the overall assessment pattern.

Individual effort and group marks

In the assessment of group activities this is particularly problematic. Some argue that in a collaborative assignment a single composite mark emphasizes the need to work together and reflects the spirit of the exercise. In a higher education system founded upon individual grading, however, there is often anxiety among diligent and high-ability students that less hard-working students will lower their grade. There is also concern among tutors that they lack sufficient information on the level of individual contributions to discriminate accurately between group members in the allocation of marks.

Whilst there is no universally applicable solution to this issue, there are practical ways forward (see Brown and Knight 1994; Brown *et al.* 1997). For those wishing to provide a group mark, the freeloader issue can be addressed by a 'card' system in which a poorly contributing member can be 'yellow-carded' if the rest of the group make a satisfactory case to the tutor. This can be rescinded if the student improves his or her performance by a certain date; if not, he or she receives a 5 per cent penalty. If the situation continues, a case can be made for a red card, which removes the student from the group and means that he or she has to submit an individual piece of work. For tutors wishing to generate individual marks, one simple solution is to provide a collective mark and multiply it by the number of students in the group. This total can then be divided up by group members themselves according to clear, pre-agreed criteria and, in an additional twist, according to their roles in the process (chair, note-taker, report writer and so on). A ground rule specifying that no individual mark can be more than 10 per cent above or below the group mark can help to make the process more acceptable to students. However, given many history students' aversion to peer grading, Nicholson and Ellis (2000) found it most successful for the tutor to divide up the composite mark and allocate individual marks. To ensure fairness they used individual portfolios, submitted by all members of the team and detailing their personal contributions, alongside a group portfolio including, for example, student ground rules, plans, minutes of meetings, indicating who attended, monitoring and self-evaluation pro formas, and a diary of critical incidents. Asking each student leader to write a report of a group-led seminar, to be assessed by the tutor, also makes it possible to generate individual marks more easily. An alternative is to viva students on the topic for a proportion of a group mark, although this is time consuming and can be intimidating. Gibbs (1992a) further suggests the possibility of making some examination questions on a course refer to a group assignment or project. In assessing online discussion, records of the quantity and quality of posted questions and responses can be an effective means of evaluating individual contributions (McConnell 2000).

Validity, reliability and moderation

There is a long and complex educational literature on the issues of reliability and validity in assessment (see Heywood 1989, 2000; Brown *et al.* 1997). Validity relates to whether the type of assessment employed measures what it is supposed to. Here the key issue is appropriateness of assessment to course objectives. Thus, for example, the ability to work with others in a group project might be more suitably assessed by self- or peer assessment than by tutors. Reliability refers to the extent to which the same assessment would be made if a teacher was to mark the same performance on more than one occasion, or if the same assignment was to be assessed by someone else. The key issue here is consistency.

Validity and reliability are clearly concerns in all forms of assessment. They can be demonstrated through proper alignment of course components, the use of clear criteria and grading systems (understood by the students), and alertness to one's prejudices and to the times during marking when accuracy diminishes. More problematic in practice in assessments such as oral presentations and seminar assessment is the issue of external verification. In a department where innovative assessment strategies are routinely employed, comparing results across courses can provide a measure of consistency. However, the fact that other examiners are not usually present is often perceived to be a problem, and video and audio recording of such sessions can be difficult to arrange as well as intimidating for students. Of course, if agreeable to students, a video of one such session might be used as general evidence of the fit between criteria and student performance, though doubts might remain about whether it is representative. Other solutions include training staff in a department so that they become familiar with such assessment activities, for as confidence in marking essays comes with experience, the same is also true of non-traditional methods. Some history departments ensure that colleagues assess such work jointly (easier on team-taught courses than those taught by an individual teacher) or try to ensure that second markers attend a sample of such sessions, and this can form a component in a wider departmental peer-observation system. Others attempt to provide second markers with a combination of self-, peer and tutor assessment to provide as wide a range of evidence as possible. This might include asking students to write a short report, including preparatory notes, handouts, audio-visual materials and other materials used, peer evaluation of the session, and tutor evaluation using a criteria checklist. Whatever the approach employed, a key factor in its success will be the quality of the feedback elicited and provided.

Obtaining feedback on student learning

It can be difficult to gauge the effects of teaching on student learning. Here the Study Processes Questionnaire (Biggs 1987) and, especially, the Approaches to Studying Inventory (Entwistle 1988), the latter also available in a shortened version (Gibbs 1992b), have proved influential, research-based tools for examining changes in students' approaches to learning. However, there are also many informative methods that can be used quickly in any history classroom to gain an impression of how well students have understood a topic, and register changes in academic and personal development. Simple observation of the level and quality of participation in class discussion or attentiveness to others' views, for example, can provide many clues about how students are learning. Active-learning techniques described in previous chapters (such as brainstorming, buzz groups, concept mapping, quizzes, letters to successors, diaries, logs and portfolios) can all generate valuable evidence. Information may also come from talking with students as their personal tutor or outside class, from formal end-of-course questionnaires and focus groups, or from comments by colleagues either informally or as part of departmental peer observation of teaching schemes. Feedback on learning is not therefore confined to information gained from marking student assignments and formal end-of-course student feedback questionnaires, but can be gathered continuously on a course. Many small-scale monitoring ('classroom assessment') techniques for the purpose of understanding student progress and providing information to improve teaching and learning have been compiled by Angelo (1991), Angelo and Cross (1993) and George and Cowan (1999). What follows draws upon these and the efforts of historians to find simple yet reliable methods to map students' learning.

Minute paper

This has been the most widely used and adapted of Angelo and Cross's techniques, largely because, as they point out, 'it is easy to explain, easy to use, and flexible to fit any class, any time' (Angelo and Cross 1993: 370). In the last five minutes of a class students are asked (anonymously unless otherwise agreed) to write for two or three minutes on 'the most important thing I learned today', and 'one issue, idea or question about which I am still unsure or confused'. Their views are collected (students can also write them on Post-its and put them on a whiteboard or wall) and are reported back on at the next class. They can also help the fine-tuning of teaching in subsequent sessions. If less time is available, a 'half-minute' paper is possible; given more time, students can discuss their responses in pairs or small groups.

Discussion log

This is a shortened and adapted version of the longer 'discussion audit' described by Brookfield (1999) and focuses, like the minute paper, on what students think they have learned. At the end of a seminar students are asked to write a few sentences on the following: 'What I know or understand as a result of participating in this discussion that I didn't before'; 'What I contributed to discussion'; and 'How could I contribute to the next seminar that would deepen my understanding of issues and ideas?' Here the focus is on the process of learning as well as on content. These can be used as a source for a report on their learning in seminars or submitted in a portfolio of work.

Mid-course review

In another minute-paper variation, students are asked to 'state the three (or more) most important ideas, concepts and facts you have learned on this period (or theme) so far, and the three things you have found most difficult to understand and do'. These can be collected in and form the basis for mid-course discussion about learning (and teaching) on the course.

Closing summary

At the end of a class, Davis (1993) suggests asking students, individually or in pairs, to summarize briefly the main points learned.

These are handed in and examined for clarity or confusion. Students can also be asked to paraphrase a key idea or concept covered. Summarizing can also be useful in student oral presentations, both to check understanding of what has been learned and to motivate students to listen actively. Or, at the start of a class, students can be asked to summarize the key ideas from the previous class.

Sample student notes

Borrowing lecture notes from a sample of volunteers can be an effective, if occasionally dispiriting, means of discovering whether students are getting from lectures what you want them to. It can provide the opportunity for discussion with students about the uses of history lectures and the best means of learning from them, and a useful starting point for a wider review of learning on a course.

Prior learning and background knowledge review

This helps both students and the teacher to explore misconceptions and preconceptions and is best conducted in the first class. In the example given by Angelo and Cross (1993: 133–4) on a course on the Americas before Columbus, the teacher gave students three questions: 'About how many people lived in North America in 1491?', 'About how long had they been on this continent by 1491?' and 'What significant achievements had they made in that time?' After five minutes she shuffled the papers and handed them back so that each student had someone else's paper. They then shared the answers and found that there was a huge range of answers to questions one and two. For question three she simply put the answers on the board until they began to repeat. She then wrote a fourth question up for discussion: 'Where did you get those three answers?' Most students realized that their impressions were not well founded. This was followed by a library exercise in which students had to check their answers, and found in the process that there were no generally accepted answers but that some answers were more plausible than others. More complex quizzes might include multiple-choice questions that could be handed in to ascertain students' levels of background knowledge.

Concept mapping

Concept maps can be used at any point in a class to check on understanding. There are many different types of concept map, from the classic 'spider' diagram with a circle for the general issue, radiating from which are connected ideas, to tree maps, flow maps and mind maps. Some of these are outlined in Heywood (2000), but any kind of sketch can help to assess where students are in their learning. If this is the first time students have encountered concept maps, it pays to have an example to explain what they look like and their value. Ask each student to draw a map of what were the main ideas, facts, issues and so on to arise in a class, and draw one yourself. The first time, show your map and ask them to share their own maps and, if time is available, explain them. Confirm important points and address misunderstandings. If time is available, suggest further reading or provide space to air misunderstandings in the next class.

All the above techniques can provide valuable feedback on learning to both teachers and students, although their success depends upon how they are implemented. In particular, the willingness of students to be honest will depend upon whether they feel comfortable in expressing their opinions openly and admitting difficulties. However, when feedback is regarded as a natural and ongoing part of the process of teaching and learning, and is of obvious practical benefit to students, it is more likely to be accepted and taken seriously.

Providing feedback on student assignments

Feedback can have as many purposes as assessment. However, in terms of improving student learning its most important function is to ensure that students recognize their existing level of knowledge, skills and understanding, know what they need to do to improve their performance, and are motivated to do so. High-quality feedback therefore constitutes 'the life-blood of learning', as Rowntree (1979: 24) puts it, and is rightly regarded as a key indicator of teaching quality. It can be achieved in many ways, from informal advice at the end of or following a class, to formal tutorials, to, most commonly, comments written in the margins and at the end of assignments or on criteria mark-sheets. All of these practices send out signals to students about the nature of the assessment system and what each tutor regards as important.

A survey of student perceptions of feedback in seventeen history departments in the United Kingdom reveals some of the general contours of feedback in the discipline. Hyland (2000) observed that written feedback on assignments was considered important by over 90 per cent of students, with mature students most consistently likely to say that it was very useful. It was perceived both to provide a sense of achievement and help in reviewing and improving performance, and three-quarters of all students surveyed believed that feedback helped them to deepen their understanding of what they had learned. Responses suggested that tutors' comments were taken seriously, were frequently read more than once by the student, and, interestingly, often by other students, and were used to help in subsequent assessment tasks. Yet while the history students in this study received comments routinely on coursework essays (though complaints about the quality of feedback were not uncommon), 70 per cent claimed never to receive feedback apart from a grade or mark on examination essays. Nor did they have a formal opportunity to discuss this work with tutors. What they make of the feedback they receive can also vary widely. Individual students respond differently to the same tutor comments, reflecting variations in personality, experience and conceptions of the disciplinary discourse and learning tasks. Thus, for example, there is strong evidence that comments on history essays such as 'too descriptive', 'not analytical enough' or 'needs better structure' are often not well understood by students, which partly reflects tensions in disciplinary discourse on writing history (see Hounsell 1987; Biggs 1988; Stockton 1995; Chanock 2000).

What then does effective feedback to students involve? Manifestly it should be prompt, clear and demonstrably fair. However, more is required if improvement in learning is to be reliably achieved. Responding to students requires careful listening, observation and empathy to encourage them to reflect critically upon their performance without becoming alienated or disillusioned. In larger classes, asking students to form an agenda by stating what aspects of their work they particularly want feedback on can help make the tutorial process more efficient. Or, if seeing all students in individual essay-tutorials is impractical, drop-in sessions where students with difficulties can talk about their work can provide an alternative. There are many time-saving ways of dealing with feedback to larger classes. These include group-feedback sessions (where students discuss comments on each other's previous work, or work together to identify common problems in undertaking history assignments), summary reports by the tutor of common errors, student self-help groups, or even the use of audio-taped rather than written comments on essays (see Gibbs 1992a). Online feedback to a whole class of common strengths and weaknesses is also effective. Indeed, as Paloff and Pratt (1999) suggest, a significant benefit of online courses is their ability to generate considerable feedback to students from tutors and peers, which can be used for self-reflection on progress.

Feedback discussion with students needs to address not only the specifics of an assignment but also conceptions of key tasks, in order to ensure as close a correspondence as possible between students' and teachers' conceptions of terms used in the discourse of disciplinary assessment (Lea and Street 2000; Ivanic *et al.* 2000). As Hyland (2000: 242) points out, 'students need to understand what their tutors mean by such terms as "structure", "argument", "analysis", "interpretation" and "evidence" in history writing, so that they know the kind of questions that historians ask when reading, and can organise their material and direct their writing to address a topic in a way that meets the particular requirements of their tutors'. This can be achieved through specific feedback comments, preferably linked to future assignments, and clear grading criteria discussed, or negotiated, with students in language with which they are familiar. These, however, need to be addressed in ways calculated to encourage improvement. This includes the recognition that students often focus on the negative in evaluating tutors' comments on their work ('where I went wrong', 'where my weaknesses lie', 'what my problems are', 'my mistakes'). Whatever the reasons for this, comments that are phrased positively and demonstrate an interest in the individual (not least by addressing them by their first name) are likely to be more effective than the most objective and rigorous critique. Finding the right balance between challenge and support can be difficult even for the most experienced teacher, but empathy and encouragement are essential. Students need to feel that their tutor is friendly and interested in their progress if they are to be willing to reflect honestly and self-critically upon their work. Effective feedback involves far more than writing comments at the end of a piece of work.

Conclusion

For students, assessment demonstrates in its starkest form what really counts on a course. If they are to be motivated to learn actively and independently, and develop higher levels of understanding, assessment techniques must be carefully aligned with course goals and teaching strategies. Constructing an assessment matrix plotting aims against assessment methods is a practical way to begin thinking about this. An assessment audit also provides the opportunity to reflect more fundamentally upon the quality of provision. Key questions for individuals and departments include:

- What is being looked for? Knowledge, mastery of skills, understanding?
- Are assignments fully aligned with course learning objectives?
- How do assignments connect with prior knowledge and experience?
- What skills and abilities are currently underrepresented in assessment?
- Do assignments encourage critical reflection by students?
- Is course workload conducive to a deep approach to learning?
- Are assessment criteria explicit, and do students understand them?
- Is marking accurate and consistent, and how is this ensured?
- Do methods encourage student involvement?
- Do assessment and evaluation techniques provide a clear and detailed picture of how students are learning?
- Is feedback understood and reflected upon by students, and how is this known?

In designing assessment strategies, educational objectives are paramount. What is assessed, and the methods used, must reflect what outcomes are considered most important and not what is easiest to measure. High-quality attributes, such as critical reflection and imaginative use of evidence, are clearly more difficult to measure as precisely as thoroughness of knowledge. However, Ramsden (1992: 212) reminds us to 'be suspicious of the objectivity and accuracy of all measures of student ability and conscious that human judgement is the most important element in every indicator of achievement'. All assessment has limitations, and varied tasks and methods are necessary in order to develop and measure the full range of student achievement and reflect the complex and multidimensional nature of learning in history. By itself, however, variety is not sufficient to improve learning. Whether methods are successful in terms of learning will depend upon how they are implemented and the whole context within which they operate, and this raises more fundamental issues. Whilst assessment can clearly have multiple purposes, from the perspective adopted here its primary purpose is to enhance students' understanding and the integration of skills and knowledge associated with this. Thus, whilst distinctions can be made between the diagnostic, summative and formative functions of assessment, in practice these are not separate entities but are part of a continuum in which the aim is improved understanding. This further reminds us that assessment is not simply something done to students at the end of a course, but rather an ongoing and integral part of the whole process of teaching and learning. It therefore needs to be considered from the outset of the planning process on a course. In the words of Brown and Knight (1994: 155): 'Assessment is at the heart of learning. Assessment is for learning. Assessment is learning.' Assessment exerts a powerful influence upon what students learn and how they engage with their subject. It also reveals in stark fashion a teacher's conceptions of history teaching and learning, and thus provides a lens through which we might examine and enhance our own practices. How such a reflective practice can be developed is considered in the final chapter.

9

DEVELOPING
UNDERSTANDING OF
TEACHING

We have had distressingly few commitments to curricular
discussions by major researchers . . . The key mission of
humanities teaching really is to apply some of the same
enthusiasm and creativity to curriculum development that
have for decades marked research.

(Stearns 1993)

Scholarship and history teaching

Encouraging students to engage critically, reflectively and
imaginatively with issues in the past, to approach their studies with
curiosity and enthusiasm, and to participate actively in their own
learning is a richly complex and challenging task. It demands rigour,
flexibility and experimentation grounded in sensitivity to student
needs as well as to teachers' own beliefs, values and experiences. As
Hutchings (1996: 1) maintains, 'teaching, like other forms of scholarly
activity, is substantive, intellectual work'. This perhaps needs
emphasizing only because in history it has too often been forgotten.
There remains an underlying belief that, for all our professional
commitment to it, teaching is somehow a less exacting, and less
exciting, form of academic endeavour than research. As Sherry (1994:
1053) remarks, 'the truth is that many of us, even among those
[historians] who prize teaching, still regard it as not only less rewarded
but less sophisticated and demanding than scholarship – simply the
easier thing to do, or otherwise less worthy of note'.

Scholarship is at the heart of historians' sense of professional
identity. It confers status and respect, and constitutes the key
determinant of career progression. It binds practitioners together and
at the same time keeps practices within accepted boundaries,
privileging some and excluding others. In his research on the nature

of academic disciplines, Becher observed that 'more historians used the phrase "community of scholars" than did respondents in any other discipline' (Becher and Trowler 2001: 187). Yet the notion of scholarship has become reserved almost exclusively for research, and for research of a particular kind – that associated with the discovery of knowledge and the creation of new historical interpretations. Greatest respect is therefore accorded to single-authored monographs and articles based upon archival research, and directed at other professional historians (Thelen 1994; Jordanova 2000; Evans 2003). Consequently, activities that focus upon the synthesis of knowledge (as in textbooks), or engage with wider audiences (as, for example, articles in popular history magazines), or rely upon evidence other than that mined from archival research, have been relegated to the ranks of lesser forms of disciplinary activity. In denying full academic esteem to a vast swathe of professional endeavour, this hierarchic model has also ensured that teaching has been relegated to the status of a secondary and derivative activity, undervalued in the discipline's systems of communication, recognition and reward, in its whole public discourse. This separation between teaching and scholarship has ensured that there is little incentive for historians interested in pedagogic issues to research their classroom practices or, still less, investigate student learning in a serious fashion. As Calder *et al.* (2002: 46) remark:

> while most of us consider ourselves to be scholars and most of us give the bulk of our time to teaching, few of us have thought to combine our dual identities and take a scholarly approach to the issues and problems that concern us as teachers. In other words, few historians inquire into teaching and learning in ways that mirror their traditional research, which is to say, in ways that are systematic, problem-based, theoretically grounded, and publicly accountable.

Today this is beginning to change. Historians in a number of countries have begun to pay serious attention to the theory and practice of history teaching and learning in higher education, and their work has been referred to throughout the preceding chapters. This emerging field of scholarship faces many challenges, not least the indifference of the mainstream, a lack of sources of research funding, and the paucity of discipline-based outlets for publication, the consequence of which is that findings are often published in educational journals, and thus remain unread by most historians.

There are, however, some encouraging signs. In the United Kingdom, for example, newly appointed lecturers today routinely have to undertake courses in teaching and learning involving some pedagogic research, and in North America many graduate programmes offer courses and mentoring in teaching development (see Stearns 1999; Brooks 2000). So, too, workshops and conferences on the teaching of history in higher education and the building of pedagogic discipline networks have become established activities in educational initiatives such as the government-funded Subject Centres for developing discipline-based teaching and learning in the United Kingdom. Key professional associations, such as the American Historical Association (AHA) and the Organization of American Historians, have also declared a commitment to encouraging scholarship in teaching and learning, and the respected *Journal of American History* has since the mid-1990s included articles on pedagogic issues. There is still much to be done, but initiatives to establish the teaching and learning of history as a serious scholarly field are gaining momentum, and the work that is emerging is helping to generate well-founded theoretical insights and practical advice about how knowledge, skills and understanding might best be promoted in the subject.

This field of enquiry has benefited greatly from attempts to formulate more flexible notions of scholarly activity. Here the work of North American educationalists such as Boyer (1990), Rice (1992) and Shulman (1989, 1993, 1998, 1999) has been particularly influential. Boyer's influential reworking of the notion of scholarship contains four distinct but interrelated dimensions: the scholarship of discovery (producing new knowledge and adding to the intellectual climate); the scholarship of integration (synthesizing views in creative ways by making connections across disciplines and putting specialisms into wider contexts); the scholarship of application (bringing together theory and practice, the academic and wider worlds); and the scholarship of teaching (nurturing and enthusing tomorrow's scholars and citizens). Recognizing that such an integrative paradigm would gain significance only if it were rooted in subject communities, in 1991 twenty professional associations were invited to reconsider existing notions of scholarship in their discipline. One of these was the AHA, whose Ad Hoc Committee on Defining Scholarly Work noted that, whilst the unequal treatment of research and teaching was not specific to history, the discipline had its specific problems:

> For history, the privilege given to the monograph in promotion and tenure has led to the undervaluing of other

activities central to the life of the discipline – writing textbooks, developing courses and curricula, documentary editing, museum exhibitions, and film projects to name but a few. Despite a number of efforts within recent years to give greater recognition to such work, a traditional, hierarchical conceptualisation of what constitutes historical scholarship, based on the German model, continues to dominate and restrict our profession's reward structure. There is little recognition of the diverse interests and talents of today's historians, or of the changes they undergo in the course of their careers.

(Diamond and Adam 1995: 26).

In reconsidering this model of scholarship the AHA outlined some of the activities that might be included within the parameters of a less rigid notion of scholarship, and how such scholarly work might be documented through, for example, portfolios of evidence, reflective writing, and peer and student review mechanisms. Its categories, drawing specifically upon the work of Eugene Rice, comprised:

- *The advancement of knowledge* (original research published in monographs and refereed journal articles, or disseminated through, for example, papers, lectures, museum exhibitions, research reports or other commissioned study).
- *The integration of knowledge* (synthesis and reintegration of knowledge as in textbooks, state of field essays, newsletters, encyclopaedia entries, edited anthologies, public lectures, museum exhibitions, film, research reports, etc.).
- *The application of knowledge* (professional practice such as public exhibitions, expert testimony, journal editing, public lectures, administration of historical organizations, writing institutional histories, creation of bibliographies and databases, contract research on policy formation and outcomes etc., directly related to an individual's specialization).
- *The transformation of knowledge through teaching* (including pedagogic innovation, development of courses, curricula, teaching materials, workshop organization, museum exhibitions, public programmes, pedagogic research and publication, and mentoring/advising students).

The task force emphasized that such a broad and overlapping definition of scholarship was not intended to diminish discovery research, which it regarded as the bedrock of the discipline, but rather to extend and enhance it. It would enable history teaching and research to be viewed as complementary and equally respected parts of an interdependent whole, and permit a more integrated and personally empowering conception of professional activity and career development. The significance of such a change, it was recognized, would be momentous. For, 'if scholarly activity is central to the work of our profession, then how we define scholarship determines what it means to be a historian and who is part of that historical community' (Diamond and Adam 1995: 26).

In the light of such efforts to outline the sorts of activity that a broader definition of scholarship might encompass, scholars in North America, Australia and Britain have attempted to clarify and refine the notion of the scholarship of teaching (see, for example, Menges and Weimer 1996; Glassick *et al.* 1997; Trigwell *et al.* 1999, 2000; Healey 2000; Kreber 2001, 2002). Whilst differences of emphasis remain, all stress that the scholarship of teaching is as much about learning as it is about teaching. They have also cast greater light upon what such a scholarship of teaching and learning might entail in terms of teacher behaviours. Some suggestions in relation to history are as follows:

1   *Engagement with the literature.* This encompasses keeping abreast not only of the findings of research in the fields of history taught, but also of key developments in subject-specific pedagogic research and the generic literature on learning and teaching.

2   *Commitment to the enhancement of learning and teaching.* This involves adopting an ongoing focus on development, particularly on improving student learning through improvements in practice, whether defined as innovations or refinements to traditional methods of subject teaching.

3   *Rigorous   enquiry into practice* founded upon critical reflection, relevant theoretical perspectives and discernibly scholarly methods in the collection, use and evaluation of evidence. This might involve standard historical or interdisciplinary methods to investigate classroom practices and place them in wider contexts, whether disciplinary, socio-cultural or historical.

4   *Communication and dissemination of practices,* including research and classroom innovations, to peers. This can operate on many levels, from conversation with or the mentoring of colleagues to formal contributions to conferences and publication. However, a commitment to community dialogue in which work is open to peer review and evaluation is essential.

The scholarship of teaching and learning, then, is not simply concerned with the publication of refereed articles or monographs containing copious footnotes, although this constitutes one aspect of it. It can encompass all four of Boyer's dimensions of scholarship, but, importantly, conforms to the standards of argument and evidence demanded in high-quality historical research. This kind of enquiry is clearly not something in which every historian will feel the desire to engage. However, it offers considerable satisfactions to those with the inclination to pursue it. It can lend rigour to teaching, refresh approaches to the subject, generate a sense of well-founded confidence in current practices, and provide a solid foundation for developing as a teacher and meeting future challenges. Above all, perhaps, it can help to make teaching more interesting and rewarding for both teachers and students

In its emphasis upon systematic, reflective enquiry, the scholarship of teaching and learning is closely linked to the notion of 'reflective practice' with its focus upon the development of professional expertise (see Eraut 1994; Beaty 1997; Moon 1999; Rowland 2000). Becoming a reflective practitioner particularly emphasizes the importance of linking actions with underlying values, assumptions and strategies – of professional development as a disciplined and practical process. It enables, in the language of educational research, the examination of 'theories-in-use' (what one is actually doing) in the light of 'espoused theories' (what one says one is doing or wants to do), and the refinement of teaching practices in the light of the results (Schon 1983, 1987). Although sometimes criticized for ignoring wider social, political and economic contexts (see Zukas and Malcolm 1999; Walker 2001), the reflective practice model can be a powerful tool for developing a spirit of scholarly enquiry into teaching and learning, one that reflects a focus on students and learning, on one's own deeply held values, on the relationship between these and pedagogic practices, and, importantly, on the connections between practice and the wider contexts within which teachers operate. In what follows are considered some broad and overlapping perspectives through which history teachers can cast light upon their pedagogic values, assumptions and practices, and the factors which influence them. They are divided for convenience into four aspects: self-observation, student perceptions, discussion with colleagues, and researching teaching and learning.

Exploring experience through self-observation

Self-reflection can occur in many contexts, both formal and informal. These include professional development events, conferences at which pedagogic issues are discussed, departmental meetings, during and after classes, and reading about teaching and student learning. There are also research-based questionnaires such as the 'approaches to teaching inventory' (Trigwell and Prosser 1999), and a host of classroom-based self-evaluation strategies (see Gibbs *et al.* 1989; Harris and Bell 1994; Brown and Race 1995). What follows are some practical, time-efficient methods by which historians and others have attempted to explore their experiences, values and practices of teaching.

Simple audit

A SWOT analysis provides a simple means of identifying perceptions and feelings about current practice. Listing one's strengths as a history teacher, perceived weaknesses, opportunities for development and threats to teaching quality can provide a sound basis for further reflection or conversation with colleagues. Some general but powerful questions can also be used to bring greater clarity to a course or module: what kinds of things do I want my students to learn (historical knowledge, historical thinking skills, disciplinary concepts, methodologies etc.)? What opportunities are provided (for example, lectures, seminars, fieldwork)? What kinds of assessment tasks are used to test the achievement of these objectives (essays, reports, examinations, projects, and so on)? Who assesses the learning (tutor, self or peers)? What do my students think are the most important things that they learn? Further questions to prompt reflection on specific teaching situations such as lectures and seminars are provided in Day *et al.* (1998).

Remembering our own histories

Knowing ourselves as history teachers is partly about exploring the relationship we have to our subject, which was considered in Chapter 4. The following are key questions: why did I become interested in the study of history? What was it in me that drew me to my particular field of expertise? How does this affect the way I see my subject? How have my research interests influenced my teaching? Palmer (1998: 21) suggests a further question: 'Which teachers influenced me most, and how did they make a difference to me?' Then, not 'What made this particular teacher great?', but 'What was it in *me* that allowed great mentoring to happen?' This makes the point that teaching and learning constitute a process that 'requires more than meeting the right teacher: the teacher must meet the right student'. Smyth (1995: 53) offers a related series of guiding questions to locate practice within broader social and political contexts: what do my practices say about my assumptions, values and beliefs about teaching? Where did these ideas come from? What social practices are expressed in these ideas? What is it that causes me to maintain my theories? What views of power do they embody? Whose interests are served by my practices? What is it that acts to constrain my views of what is possible in teaching?

Using video and audio recordings

Recording teaching sessions can be an illuminating means of gathering information on classroom dynamics, particular incidents and students' and one's own behaviour. Recordings can also be used for discussion with students to explore how they are responding to teaching methods and materials, and for improving their own skills of self-evaluation. Davis (1993) provides concise, practical guidance on using video to observe teaching, along with a checklist of items covering preparation, presentation, questioning skills, student participation and interest, discussion, and classroom climate. More generally, she suggests the following guiding questions: What specific things did I do well? What specific things could I have done better? What did students seem to enjoy the most? What did they seem to enjoy the least? If I could do this session again, what three things would I change? How would I go about making those changes?

Critical incidents and ideology critique

Tripp (1993) advocates the use of critical incident analysis as a systematic means of interrogating routine ways of working to uncover deeper ideological processes. He calls this 'ideology critique'. What is critical here is not the incident, but the mode of analysis which enables incidents to be grounded in wider social and political contexts. The teacher investigates an aspect of teaching or learning (for example, the role of history essays or seminar discussion) in four stages. First, describe the phenomenon and attribute meaning and significance to it in terms of the accepted or dominant view. Second, analyse and examine that view for internal inconsistencies, paradoxes, contradictions and counter-instances, including what is being omitted from the viewpoint. Third, look for reasons to explain why the dominant view ignores these anomalies, and suggest whose interests are best served by it and who is most disadvantaged. Fourth, try to create an alternative structure or process that is more rational and socially just.

Reflective diaries

Diaries can help to facilitate understanding of approaches and reactions to common teaching situations over time and to pinpoint development needs. They can take many forms, including descriptions of thoughts and feelings on teaching sessions (what I wanted to do; what actually happened; what I feel about this); critical incident files, describing particular events or issues in more detail, and observations on these (what were the key features, or significant factors; what was learned; what was or might be done); general observations on teaching or reflections on reading about teaching (linking these to one's own practices); and reflections on student feedback, ideas from educational development workshops, etc. Revisiting entries at a later date often creates awareness of changes in viewpoint, generates new perspectives and prompts new strategies. As with any diary keeping, the key is to persuade oneself that sufficient time is available, to think in terms of the benefits, and to create a regular space in the day or week to write entries. Focusing upon questions that one really wants to answer (rather than trying to cover everything) is also important, as is not attempting to act on everything that arises. Heiss (1998: 35) observes that on her course on twentieth-century American diplomatic history, 'reflecting on the weekly progress of the course was definitely a valuable experience, as it afforded me the kind of introspection that can only come from putting one's thoughts into words. It did not take all that much time, so it was not much of a burden, and was definitely time well spent.' She notes the influence of the diary in providing a reference point and benchmark for future teaching, but especially in prompting reflection on how choices of content, structure and teaching methods were made, and how such decisions were often done almost automatically and reflected her own long-embedded views of the field. As she concludes: 'It has given me the chance to see my teaching as a much more intellectual enterprise than I had earlier, given me a new appreciation for the exciting nature of my field, and ultimately made me a more thoughtful instructor' (38).

Teaching portfolios

Material from a teaching diary, perhaps condensed as an autobiographical commentary, can form part of a broader teaching portfolio on a course or, indeed, one's academic work as a whole. Teaching portfolios can be used for tenure or promotion purposes and to support job applications, as well as for reflection across the whole range of professional activities. They can therefore take different forms, but commonly contain statements of teaching philosophy, teaching materials, examples of student evaluations, and testimony by others. They might also include sections on innovations, and evidence of presentations and publications on teaching. There are many ways of organizing material (see Edgerton *et al.* 1991; O'Neill and Wright 1993; Anderson 1993; Hutchings 1998). Gibbs (1988) suggests a simple six-fold structure for a general portfolio, including educational aims and objectives, teaching and learning methods, assessment, evidence of the outcomes of teaching, evaluation evidence, and evidence of the continued study of teaching and learning. Cerbin (1994) emphasizes particularly the need to focus on the relationship between teaching and student learning. He suggests that the core of a course portfolio might focus around the following: a teaching statement related to intended learning outcomes, and practices to accomplish them, including a rationale connecting these; analysis of student learning through examination of one or two representative assignments; analysis of student feedback related to how students perceive that teaching affects their learning; and a summary of the strengths and weaknesses of the course in terms of student learning. In an account of an introductory survey course in American history, Cutler (1998) describes his use of a course portfolio to understand better what he was trying to achieve, and how successfully. At its core was a narrative exploring content, teaching methods and the 'general rhythms' of teaching on the course, supported by hard evidence drawn from syllabi, handouts, samples of student work, examination feedback and so on. Whilst putting the substantial portfolio together took about an hour a week, mostly on the course narrative, the benefits of an ongoing record for future fine-tuning and for better understanding of student learning were considerable. He notes that a course portfolio 'can help teachers of history (or any discipline) think more carefully about what their students are learning and how that learning relates to the content and methods of instruction' (23). Indeed, simply writing a one-page personal statement of one's teaching philosophy for a teaching portfolio can provoke in-depth reflection on what constitute the essentials of one's practice and the origins of the beliefs, values and assumptions that underpin them.

Seeing ourselves through students' eyes

Today student evaluation of teaching is ubiquitous. Students provide a powerful perspective through which to view teaching from the point of view of the consumer. By listening to student voices one can become more aware not only of their needs and interests but also of any dissonance between their perceptions and one's own. Sharing these perceptions with students so that they can reflect on their own values provides a powerful platform for constructive dialogue. Many of the methods of teaching and evaluation described in Chapters 6 to 8, such as student journals, letter to successors and minute paper, can generate valuable information about how students interpret our actions as well as how deeply they understand a topic. Here, therefore, discussion is confined to a few of the most common means for gathering student feedback on teaching.

Student feedback questionnaires

There is a vast literature on the uses and abuses of student ratings, particularly in North America, where they have long been a prime determinant in assessing instructional effectiveness (see Davis 1993; Braskamp and Ory 1994; Cashin 1995; Hoyt and Pallett 1999). A common problem is poor construction, especially asking questions about teacher performance rather than student learning and providing inadequate opportunity for substantive comment. Moreover, such questionnaires all too often become a matter of routine with little thought going into their completion or analysis. In such circumstances, employing them as the primary 'objective' measure of good teaching is pointless. Nonetheless, well-designed student feedback questionnaires can generate valuable insights into the student learning experience. Davis (1993), Centra (1993) and Hounsell *et al.* (1997) provide straightforward advice on design, noting especially the importance of brevity, clarity of goals and a focus on learning. Although tick-box questions are ubiquitous, and quick to process, in my own experience simple, open-ended questions ('What worked best in terms of helping you learn on this course?', 'What might be improved?') generate far more useful information in terms of teaching development. Issues concerning the kinds of information to be collected, how, when and by whom it is to be gathered, and how the information is to be presented to maximize critical reflection, also need to be addressed at an early stage of planning. Students particularly need to be persuaded that the exercise should be taken seriously, and that anonymity will be preserved, if worthwhile comments are to be forthcoming. Discussing with students what will change on a course as a result of feedback provides credibility. It is also useful to discuss why some suggestions for change have not been adopted. Teachers also need to accept that some negative feedback is inevitable given students' diverse conceptions of learning in history, and that this can be used creatively to reflect upon student needs and how the learning environment might be adjusted to address them.

Critical incident questionnaires

Critical incident questionnaires can help students to become more reflective and to identify resistance points to learning, as well as alerting teachers to their own habits, assumptions and mistakes. Brookfield (1995) makes the point that most feedback questionnaires are summative judgements employed at the end of a course. He offers an alternative, based upon Tripp's (1993) critical incident analysis, which can be handed out to students in the last few minutes of each class. Five questions are asked on carbon sheets so that students can retain a copy.

- At what moment in class did you feel most engaged in what was happening?
- When did you feel most distanced?
- What action that anyone (teacher or student) took in this class was most affirming and helpful to you?
- What action did you find most confusing?
- What about the class surprised you the most? This could be something about your own reactions to something, something someone did, or anything else.

Students are also expected to hand in a summary of their responses at the end of the course, and this might be built into a student learning portfolio by asking students to analyse the major themes in what and how they learned on a course. The critical incident questionnaire is ideal for groups of around twenty students, where any issues relating to the teacher's actions can be quickly identified. In larger classes a sample of responses can be read, or the questionnaire completed every few weeks. In very small classes students might be asked to work in small groups and submit a collective summary form to ensure anonymity. Of course, in this type of analysis criticism is inevitable, which is always painful for the conscientious teacher. The point, however, as Brookfield (1995: 139) observes, is not to score a perfect ten in student satisfaction, but 'to situate your teaching in an understanding of the emotional, cognitive, and political ebbs and flows of group learning that make achieving such a score an impossibility'.

Structured group discussion

The views obtained through face-to-face discussion with students often differ significantly from those raised in ratings questionnaires, partly because students have more time to reflect and can work through their initial thoughts with others. Informal group discussion can generate valuable information but systematic procedures can be still more revealing. Ensuring a non-threatening atmosphere, the clear expression of goals, allowing students time to reflect and ensuring everyone contributes are essential preconditions. 'Structured group discussion' takes about an hour with up to seventy students, and allows everyone to contribute. Students are asked to work individually on the most and least successful aspects of the course for about five minutes. They are then divided into small groups, each group compiling a list of agreed strengths and weaknesses of the course as a whole, the teaching, and the learning experience. This takes about fifteen minutes. The points raised are listed on a board or flip chart. This is followed by whole group discussion to ensure that the list is complete, and constitutes an accurate reflection of views. In a variant of this group process, the 'nominal group technique', participants are allowed ten minutes to write their individual responses to a question or issue (for example, the best/worst things about the seminars on a course). Each then provides one item to be written on the board or OHT. Students check to see if the items make sense, and re-cast items until a master list is generated. Items are then evaluated as more/less important, or more finely ranked in terms of importance. Voting is the quickest way to achieve this, and the ways in which problem issues might be overcome are discussed. Whilst it can be a more protracted process, this method is valuable because it involves students in addressing as well as identifying problem issues.

Discussion with colleagues

If student evaluation of teaching is now a routine part of course management, in history collegial conversation about teaching is a less standard practice. As Calder *et al.* (2002: 53) remark:

> 'Off the record' and 'off limits' describe very well the average history professor's classroom. His or her teaching is rarely scrutinized by granting agencies or governmental bodies. If colleagues or an administrator visit a class, it is a rare occurrence and not for a rigorous examination of the order of juried peer review. No teacher ever opens a professional journal to read with fear and trembling a review of his or her latest history course.

This is changing as demands for transparency and accountability become more insistent, and as the experience of peer review of teaching reduces concerns about individual autonomy. Conversation with colleagues enables us to see our actions from the perspective of fellow professionals who are likely to empathize with our difficulties, and be able to provide ideas from their own experience. Such conversations can also, if properly conducted, foster a sense of the department as a supportive, enquiring, scholarly community. Whilst such dialogue tends to be informal, and this is a valuable means of increasing insight, what follows are suggestions for more formal means of fostering peer discussion of teaching and learning.

Mentors and critical friends

Formal mentoring for new staff is now routine practice in many history departments. Mentoring, in a simple definition, is 'a confidential, one-to-one relationship in which an individual uses a more experienced, usually senior person as a sounding board and for guidance . . . a protected, non-judgmental relationship which facilitates a wide range of learning, experimentation and development' (Industrial Society 1995: 3). There are several roles a mentor can play. These include information provider (for example, about departmental regulations, practices and procedures); career guide or coach (how to get published, pursue one's personal development plan, prioritize key elements, etc.); academic guide (for example, observing teaching and advising on teaching issues, relevant literature); professional friend (providing emotional support, help with problems, offering a different perspective, etc.). Sharing the reasons one became a history teacher, successes and failures, principles for success or 'the five things I wish somebody had told me when I first started at this institution' can be a powerful stimulus to reflection. As a mentor it is best to ask precise questions (such as 'What kind of outcomes are you looking for in class?' or 'How do you know when it is time to intervene in a student group discussion?'), as these encourage more systematic reflection than general comments about teaching. Weimer (1990) and Brockbank and McGill (1998) provide advice on creating a positive context for mentoring, based upon regularly scheduled meetings (more frequent in the first semester), clarity about availability, explicitness of purposes and expectations, and an equal and non-judgmental relationship in which topics to be discussed are decided jointly. Establishing ground rules is essential to create such a climate of openness, encouragement and confidentiality. Mentees should be able to choose their own mentor, and Fullerton (1999) recommends that line managers should generally be avoided. Mentors must be willing to listen sensitively to ideas that differ from their own practice, and to learn from these. An external mentor or 'critical friend' can also help individuals and departments to focus more clearly on the process of teaching rather than subject content. Hyland (1996b) notes how using a critical friend from an education department provided a means of helping history colleagues to pursue a research project on student assessment by providing support, technical advice and reflective feedback on the process as the project proceeded. A critical friend can also be used in a peer observation of teaching scheme to feed back common issues to the department.

Peer observation

Schemes in which colleagues observe each other's teaching for developmental purposes are becoming increasingly common in history departments. Whilst peer observation can be employed as an instrument for measuring teaching quality in a department, here the emphasis is upon observation as a basis for reflection and collegial discussion of teaching and learning. In a report on the experience of a pilot departmental peer-observation scheme in history, two colleagues observed that whilst their classroom methods had not altered greatly as a result, the experience had made them feel that their differing approaches to teaching had been validated. Exchanging perspectives had also made them think more carefully about what they valued and why. One commented:

A lot of my colleagues here are very experienced classroom teachers; they've been at it for twenty-five years or longer. Not surprisingly, some of them take the position that teaching is something they already know how to do, and they don't need to think about how to do it better . . . My feeling is that after a while you get into a rut, and it's good to examine what you're doing. If you don't find a way to examine some of the strategies and approaches you've adopted, you risk communicating to students a lack of enthusiasm and commitment. So it's a good idea no matter how experienced you are, and how well things seem to be working in the classroom, to step back and examine your teaching and your students' learning. That's one of the things that Howard's and my visits and conversations together reinforced.

(Hutchings 1996: 19)

Whilst benefits can be considerable in terms of sharing ideas, providing reassurance and pinpointing issues of vague concern, careful implementation is necessary to ensure that peer observation feels safe to participants yet is sufficiently challenging to ensure that substantive reflection is encouraged (see Blackwell and McLean 1996). In particular, such schemes require a supportive and non-judgemental framework. This will normally involve rules about the confidentiality of all materials, discussions and findings, an emphasis upon developing reflection (not the judgement of individuals), and separation from the promotion or staff appraisal process. It is essential for the colleague being observed to make it clear in a pre-observation meeting what the objectives of the teaching session are and what the observer should particularly focus upon, as this makes targeted feedback much easier and a productive exchange more likely. The organization of the programme also needs to take account of preparation and feedback time in order to ensure that these take place in a logical sequence or cycle of reflection. Sensitivity is vital, for colleagues may initially be nervous about being observed and receiving feedback on their teaching, and asking each partner to select the sessions that they wish to be observed can provide reassurance. The observer can help by recognizing that, in the processes of observation and reflection, they too are learners whose views and actions are no less subject to critical examination than are those of their colleague. Feedback needs to be provided as soon as possible after the observation, to pinpoint specific issues related to the goals of the session, to focus on matters within the tutor's control, and to allow for open expression of feelings about how it went. It is also important to be positive and remember that it is not only what is said but how it is said that will condition whether the experience is perceived as positive or negative.

Teaching circles

A small group of tutors meeting to discuss particular aspects of teaching can provide a solid platform for exploring experiences, beliefs and values. In order to provide clarity of focus, each member can bring an issue for discussion by the whole group or an agenda can be formulated at the beginning of the meeting. Frederick (1999b) suggests a range of issues and questions for encouraging active reflection with colleagues in history departments, including:

- Critical incidents. What event in a recent class has been particularly challenging or had a particular resonance for you?
- Working with cases. Design a case that captures an important institutional issue about learning and teaching, or the curriculum, or interpreting student feedback, or mentoring or the changing nature of the student profile, etc.
- Your own experience of learning. Tell a story when you learned something new. How did you learn it? When and where? How did it feel? How did you know when you had learned it? What are the implications for your teaching?
- Exchanging and analysing successes. What have you done that really seems to work well in class? Why do you think that is?
- Listening to students. What are your students telling you about what helps and hinders their learning? How do you find this out, and what do you do with what you learn? Inviting a student representative along to contribute can help here.
- Metaphors and images. What is your metaphor for how you teach, and for how students learn? What visual image best captures your sense of an effective learning environment?

Many of these involve sharing personal narratives, and Alterio (1999) describes a project in which formalized storytelling is used to promote structured reflection. One person recounts a teaching experience to a colleague or group of colleagues. These are not allowed to make comments or introduce personal material from their own experience, as the discussion has to focus upon the storyteller. However, 'by asking questions about the situation, perhaps the teaching style used or the character of the group of students, the listener can explore the problem at a greater level' (30), and gain insights that might be missed in a more spontaneous conversation. Such storytelling sessions can also be transcribed and the results re-read to allow for individual reflection, followed by a further meeting for discussion and clarification if time is available. Brookfield (1995) advocates a 'three role structure' similar to the triad work used with students and described in Chapter 7. Here the teacher relates a puzzling or problematic incident, and the other participants ask questions to provide details that can help them to see the incident better through the eyes of the narrator. They then report back on what assumptions they think the narrator holds and put forward their own interpretation of the events, and the storyteller can ask them to elaborate their reasons for making such an interpretation. Finally, all discuss what they have learnt from the conversation and what it means for future action. Brookfield further notes that it can be helpful to appoint an umpire to ensure that personal judgements are not voiced and to comment on the quality of listening and contributing.

Such in-depth, personal reflection and revelation, however, are most easily achieved in departments where there exists a high degree of trust, consensus over goals and interaction between staff. Quinlan and Akerlind (2000) provide the example of a history department with no tradition of formal collegial discussion of teaching, and with a typical range of internal tensions. Here teaching circles were organized around a series of free-standing topics chosen at an initial meeting, to which all faculty were invited. Six topics relating to teaching were decided upon for discussion over an eight-month period. These were breadth versus depth in the history survey; required courses for majors; using graduate teaching assistants in large classes; teaching writing; the relationship between research and teaching; and race, gender and classroom climate. Each session was approximately an hour in length and limited to twelve people (who signed up on a sheet situated near staff pigeonholes) in order to keep discussion manageable. Although the core beliefs of participants remained little altered by the experience, many benefits were noted, not least the sharing of good ideas and practices on handling certain situations, and, for newer staff, the identification of sources of expertise on particular issues. In a similar experiment, another history department scheduled hour-and-a-half sessions in the late afternoon with refreshments to discuss teaching issues. To avoid too much generalized chatting about teaching, each session had clear goals, agreed by participants, and an agenda focused upon issues of concrete, practical concern to history teachers and designed to help them take more informed action. The benefits reported lay not only in sharing insights that enabled members to refine their own teaching, but also in fostering greater collegiality. As one of the organizers put it: 'They've put important teaching topics on the table and changed the way people relate to one another. The dialogue about teaching has really started' (Hutchings 1996: 9).

Successful teaching circles depend upon a sense of ownership and relevance to immediate staff concerns. Quinlan and Akerlind also suggest that the involvement of an outside consultant can help facilitate discussion and the handling of difficult people or situations, as well as provide well-founded advice grounded in the literature of teaching and learning. In history, experience suggests that teaching circles which require little long-term commitment and encourage the sharing of practical examples of practice are most likely to succeed. Discussion of general issues rather than personal 'problems' also tends to make participants feel more comfortable. The success of collegial dialogue, however, is founded upon many factors, perhaps most notably departmental leadership. Although there is insufficient space to explore this here, Centra (1993), Ramsden (1998) and Knight and Trowler (1999, 2000, 2001) provide a range of practical strategies by which academic leaders can create a positive context. Frederick (1991) also provides insights into how conversations with staff as part of career appraisal were used to create a sense of collegiality and purposeful reflection in a history department. All emphasize the importance of creating an atmosphere of trust, openness and support for teaching development within departments. This can be achieved through the demonstration by heads of department of a personal commitment to teaching, an emphasis on the need for active reflection on teaching in career interviews, a recognition of the need for public discussion of teaching issues, and support for innovation and pedagogic research and publication.

Researching teaching and learning

Research into history teaching and learning in higher education is a field which, although still relatively small, is growing quickly in scale and sophistication. A major challenge lies in its apparent proximity to educational research, often dismissed by historians as either commonsensical or jargon-ridden and whose methods most feel unqualified to evaluate. It is therefore important for researchers to find an accessible language for addressing pedagogy, one 'defined by the respect it shows for disciplinary languages and disciplinary standards for what constitutes a convincing argument' (Calder et al. 2002: 55). The course between educational theory and methods (which historians rarely read) and anecdotal accounts of classroom practices (which can be dismissed as simplistic, common sense and unscholarly) is not easy to steer. However, those investigating the history classroom have begun to navigate it more surely, demonstrating a growing confidence in the educational literature and educational research methods, whilst maintaining a commitment to the argument cum narrative-driven discourse, based on supporting examples and quotations, that characterizes professional historical writing.

If some of the more scientifically driven methods and concepts of educational research (such as experimental or correlational research) are unfamiliar to historians trained in documentary analysis, many demand exactly the kinds of skills that historians are trained to bring to bear. Indeed, as Cohen and Manion (1994) point out, historical research is itself a valued part of educational research, whether in charting developments in teaching and learning, mapping the current state of practice or surveying the literature on pedagogy. However, let us briefly consider a method unfamiliar to most historians yet common in research into classroom practices. Action research is widely used in education to describe a process whereby teachers engage in researching their practice with the aim of changing it. It is not an uncontested or uncomplicated concept; rather, as Reason and Bradbury (2001: xxiv) note, 'the action research family includes a whole range of approaches and practices, each grounded in different traditions, in different philosophical and psychological assumptions, pursuing different political commitments'. Carr and Kemmis (1986) outline three broad models of educational action research. These they call the *technical* (the testing of established research findings in the practices of teachers aimed at efficient and effective practice, and judged by criteria often imported from outside rather than the self-reflection of practitioners); the *practical* (also aimed at effective practice but involving practitioners more in planning, monitoring mechanisms and reflection on the process and outcomes, usually with the help of a facilitator); and the *emancipatory* (involving a group of practitioner-researchers who act together as a critical community in an open-minded process which explores practices and incidents not merely as individual occurrences but within wider relationships of power, and aims at individual, educational and social transformation). Although the various kinds of action research differ in the extent to which they are influenced by critical theory, they possess some features in common (see Stenhouse 1975; Elliot 1991; McKernan 1991; McNiff 1992; McNiff et al. 1996; Zuber-Skerritt 1992; Kember 2000). Thus educational action research is generally accepted to be:

- concerned with educational practice as socially constructed (that is, existing in complex social interactions, such as those between teachers and students, and within wider departmental, institutional, disciplinary and socio-cultural contexts);
- action-oriented (about generating knowledge for, and from, action, rather than accumulating knowledge);
- aimed at improvement, whether defined in relation to a teacher's own practice or wider social change;
- rigorous and systematic, following a research cycle of planning, action, observation and reflection, usually over at least two cycles, with a coherent evaluation process leading to outcomes made public;
- participative (controlled by teachers themselves, whether as individuals or in groups, who take the key role as researchers).

Whilst all this may at first sight seem remote from the practices of historical scholarship, action-research projects are generally founded upon a four-stage cycle of reflection/action (corresponding to Kolb's model of experiential learning outlined in Chapter 7), that is in alignment with the investigative and reflective process of historical research. Similar stages are in evidence, notably planning (finding a topic, reading the literature), investigation (archive or library searches), evaluation of evidence (close reading and interpretation) and reflection on meaning in order to make generalizations, leading to further investigation. As Kemmis (1988: 184) suggests:

the techniques for generating and accumulating evidence about practices, and the techniques for analyzing and interpreting the evidence more closely resemble the techniques employed by interpretative researchers (ethnographers, case study researchers, historians) than empirical-analytic researchers (correlational analysis, comparative experiments, etc.). This is so primarily because the 'objects' of research are actions (practices) and the viewpoints and historical circumstances that gave these actions meaning and significance.

The historian's skills of rigorous sifting, analysis and interpretation of large bodies of complex information can greatly illuminate the results of interviews with, or observation of, students and staff, just as they do an eighteenth-century letter or manuscript. A basic educational evaluation method such as triangulation – the process of comparing and justifying evidence from one evaluation method against that from another, for example, a class situation recorded through the views of students, teacher and an observer – bears a close resemblance to the practice of checking a primary source against a variety of other sources as a means of establishing reliability. Historians need not feel ill-equipped to undertake research into the teaching and learning of their discipline, and for the first-time researcher well-grounded, straightforward advice on educational trends and methods is available (see, for example, Brookfield 1995; Bennett *et al.* 1996; Jones *et al.* 1997).

Conclusion

Adopting a scholarly approach to teaching involves applying the same intellectual rigour to one's practices in relation to student learning as to any other form of academic activity, in a process aimed at improvement in one's practice. A key challenge, as one historian puts it, is

> to overcome the perceived dichotomy between disciplinary scholarship and pedagogical scholarship in order to integrate my professional responsibilities. I believe that my focus on student learning is helping me to create a unified scholarly discourse. Whether I am examining the methodologies of history as ways of thinking, exploring theories of adult learning and development for insights into my students, or whether we as a faculty and staff are carrying out formal and informal empirical studies of our students' learning, I see myself engaged in a common scholarship of teaching that has a direct impact on the learning environment.
>
> (quoted in Mentkowski 2000: 268–9)

Integral to this is a spirit of curiosity about student learning, and an approach that is 'systematic, grounded in evidence, informed by relevant theory, mindful of . . . [the] discipline's standards for what constitutes convincing claims to knowledge, and accountable to public review' (Calder *et al.* 2002: 55). This kind of disciplined enquiry involves a process that is at once intellectual and practical, reflective and action-oriented, and through which a teacher's own insights can be powerfully illuminated and challenged by the perspectives of students, colleagues and other researchers. Nonetheless, returning systematically to experience, and to the assumptions that underpin one's practices, provides the starting point for developing the understanding that can lead to significant improvements in student learning.

Developing as a history teacher is a long-term, ongoing process in which mastery is never complete; for each class is different and no teaching is ever perfect given the diverse nature of students' experience, abilities and approaches to learning. It is also an endeavour that concerns more than the individual historian, for classroom teaching and learning are part of an interconnected system that includes the institution, disciplinary community and the wider socio-cultural forces impinging upon them. Historians, whose professional livelihood is the analysis of change in all its forms, are particularly well placed to understand these forces, and to appreciate that what is regarded as good practice today will change in the light of further enquiry and reflection. In the face of pressures on time and resource constraints, of course, it is easy to do nothing and blame others for making life difficult, or fall back too readily upon the latest teaching 'tips'. Approaching teaching in a scholarly fashion (with the same spirit of intrinsic interest, curiosity and engagement as in research) not only inspires confidence that the skills, knowledge and understanding that one intends are being fostered, but also makes teaching (and learning) more interesting and more fun. At a time when an 'accountability' mentality is in the ascendant across higher education, such an opportunity to enlarge our professional aspirations and enhance our enjoyment is to be highly prized.

REFERENCES

The following abbreviations are used in this section:

ASHE-ERIC   Association for the Study of Higher Education-Educational
               Resources Information Centre
CVCP   Committee of Vice-chancellors and Principals
HESDA   Higher Education Staff Development Association
HUDG   History at the Universities Defence Group
LTSN   Learning and Teaching Support Network
NIACE   National Institute for Adult Continuing Education
SEDA   Staff and Educational Development Association
UCoSDA   Universities and Colleges Staff Development Association

Abbott, M. (ed.) (1996) *History Skills: a student's handbook,* London: Routledge.
Adams, D. (2000) 'Views of academic work', *Teacher Development,* 4: 65–78.
Allen, J. and Lloyd-Jones, R. (1998) *The Assessment of Group Work and Presentations in the Humanities,* Sheffield: Sheffield Hallam University.
Alterio, M. (1999) 'Tell your side of the story', *Times Higher Education Supplement,* 16 April: 30–31.
Anderson, C. (1997) 'Enabling and shaping understanding through tutorials', in F. Marton, D. Hounsell and N. Entwistle, (eds) *The Experience of Learning,* Edinburgh: Scottish Academic Press.
Anderson, E. (ed.) (1993) *Campus Use of the Teaching Portfolio,* Washington, DC: American Association for Higher Education.
Anderson, J. and Adams, M. (1992) 'Acknowledging the learning styles of diverse student populations: implications for instructional design', in L. Border and N. Chism (eds) *Teaching for Diversity,* San Francisco: Jossey-Bass.
Andress, D. (1998) 'Truth, ethics and imagination', in J. Arnold, K. Davies and S. Ditchfield (eds) *History and Heritage: consuming the past in contemporary culture,* Dorset: Donhead.
Angelo, T. (1991) 'Ten easy pieces: assessing higher learning in four dimensions', in T. Angelo, *Classroom Assessment Techniques: early lessons from success,* San Francisco: Jossey-Bass.

Angelo, T. (1993) 'A teacher's dozen: fourteen general, research-based principles for improving higher learning in our classrooms', *Bulletin of the American Association of Higher Education*, April: 3–13.

Angelo, T. and Cross, P. (1993) *Classroom Assessment Techniques: a handbook for college teachers*, San Francisco: Jossey-Bass.

Appleby, J., Hunt, L. and Jacob, M. (1994) *Telling the Truth about History*, New York: Norton.

Arthur, J. and Phillips, R. (eds) (2000) *Issues in History Teaching*, London: Routledge.

Ashby, R. and Lee, P. (1987) 'Children's concepts of empathy and understanding', in C. Portal (ed.) *The History Curriculum for Teachers*, Lewes: Falmer.

Atkins, M., Beattie, J. and Dockrell, W. (1993) *Assessment Issues in Higher Education*, London: Department of Employment.

Bailey, D., De Vinny, G. and Gordon, C. (2000) 'AIDS and American history: four perspectives on experiential learning', *Journal of American History*, 86: 1721–33.

Bain, R. (2000) 'Into the breach: using research and theory to shape history instruction', in P. Stearns, P. Seixas and S. Wineburg (eds) *Knowing, Teaching and Learning History*, New York: New York University Press.

Baldwin, C. (1992) 'How I got my first in history', in H. Arksey (ed.) *How to Get a First Class Degree*, Lancaster: Centre for Innovation, Lancaster University.

Barker, A. (1997) 'University history 1997', *History Today*, 47(8): 58–61.

Barker, H., McLean, M. and Roseman, M. (2000) 'Re-thinking the history curriculum: enhancing students' communication and group-work skills', in A. Booth and P. Hyland (eds) *The Practice of University History Teaching*, Manchester: Manchester University Press.

Barnet, R. (1997) *Higher Education: a critical business*, Buckingham: Open University Press.

Bartul, J. (1999) 'Teaching the value of inquiry through the essay question', in S. Gillespie (ed.) *Perspectives on Teaching Innovations: teaching to think historically*, Washington, DC: American Historical Association.

Bates, D. (1999) 'Undergraduate history 1999', *History Today*, 49(8): 54–60.

Baume, C. and Baume, D. (1992) *Course Design for Active Learning*, Sheffield: CVCP.

Beaty, L. (1997) *Developing Your Teaching Through Reflective Practice*, SEDA Special no. 5.

Becher, T. and Trowler, P. (2001, 2nd edn) *Academic Tribes and Territories: intellectual enquiry and the cultures of disciplines*, Buckingham: Open University Press.

Belenky, M., Clinchy, B., Goldberger, N. and Tartule, J. (1986) *Women's Ways of Knowing: the development of self, voice and mind*, New York: Basic Books.

Bender, T. (1994) 'Venturesome and cautious: American history in the 1990s', *Journal of American History*, 81: 992–1003.

Bennett, C., Foreman-Peck, L. and Higgins, C. (1996) *Researching into Teaching Methods in Higher Education*, London: Kogan Page.

Berkhofer, R. (1999) 'Demystifying historical authority: critical textual analysis in the classroom', in S. Gillespie (ed.), *Perspectives on Teaching Innovations: teaching to think historically*, Washington, DC: American Historical Association.

Bevir, M. (1994) 'Objectivity in history', *History and Theory*, 33: 328–44.

Biggs, J. (1987) *Student Approaches to Learning and Studying*, Hawthorn, Victoria: Australian Council for Educational Research.

REFERENCES

Biggs, J. (1988) 'Approaches to learning and essay writing', in R. Schmeck (ed.) *Learning Strategies and Learning Styles*, New York: Plenum.

Biggs, J. (1999) *Teaching for Quality Learning at University*, Buckingham: Open University Press.

Biggs, J. and Collis, K. (1982) *Evaluating the Quality of Learning: the SOLO taxonomy*, New York: Academic Press.

Black, J. and MacRaild, D. (1997) *Studying History*, London: Macmillan.

Blackey, R. (1997) 'New wine in old bottles: revitalizing the traditional history lecture', *Teaching History: a journal of methods*, 22: 3–25.

Blackey, R. (1999) 'Introduction', in S. Gillespie (ed.) *Perspectives on Teaching Innovations: teaching to think historically*, Washington, DC: American Historical Association.

Blackwell, R. and McLean, M. (1996) 'Peer observation of teaching and staff development', *Higher Education Quarterly*, 50: 156–71.

Bligh, D. (ed.) (1986) *Teach Thinking by Discussion*, Guildford: Society for Research into Higher Education.

Bligh, D. (1998) *What's the Use of Lectures?*, Exeter: Intellect Press.

Bloxham, S. (1997) 'Improving learning skills: an evaluation', in G. Gibbs and C. Rust (eds) *Improving Student Learning through Course Design*, Oxford: Oxford Centre for Staff and Learning Development.

Bonwell, C. and Eison, J. (1991) *Active Learning: creating excitement in the classroom*, Washington, DC: ASHE-ERIC Higher Education Report.

Booth, A. (1993) 'Learning history in university: student views on teaching and assessment', *Studies in Higher Education*, 18: 227–35.

Booth, A. (1996a) 'Changing assessment to improve learning', in A. Booth and P. Hyland (eds) *History in Higher Education*, London: Blackwell.

Booth, A. (1996b) 'Assessing group work', in A. Booth and P. Hyland (eds) *History in Higher Education*, London: Blackwell.

Booth, A. (1997) 'Listening to students: experiences and expectations in the transition to a history degree', *Studies in Higher Education*, 22: 205–20.

Booth, A. (2000) 'Creating a context to enhance student learning in history', in A. Booth and P. Hyland (eds) *The Practice of University History Teaching*, Manchester: Manchester University Press.

Booth, A. (2001) 'Developing students' study skills in the transition to university', *Teaching in Higher Education*, 6: 487–502.

Booth, A. and Hyland, P. (eds) (1996) *History in Higher Education: new directions in teaching and learning*, Oxford: Blackwell.

Booth, A. and Hyland, P. (eds) (2000) *The Practice of University History Teaching*, Manchester: Manchester University Press.

Border, L. and Chism, N. (eds) (1992) *Teaching for Diversity*, San Francisco: Jossey-Bass.

Bosworth, S., Gossweiler, R. and Slevin, K. (2000) 'Assessing learning outcomes: tests, gender and the assessment of historical knowledge', in A. Booth and P. Hyland (eds) *The Practice of University History Teaching*, Manchester: Manchester University Press.

Boud, D. (1990) 'Assessment and the promotion of academic values', *Studies in Higher Education*, 15: 101–11.

Boud, D. (ed.) (1995a, 2nd edn) *Developing Student Autonomy in Learning*, London: Kogan Page.

Boud, D. (ed.) (1995b) *Enhancing Learning through Self-assessment*, London: Kogan Page.

Boud, D. and Falchikov, N. (1989) 'Quantitative studies of student self-assessment in higher education', *Higher Education*, 18: 529–49.

Boud, D. and Falchikov, N. (1995) 'What does research tell us about self-assessment?', in D. Boud (ed.) *Enhancing Learning through Self-assessment*, London: Kogan Page.

Boulton-Lewis, G. (1995) 'The SOLO taxonomy as a means of shaping and assessing learning in higher education', *Higher Education Research and Development*, 14: 143–54.

Boyer, E. (1990) *Scholarship Reconsidered: priorities of the professoriate*, Princeton, NJ: Carnegie Foundation for the Advancement of Teaching.

Boys, C., Brennan, J., Henkel, M., Kirkland, J., Kogan, M. and Youll, P. (1988) *Higher Education and the Preparation for Work*, London: Jessica Kingsley.

Bradford, M. and O'Connell, C. (1998) *Assessment in Geography*, Cheltenham: Geography Discipline Network.

Braskamp, L. and Ory, J. (1994) *Assessing Faculty Work: enhancing individual and institutional performance*, San Francisco: Jossey-Bass.

Brecher, B. and Hickey, T. (1990) 'Teaching skills through history', *PUSH Newsletter*, 1: 13–20.

Brew, A. (1995) 'Self-assessment in different domains', in D. Boud (ed.) *Enhancing Learning through Self-assessment*, London: Kogan Page.

Brockbank, A. and McGill, I. (1998) *Facilitating Reflective Learning in Higher Education*, Buckingham: Open University Press.

Bromwick, R. and Swallow, B. (1999) 'I like being who I am: a study of young people's ideals', *Educational Studies*, 25: 117–28.

Brookfield, S. (1995) *Becoming a Critically Reflective Teacher*, San Francisco: Jossey-Bass.

Brookfield, S. (1999) *Discussion as a Way of Teaching*, Buckingham: Open University Press.

Brooks, C. (2000) 'Teaching and the academic career', in A. Booth and P. Hyland (eds) *The Practice of University History Teaching*, Manchester: Manchester University Press.

Brown, G. and Atkins, M. (1990) *Effective Teaching in Higher Education*, London: Routledge.

Brown, G., Bull, J. and Pendlebury, M. (1997) *Assessing Student Learning in Higher Education*, London: Routledge.

Brown, M., Harding, D. and Rogers, G. (2001) 'The virtual learning environment as a pedagogic tool', in R. Hall and D. Harding (eds) *Chic Project Case Studies: managing ICT in the curriculum*, Middlesbrough: Courseware for History Implementation Consortium.

Brown, S. and Knight, P. (1994) *Assessing Learners in Higher Education*, London: Kogan Page.

Brown, S. and Race, P. (1995) *Assess Your Own Teaching Quality*, London: Kogan Page.

Brown, S. and Race, P. (2002) *Lecturing: a practical guide*, London: Kogan Page.

Brown, S., Rust, C. and Gibbs, G. (1994) *Strategies for Diversifying Assessment in Higher Education*, Oxford: Oxford Centre for Staff Development.

Brown, S., Thompson, G. and Armstrong, S. (eds) (1998) *Motivating Students*, London: Kogan Page.

Bruce, C. and Gerber, R. (1995) 'Towards lecturers' conceptions of student learning', *Higher Education*, 29: 442–58.

Bruley, S. (1996) 'Women's history, oral history and active learning: an experience from southern England', *Women's History Review*, 5: 111–27.

Bruner, J. (1996) *The Culture of Education*, Cambridge, MA: Harvard University Press.

Burke, P. (ed.) (1991) *New Perspectives on Historical Writing*, Oxford: Polity Press.

Burke, P. (2001) *Eyewitnessing: the uses of images as historical evidence*, Ithaca, NY: Cornell University Press.

Buzan, T. (1995) *Use Your Head*, London: BBC.

Calder, L. (2002) 'Looking for learning in the history survey', *Perspectives*, 40: 43–4.

Calder, L., Cutler, W. and Kelly, T. (2002) 'History lessons: historians and the scholarship of teaching and learning', in M. Huber and S. Morreale (eds) *Disciplinary Styles in the Scholarship of Teaching: exploring common ground*, Washington, DC: American Association for Higher Education.

Cameron, S. (2002) 'Using the world wide web to teach history, classics and archaeology', LTSN Subject Centre for History, Classics and Archaeology, Briefing Paper no. 7.

Carr, W. and Kemmis, S. (1986) *Becoming Critical: education, knowledge and action research*, Lewes: Falmer.

Cashin, W. (1995) 'Student ratings of teaching: the research revisited', IDEA paper no. 32.

Cassity, M. (1994) 'History and the public purpose', *Journal of American History*, 81: 968–76.

Centra, J. (1993) *Reflective Faculty Evaluation: enhancing teaching and determining faculty effectiveness*, San Francisco: Jossey-Bass.

Cerbin, W. (1994) 'The course portfolio as a tool for continuous improvement of teaching and learning', *Journal of Excellence in College Teaching*, 5: 95–105.

Chanock, K. (2000) 'Comments on essays: do students understand what tutors write?', *Teaching in Higher Education*, 5: 95–105.

Chickering, A. and Gamson, Z. (1987) 'Seven principles for good practice in undergraduate education', *The Wingspread Journal*, 9: 1–3.

Chickering, A. and Reisser, L. (1993, 2nd edn) *Education and Identity*, San Francisco: Jossey-Bass.

Church, C. (1976) 'Disciplinary dynamics', *Studies in Higher Education*, 1: 101–18.

Church, C. (1978) 'Constraints on the historian', *Studies in Higher Education*, 3: 127–38.

Clare, J. (1998) 'Oxford graduates have "degree of ignorance" about history', *Daily Telegraph*, 27 October.

Clark, C. and de Groot, J. (1992) 'Group project work in undergraduate history', Submission for the Cadbury Schweppes Prize for Innovative Teaching and Learning.

Clarke, P. and Associates (1994) 'Men's and women's performance in tripos examinations, 1980–1993', History Faculty Gender Working Party Report, University of Cambridge.

Cohen, L. and Manion, L. (1994, 4th edn) *Research Methods in Education*, London: Routledge.

Collier, G. (ed.) (1983) *The Management of Peer-Group Learning*, Guildford: Society for Research into Higher Education.

Collingwood, R. (1946) *The Idea of History*, Oxford: Clarendon Press.

Counsell, C. (2000) 'Historical knowledge and historical skills', in J. Arthur and R. Phillips (eds) *Issues in History Teaching*, London: Routledge.

Cowan, A. (1994) 'Using original sources in a history course', in J. Wisdom and G. Gibbs (eds) *Course Design for Resource Based Learning: Humanities*, Oxford: Oxford Centre for Staff Development.

Cowan, A. (1996) 'Planning a history curriculum', in A. Booth and P. Hyland (eds) *History in Higher Education*, London: Blackwell.

Creme, P. (2000) 'The personal in university writing: uses of reflective learning journals', in M. Lea and B. Stirer (eds) *Student Writing in Higher Education: new contexts*, Buckingham: Open University Press.

Crooks, T. (1988) *Assessing Student Performance*, Kensington, NSW: Higher Education Research and Development Society of Australasia.

Crozier, W. (1997) *Individual Learners: personality differences in education*, London: Routledge.

Cruse, J. (1994) 'Practising history: a high school teacher's reflections', *Journal of American History*, 81: 1064–74.

Currie, J. (2000) 'Exploit your experience', *Times Higher Educational Supplement*, 31 March: 40–41.

Cutler, W. (1998) 'Writing a course portfolio for an introductory course in American history', in P. Hutchings (ed.) *The Course Portfolio*, Washington, DC: American Association for Higher Education.

Dall'Alba, G. (1991) 'Foreshadowing conceptions of teaching and learning', *Research and Development in Higher Education*, 13: 293–7.

Davies, P. (2000) 'Imaginative ideas for teaching and learning', in A. Booth and P. Hyland (eds) *The Practice of University History Teaching*, Manchester: Manchester University Press.

Davis, B. (1993) *Tools for Teaching*, San Francisco: Jossey-Bass.

Davison, R. (1993) 'Teaching history with song and doggerel', in R. Blackey (ed.) *History Anew: innovations in the teaching of history*, Long Beach, CA: California State University Press.

Dawson, I. (1990) 'The use of role-play in history teaching at degree level', *PUSH Newsletter*, 2: 34–8.

Dawson, I. and de Pennington, J. (2000) 'Fieldwork in history teaching and learning', in A. Booth and P. Hyland (eds) *The Practice of University History Teaching*, Manchester: Manchester University Press.

Day, K., Grant, R. and Hounsell, D. (1998) *Reviewing Your Teaching*, Edinburgh: Centre for Teaching, Learning and Assessment.

De Bono, E. (1986) 'Brainstorming', in D. Bligh (ed.) *Teach Thinking by Discussion*, Guildford: Society for Research into Higher Education.

Demos, J. (2002) 'Using self, using history', *Journal of American History*, 88: 37–42.

Denicolo, P., Entwistle, N. and Hounsell, D. (1992) *What is Active Learning?*, Sheffield: CVCP.

Diamond, R. (1989) *Designing and Improving Courses and Curricula in Higher Education*, San Francisco: Jossey-Bass.

Diamond, R. and Adam, B. (eds) (1995) *The Disciplines Speak: rewarding the scholarly, professional, and creative work of faculty*, Washington, DC: American Association for Higher Education.

Dickinson, A. and Lee, P. (eds) (1978) *History Teaching and Historical Understanding*, London: Heinemann.

Donovan, B. (1998) 'Service learning as a tool of engagement: from Thomas Aquinas to Che Guevara', in I. Harkavy and B. Donovan (eds) *Connecting Past to Present: concepts and models for service-learning in history*, Washington, DC: American Association for Higher Education.

Donovan, T. (1973) *Historical Thought in America: postwar patterns*, Oklahoma: University of Oklahoma Press.

Doran, S., Durston, C., Fletcher, A. and Longmore, J. (2000) 'Assessing students in seminars: an evaluation of current practice', in A. Booth and P. Hyland (eds) *The Practice of University History Teaching*, Manchester: Manchester University Press.

Doughty, G. (1996) 'Computers for teaching and learning', in J. Tait and P. Knight (eds) *The Management of Independent Learning*, London: Kogan Page.

Dunkin, M. (ed.) (1991) *Award Winning University Teachers: talking about teaching*, Sydney: Centre for Teaching and Learning, University of Sydney.

Eble, K. (1988) *The Craft of Teaching*, San Francisco: Jossey-Bass.

Edgerton, R., Hutchings, P. and Quinlan, K. (1991) *The Teaching Portfolio: capturing scholarship in teaching*, Washington, DC: American Association for Higher Education.

Ellington, H., Addinall, E. and Percival, F. (1982) *A Handbook of Game Design*, London: Kogan Page.

Elliot, J. (1991) *Action Research for Educational Change*, Buckingham: Open University Press.

Elton, G. (1967) *The Practice of History*, London: Methuen.

Entwistle, N. (1988) *Styles of Learning and Teaching: an integrated outline of educational psychology*, London: Fulton.

Entwistle, N. (1992) *The Impact of Teaching on Learning Outcomes in Higher Education: a literature review*, Sheffield: CVCP.

Entwistle, N. (1995) 'Frameworks for understanding as experienced in essay writing and in preparing for examinations', *Educational Psychologist*, 30: 47–54.

Entwistle, A. and Entwistle, N. (1992) 'Experiences of understanding in revising for degree examinations', *Learning and Instruction*, 2: 1–22.

Entwistle, N. and Entwistle, A. (1997) 'Revision and the experience of understanding', in F. Marton, D. Hounsell and N. Entwistle (eds) *The Experience of Learning*, Edinburgh: Scottish Academic Press.

Entwistle, N. and Marton, F. (1994) 'Knowledge objects: understandings constituted through intensive academic study', *British Journal of Educational Psychology*, 64: 161–78.

Entwistle, N. and Ramsden, P. (1983) *Understanding Student Learning*, London: Croom Helm.

Entwistle, N., Thompson, S., Tait, H. (1992) *Guidelines for Promoting Effective Learning in Higher Education*, Edinburgh: Centre for Research on Learning and Instruction.

Entwistle, N., Boys, C., Brennan, J., Henkel, M., Kirkland, J., Kogan, M. and Youll, P. (1989) *The Performance of Electrical Engineering Students in Scottish Higher Education*, Edinburgh: Centre for Research on Learning and Instruction.

Eraut, M. (1992) 'Developing the knowledge base: a process perspective on professional education', in R. Barnet (ed.) *Learning to Effect*, Buckingham: Open University Press.

Eraut, M. (1994) *Developing Professional Knowledge and Competence*, London: Falmer.

Eraut, M. (2000) 'Non-formal learning and tacit knowledge in professional work', *British Journal of Educational Psychology*, 70: 113–36.

Erikson, E. (1965) *Childhood and Society*, London: Penguin.

Evans, C. and Brown, T. (1998) 'Teaching the history survey course using multimedia techniques', *Perspectives*, 36: 17–20.

Evans, E. (2003) 'University history and school history', in M. Riley and R. Harris (eds) *Past Forward: a vision for school history 2002–2012,* London: Historical Association.

Evans, R. (1988) 'Lessons from history: teacher and student conceptions of the meaning of history', *Theory and Research in Social Education*, 16: 203–25.

Evans, R. (1989) 'Teacher conceptions of history', *Theory and Research in Social Education*, 17: 210–40.

Evans, R. (1994) 'Educational ideologies and the teaching of history', in G. Leinhardt, I. Beck and C. Stainton (eds) *Teaching and Learning in History*, Hillsdale, NJ: Lawrence Erlbaum.

Evans, R. J. (1997) *In Defence of History*, London: Granta.

Ferguson, N. (ed.) (1998) *Virtual History: alternatives and counterfactuals*, London: Macmillan.

Fitzgerald, I. and Hingley, V. (1996) 'University history today', *History Today*, 46 (8): 50–54.

Fitzgerald, I. and Hodgkinson, K. (1994) 'British university history now', *History Today*, 44 (8): 53–7.

Fox, D. (1983) 'Personal theories of teaching', *Studies in Higher Education*, 8: 151–63.

Francis, B., Robson, J. and Read, B. (2001) 'An analysis of undergraduate writing styles in the context of gender and achievement', *Studies in Higher Education*, 26: 313–26.

Frank, D., Schofer, E. and Torres, J. (1994) 'Rethinking history: changes in the university curriculum 1910–90', *Sociology of Education*, 67: 231–42.

Frederick, P. (1981) 'The dreaded discussion – ten ways to start', *College Teaching*, 29: 109–14.

Frederick, P. (1986) 'The lively lecture – eight variations', *College Teaching*, 34: 43–50.

Frederick, P. (1991) 'Changing collegial conversation', *The Department Advisor*, 6: 1–5.

Frederick, P. (1995) 'Walking on eggs – mastering the dreaded diversity discussion', *College Teaching*, 43: 83–92.

Frederick, P. (1999a) 'Motivating students by active learning in the history classroom', in S. Gillespie (ed.) *Perspectives on Teaching Innovations: teaching to think historically*, Washington, DC: American Historical Association.

Frederick, P. (1999b) 'Working with colleagues: creating a culture for learning', unpublished paper.

Frederick, P. (2000) 'Approaches to teaching diversity', *Bulletin of the National Education Association*, 17: 5–8.

Frederick, P. (2001a) 'Learning from the inside out', in H. Edwards, B. Smith and G. Webb (eds) *Lecturing: case studies, experience and practice*, London: Kogan Page.

Frederick, P. (2001b) 'Four reflections on teaching and learning', *Perspectives*, 39: 28–30.

Frederick, P. and Jeffrey, J. (2002) *American History in a Box*, London: Longman.

French, D., Hale, C., Johnson, C. and Farr, G. (eds) (1999) *Internet Based Learning: an introduction and framework for higher education and business*, London: Kogan Page.

Fry, H., Ketteridge, S. and Marshall, S. (eds) (1999) *A Handbook for Teaching and Learning in Higher Education*, London: Kogan Page.

Fullerton, H. (1999) 'Get mentoring to work well', *Times Higher Educational Supplement*, 14 May: 36–7.

Gallman, J. (1998) 'Service-learning and history: training the metaphorical mind', in I. Harkavy and B. Donovan (eds) *Connecting Past to Present: concepts and models for service-learning in history*, Washington, DC: American Association for Higher Education.

Games, G. (1996) 'Lectures versus seminars: getting to grips with teaching', in D. Allan (ed.) *In at the Deep End: first experiences of university teaching*, Lancaster: Centre for Innovation, Lancaster University.

Gardner, H. (1999) *Intelligence Reframed: multiple intelligences for the 21st century*, New York: Basic Books.

Gardner, H. and Boix-Manilla, V. (1994) 'Teaching for understanding in the disciplines – and beyond', *Teachers College Record*, 96: 198–218.

George, J. and Cowan, J. (1999) *A Handbook of Techniques for Formative Education*, London: Kogan Page.

Gibbs, G. (1981) *Teaching Students to Learn*, Buckingham: Open University Press.

Gibbs, G. (1988) *Creating a Teaching Portfolio*, Bristol: Technical and Educational Services.

Gibbs, G. (1992a) *Assessing More Students*, Oxford: Oxford Centre for Staff Development.

Gibbs, G. (1992b) *Improving the Quality of Student Learning*, Bristol: Technical and Educational Services.

Gibbs, G. (1992c) *Discussion with More Students*, Oxford: Oxford Centre for Staff Development.

Gibbs, G. (1992d) 'Improving the quality of learning through course design', in R. Barnet (ed.) *Learning to Effect*, Buckingham: Open University Press.

Gibbs, G. (1995) 'Research into student learning', in B. Smith and S. Brown (eds) *Research, Teaching and Learning in Higher Education*, London: Kogan Page.

Gibbs, G. and Habeshaw, T. (1990) 253 *Ideas for Your Teaching*, Bristol: Technical and Educational Services.

Gibbs, G., Habeshaw, S. and Habeshaw, T. (1989) 53 *Interesting Ways to Appraise Your Teaching*, Bristol: Technical and Educational Services.

Gibbs, G., Rust, C., Jenkins, A. and Jaques, D. (1994) *Developing Students' Transferable Skills*, Oxford: Oxford Centre for Staff Development.

Gillespie, S. (ed.) (1999) *Perspectives on Teaching Innovations: teaching to think historically*, Washington, DC: American Historical Association.

Gilligan, C. (1986) *In a Different Voice: psychological theory and women's development*, Cambridge, MA: Harvard University Press.

Glasfurd, G. and Winstanley, M. (2000) 'History in cyberspace: challenges and opportunities of internet-based teaching and learning', in A. Booth and P. Hyland (eds) *The Practice of University History Teaching*, Manchester: Manchester University Press.

Glassick, C., Huber, M. and Maeroff, G. (1997) *Scholarship Assessed: evaluation of the professoriate*, San Francisco: Jossey-Bass.

Goldshmid, B. and Goldshmid, M. (1976) 'Peer teaching in higher education: a review', *Higher Education*, 5: 9–33.

Gonzalez, M. (2001) 'Learning independently through project work', in M. Walker (ed.) *Reconstructing Professionalism in University Teaching*, Buckingham: Open University Press.

Goodlad, S. (ed.) (1995) *Students as Tutors and Mentors*, London: Kogan Page.

Goodlad, S. and Hirst, B. (1989) *Peer Tutoring: a guide to learning by teaching*, London: Kogan Page.

Gould, P. (1973) 'The open geographic curriculum', in R. Chorley (ed.) *Directions in Geography*, London: Methuen.

Graff, J. (1991) *New Life for the College Curriculum*, San Francisco: Jossey-Bass.

Graham, J. (1999) 'Individual effort, collective outcome: a case study of group teaching strategies in history', *Innovations in Education and Training International*, 36: 205–18.

Gutierrez, C. (2000) 'Making connections: the interdisciplinary community of teaching and learning history', in P. Stearns, P. Seixas and S. Wineburg (eds) *Knowing, Teaching and Learning History*, New York: New York University Press.

Hall, R. and Harding, D. (eds) (2001) *Chic Project Case Studies: managing ICT in the curriculum*, Middlesbrough: Courseware for History Implementation Consortium.

Hall, R., Holden, K. and Rogers, G. (2001) 'Supporting students' critical reflection through web-based pedagogic innovation', in R. Hall and D. Harding (eds) *Chic Project Case Studies: managing ICT in the curriculum*, Middlesbrough: Courseware for History Implementation Consortium.

Hallas, C. (1996) 'Learning from experience: field trips and work placements', in A. Booth and P. Hyland (eds) *History in Higher Education*, London: Blackwell.

Hallden, O. (1986) 'Learning history', *Oxford Review of Education*, 12: 53–66.

Hallden, O. (1994) 'On the paradox of understanding history in an educational setting', in G. Leinhardt, I. Beck and C. Stainton (eds) *Teaching and Learning in History*, Hillsdale, NJ: Lawrence Erlbaum.

Hannam, J. and Swain, G. (1990) 'Variations on the essay theme: an alternative approach to assessment', *PUSH Newsletter*, 2: 41–7.

Harris, D. (1999) 'Creating a complete learning environment', in D. French, C. Hale, C. Johnson and G. Farr (eds) *Internet Based Learning: an introduction and framework for higher education and business*, London: Kogan Page.

Harris, D. and Bell, C. (1994) *Evaluating and Assessing for Learning*, London: Kogan Page.

Harrison, B. (1968) 'History at the universities', *History*, 53: 357–80.

Hartley, J. (1998) *Learning and Studying: a research perspective*, London: Routledge.

Hartley, J. and Greggs, M. (1997) 'Divergent thinking in arts and science students', *Studies in Higher Education*, 22: 93–7.

Hayes, K. and Richardson, J. (1995) 'Gender, subject and context as determinants of approaches to studying in higher education', *Studies in Higher Education*, 20: 215–21.

Head, J. (1997) *Working with Adolescents: constructing identity*, London: Falmer.

Healey, M. (2000) 'Developing the scholarship of teaching in higher education: a discipline-based model', *Higher Education Research and Development*, 19: 169–89.

Heiss, M. (1998) 'A course portfolio for a colloquium in twentieth-century American foreign relations', in P. Hutchings (ed.) *The Course Portfolio*, Washington, DC: American Association for Higher Education.

Henry, J. (1994) *Teaching through Projects*, London: Kogan Page.

Heron, J. (1995) 'Assessment revisited', in D. Boud (ed.) *Developing Student Autonomy in Learning*, London: Kogan Page.

Heywood, J. (1989) *Assessment in Higher Education*, Chichester: Wiley.

Heywood, J. (2000) *Assessment in Higher Education: student learning, teaching, programmes and institutions*, London: Jessica Kingsley.

Hibberd, B. (2002) 'It's a lot harder than politics: students' experience of history at Advanced level', *Teaching History*, 109: 39–43.

Higher Education Funding Council for England (1994) *Subject Overview Report: quality assessment of history*, Bristol: Higher Education Funding Council.

Hill, K. (1996) 'My first seminars', in D. Allan (ed.) *In at the Deep End: first experiences of university teaching*, Lancaster: Centre for Innovation, Lancaster University.

History Benchmarking Group (2000) Subject Benchmark Statement: academic standards – history, Gloucester: Quality Assurance Agency for Higher Education.

History at the Universities Defence Group (1998a) *Standards in History: final report to the quality assurance agency*, London: HUDG.

History at the Universities Defence Group (1998b) Submission to the National Committee of Inquiry into Higher Education, London: HUDG.

Hitchcock, T., Shoemaker, R. and Tosh, J. (2000) 'Skills and the structure of the history curriculum', in A. Booth and P. Hyland (eds) *The Practice of University History Teaching*, Manchester: Manchester University Press.

Hoberman, L. (1999) 'The immigrant experience and student-centred learning: an oral history video project', in S. Gillespie (ed.) *Perspectives on Teaching Innovations: teaching to think historically*, Washington, DC: American Historical Association.

Hodges, M. (1998) 'Explorations in teaching inspiration: a seminar for students beginning dissertations', *Journal of American History*, 84: 1439–46.

Hodgson, V. (1997) 'Lectures and the experience of relevance', in F. Marton, D. Hounsell and N. Entwistle (eds) *The Experience of Learning*, Edinburgh: Scottish Academic Press.

Holden, K. (2001) 'Webs of learning: the role of new technology in teaching history at the University of the West of England', HESDA briefing paper no. 89.

Holt, T. (1990) *Thinking Historically: narrative, imagination and understanding*, New York: College Entrance Examination Board.

Honey, P. and Mumford, A. (1992) *The Manual of Learning Styles*, Maidenhead: P. Honey.

Hounsell, D. (1987) 'Essay-writing and the quality of feedback', in J. Richardson, M. Eysenck and D. Warren-Piper (eds) *Student Learning: research in education and cognitive psychology*, Buckingham: Open University Press.

Hounsell, D. (1997) 'Contrasting conceptions of essay-writing', in F. Marton, D. Hounsell and N. Entwistle (eds) *The Experience of Learning*, Edinburgh: Scottish Academic Press.

Hounsell, D. (2000) 'Reappraising and recasting the history essay', in A. Booth and P. Hyland (eds) *The Practice of University History Teaching*, Manchester: Manchester University Press.

Hounsell, D., McCulloch, M. and Scott, M. (eds) (1996) *The ASHE Inventory: changing assessment practices in Scottish higher education*, Edinburgh: Centre for Teaching, Learning and Assessment.

Hounsell, D., Tait, H. and Day, K. (1997) *Support for Course Organisation: feedback on courses and programmes of study*, Edinburgh: Centre for Teaching, Learning and Assessment.

Hoyt, D. and Pallett, W. (1999) 'Appraising teaching effectiveness: beyond student ratings', *IDEA Paper* no. 36.

Hughes-Warrington, M. (1996) 'How good an historian should I be?: R G Collingwood on education', *Oxford Review of Education*, 22: 217–35.

Humphreys, D. (2000) 'New research on faculty attitudes on the benefits of diverse learning environments', *Diversity Digest*, Spring/Summer: 3–32.

Hunter, L. (1998) 'The future of teaching history research methods classes in the electronic age', in D. Trinkle (ed.) *Writing, Teaching, and Researching History in the Electronic Age*, New York: M.E. Sharpe.

Husbands, C. (1996) *What is History Teaching?: language, ideas and meaning in learning about the past*, Buckingham: Open University Press.

Hutchings, P. (1996) *Making Teaching Community Property: a menu for peer collaboration and peer review*, Washington, DC: American Association for Higher Education.

Hutchings, P. (ed.) (1998) *The Course Portfolio: how faculty can examine their teaching to advance practice and improve student learning*, Washington, DC: American Association for Higher Education.

Hutchings, P. (2000) 'Windows on practice: cases about teaching and learning', *Change*, 25: 14–21.

Hvolbek, R. (1993) 'History and humanities: teaching as destructive certainty', in R. Blackey (ed.) *History Anew: innovations in the teaching of history today*, Long Beach, CA: California State University Press.

Hyland, P. (1994) 'A divisional initiative to move all courses to resource-based learning', in J. Wisdom and G. Gibbs (eds) *Course Design for Resource Based Learning: humanities*, Oxford: Oxford Centre for Staff Development.

Hyland, P. (1996a) 'Examining action research to improve seminars through assessment', in G. Gibbs (ed.) *Improving Student Learning: using research to improve student learning*, Oxford: Oxford Centre for Staff and Learning Development.

Hyland, P. (1996b) 'Measuring and improving the quality of teaching', in A. Booth and P. Hyland (eds) *History in Higher Education*, London: Blackwell.

Hyland, P. (2000) 'Learning from feedback on assessment', in A. Booth and P. Hyland (eds) *The Practice of University History Teaching*, Manchester: Manchester University Press.

Industrial Society (1995) *Managing Best Practice: mentoring*, London: Industrial Society.

Ivanic, R., Clark, R. and Rimmershaw, R. (2000) 'What am I supposed to make of this? The messages conveyed to students by tutors' written comments', in M. Lea and B. Stierer (eds) *Student Writing in Higher Education: new contexts*, Buckingham: Open University Press.

Jaques, D. (1991, 2nd edn) *Learning in Groups*, London: Kogan Page.

Jenkins, K. (1991) *Rethinking History*, London: Routledge.

REFERENCES

Jenkins, K. (1996) 'Teaching history theory: a radical introduction', in A. Booth and P. Hyland (eds) *History in Higher Education*, London: Blackwell.

Jenkins, K. (1997) *The Postmodern History Reader*, London: Routledge.

Jenkins, K. (2003) *Refiguring History*, London: Routledge.

Johnson, D., Johnson, R. and Smith, K. (1994) *Active Learning: co-operation in the college classroom*, Edina, MN: Interaction Book Company.

Johnson, D., Johnson, R. and Smith, K. (1998) 'Co-operative learning returns to college: what evidence is there that it works?', *Change*, 30: 26–35.

Jones, K. (1994) *Icebreakers: a sourcebook of games, exercises and simulations*, London: Kogan Page.

Jones, M., Siraj-Blatchford, J. and Ashcroft, K. (1997) *Researching into Student Learning in Higher Education*, London: Kogan Page.

Jordanova, L. (2000) *History in Practice*, London: Arnold.

Joyce, P. (1998) 'The return of history: postmodernism and the problem of academic history', *Past and Present*, 158: 207–35.

Kaldeway, K. and Korthaven, F. (1995) 'Training in studying in higher education: objectives and effects', *Higher Education*, 30: 81–97.

Keirn, T. (1999) 'Starting small: the creation of a year fourteen history standard', *Organization of American Historians Newsletter*, November: 9–10.

Kember, D. (1997) 'A reconceptualisation of the research into university academics' conceptions of teaching', *Learning and Instruction*, 7: 255–75.

Kember, D. (2000) *Action Learning and Action Research: improving the quality of teaching and learning*, London: Kogan Page.

Kember, D. and Gow, L. (1994) 'Orientations to teaching and their effect on the quality of student learning', *Journal of Higher Education*, 65: 58–74.

Kemmis, S. (1988) 'Action research', in J. Reeves (ed.) *Educational Research, Methodology, and Measurement: an international handbook*, Oxford: Pergamon.

King, P. and Kitchener, K. (1994) *Developing Reflective Judgement: understanding and promoting intellectual growth and critical thinking in adolescents and adults*, San Francisco: Jossey-Bass.

Kitson-Clark, G. (1973) 'A hundred years of the teaching of history at Cambridge 1873–1973', *Historical Journal*, 16: 535–53.

Knight, P. (2002) *Being a Teacher in Higher Education*, Buckingham: Open University Press.

Knight, P. and Trowler, P. (1999) 'It takes a village to raise a child: mentoring and the socialisation of new entrants to the academic professions', *Mentoring and Tutoring*, 7: 23–34.

Knight, P. and Trowler, P. (2000) 'Departmental-level cultures and the improvement of learning and teaching', *Studies in Higher Education*, 25: 70–83.

Knight, P. and Trowler, P. (2001) *Departmental Leadership in Higher Education*, Buckingham: Open University Press.

Knowles, M. (1975) *Self-directed Learning: a guide for learners and teachers*, New York: Associated Press.

Knowles, M. (1986) *Using Learning Contracts*, San Francisco: Jossey-Bass.

Kolb, D. (1984) *Experiential Learning: experience as the source of learning and development*, Englewood Cliffs, NJ: Prentice-Hall.

Koman, R. (1999) 'Historic places: their use in teaching and learning', in S. Gillespie (ed.) *Perspectives on Teaching Innovations: teaching to think historically*, Washington, DC: American Historical Society.

Kornblith, G. and Lasser, C. (2001) 'Teaching the American history survey at the opening of the twenty-first century: a round table discussion', *Journal of American History*, 87: 1409–41.

Kornfeld, E. (1993) 'Representations of history: role-playing debates in college history courses', in R. Blackey (ed.) *History Anew: innovations in the teaching of history*, Long Beach, CA: California State University Press.

Kreber, C. (ed.) (2001) *Revisiting Scholarship: perspectives on the scholarship of teaching*, San Francisco: Jossey-Bass.

Kreber, C. (2002) 'Controversy and consensus on the scholarship of teaching', *Studies in Higher Education*, 27: 152–67.

Kuh, G. (1994) *The Student Learning Imperative: implications for student affairs*, Indianapolis, IN: American College Personnel Association.

Kuh, G. (1995) 'The other curriculum: out-of-class experiences associated with student learning and personal development', *Journal of Higher Education*, 66: 124–55.

Lang, S. (1991) *A Level History: the case for change*, London: Historical Association.

Langer, E. (1997) *The Power of Mindful Learning*, Reading, MA: Addison-Wesley.

Langer, J. (1992) 'Speaking of knowing: conceptions of understanding in academic disciplines', in A. Herrington and C. Moran (eds) *Writing, Teaching and Learning in the Disciplines*, New York: Modern Language Association of America.

Laurillard, D. (1994) *Rethinking University Teaching: a framework for the effective use of educational technology*, London: Routledge.

Lea, M. and Street, B. (2000) 'Student writing and staff feedback in higher education: an academic literacies approach', in M. Lea and B. Stierer (eds) *Student Writing in Higher Education: new contexts*, Buckingham: Open University Press.

Lee, P. (1970) 'History at the universities: the consumers' view: 1. Oxford University', *History*, 55: 327–36.

Lee, P. (1994) 'Historical knowledge and the national curriculum', in H. Bourdillon (ed.) *Teaching History*, Buckingham: Open University Press.

Lee, P., Ashby, R. and Dickinson, A. (1996) 'Progression in children's ideas about history', in M. Hughes (ed.) *Progression in Learning*, Clevedon: Multilingual Matters.

Leinhardt, G. (1994) 'History: a time to be mindful', in G. Leinhardt, I. Beck and C. Stainton (eds) *Teaching and Learning in History*, Hillsdale, NJ: Lawrence Erlbaum.

Leinhardt, G. (2000) 'Lessons on teaching and learning in history from Paul's pen', in P. Stearns, P. Seixas and S. Wineburg (eds) *Knowing, Teaching and Learning History*, New York: New York University Press.

Leinhardt, G., Beck, I. and Stainton, C. (eds) (1994) *Teaching and Learning in History*, Hillsdale, NJ: Lawrence Erlbaum.

Lewis, E. and Theoharris, J. (1996) 'Race in a world of overlapping diasporas: the history curriculum', in A. Booth and P. Hyland (eds) *History in Higher Education*, London: Blackwell.

Light, G. and Cox, R. (2001) *Learning and Teaching in Higher Education: the reflective professional*, London: Paul Chapman.

Lowenthal, D. (2000) 'Dilemmas and delights of learning history', in P. Stearns, P. Seixas and S. Wineburg (eds) *Knowing, Teaching and Learning History: national and international perspectives*, New York: New York University Press.

Lubelska, K. (1996) 'Gender in the curriculum', in A. Booth and P. Hyland (eds) *History in Higher Education*, London: Blackwell.

Luker, P. (1987) 'Some case studies of small group teaching', unpublished PhD thesis, University of Nottingham.

Maassen, P. and Van Vught, F. (eds) (1996) *Inside Academia: new challenges for the academic profession*, Utrecht: Centre for Higher Education Policy Studies.

McAleavy, T. (1998) 'The use of sources in school history 1910–1998: a critical perspective', *Teaching History*, 91: 10–16.

McConnell, D. (2000, 2nd edn) *Implementing Computer Supported Co-operative Learning*, London: Kogan Page.

McDrury, J. and Alterio, M. (2001) 'Achieving reflective learning using storytelling pathways', *Innovations in Education and Teaching International*, 38: 63–73.

McGill, I. and Beaty, L. (1995) *Action Learning: a guide for professional managers and educational developers*.

McGivney, V. (1996) *Staying or Leaving the Course: non-completion and retention of mature students in further and higher education*, Leicester: NIACE.

McKeachie, W. (1994), *Teaching Tips: a guidebook for the beginning college teacher*, Lexington, MA: D.C. Heath.

McKernan, J. (1991) *Curriculum Action Research: a handbook of methods and resources for the reflective practitioner*, London: Kogan Page.

McMichael, A. (1998) 'The historian, the internet, and the web: a reassessment', *Perspectives*, 36: 29–32.

McNiff, J. (1992) *Action Research: principles and practice*, London: Routledge.

McNiff, J., Lomax, P. and Whitehead, J. (1996) *You and Your Action Research Project*, London: Routledge.

Malseed, J. (1992) *Forty-Eight Warm-ups for Group Work*, Lancaster: Centre for Innovation in Higher Education, Lancaster University.

Marchand, R. (1999) 'Further comment on Daniel Trifan's "active learning: a critical examination" ', in S. Gillespie (ed.) *Perspectives on Teaching Innovations: teaching to think historically*, Washington, DC: American Historical Society.

Marsh, H. (1987) 'Students' evaluations of university teaching: research findings, methodological issues and directions for future research', *International Journal of Educational Research*, 11: 253–388.

Martin, E. and Ramsden, P. (1987) 'Learning skills or skill in learning', in J. Richardson, M. Eysenck and D. Warren-Piper (eds) *Student learning: research in education and cognitive psychology*, Buckingham: Open University Press.

Martin, E., Prosser, M., Trigwell, K., Lueckenhausen, G. and Ramsden, P. (2001) 'Using phenomenography and metaphor to explore academics' understanding of subject matter and teaching', in C. Rust (ed.) *Improving Student Learning*, Oxford: Oxford Centre for Staff and Learning Development.

Martin, M. (1997) 'Emotional and cognitive effects of examination proximity in female and male students', *Oxford Review of Education*, 23: 479–86.

Marton, F. and Saljo, R. (1976a) 'On qualitative differences in learning I: outcome and process', *British Journal of Educational Psychology*, 46: 4–11.

Marton, F. and Saljo, R. (1976b) 'On qualitative differences in learning II: outcome as a function of the learner's conception of the task', *British Journal of Educational Psychology*, 46: 115–27.

Marton, F., Dall'Alba, G. and Beaty, L. (1993) 'Conceptions of learning', *International Journal of Educational Research*, 19: 277–300.

Marton, F., Hounsell, D. and Entwistle, N. (eds) (1997, 2nd edn) *The Experience of Learning: implications for teaching and studying in higher education*, Edinburgh: Scottish Academic Press.

Marty, M. (1994) 'Historians' crafts: common interests in a diverse profession', *Journal of American History*, 81: 1078–87.

Marwick, A. (1996) 'Structured distance learning', in A. Booth and P. Hyland (eds) *History in Higher Education*, London: Blackwell.

Marwick, A. (2001) *The New Nature of History: knowledge, evidence, language*, London: Palgrave.

Mattheisen, D. (1993) 'Finding the right film for the history classroom', in R. Blackey (ed.) *History Anew: innovations in the teaching of history*, Long Beach, CA: California State University Press.

Matthews, R. (1996) 'Collaborative learning: creating knowledge with students', in R. Menges and M. Weimer (eds), *Teaching on Solid Ground: using scholarship to improve practice*, San Francisco: Jossey-Bass.

Melton, R. (1997) *Objectives, Competencies and Learning Outcomes: developing instructional materials in open and distance learning*, London: Kogan Page.

Menges, R. and Weimer, M. (eds) (1996) *Teaching on Solid Ground: using scholarship to improve practice*, San Francisco: Jossey-Bass.

Mentkowski, M. (2000) *Learning that Lasts: integrating learning, development and performance in college and beyond*, San Francisco: Jossey-Bass.

Meyers, C. (1986) *Teaching Students to Think Critically*, San Francisco: Jossey-Bass.

Meyers, C. and Jones, T. (1993) *Promoting Active Learning: strategies for the college classroom*, San Francisco: Jossey-Bass.

Miller, C. and Parlett, M. (1974) *Up to the Mark: a study of the examinations game*, London: Society for Research into Higher Education.

Moon, J. (1995) 'Writing learning outcomes for modules in higher education', UCoSDA Briefing Paper Twenty-Eight.

Moon, J. (1999) *Reflection in Learning and Professional Development*, London: Kogan Page.

Moxley, D., Najor-Durack, A. and Dumbrigue, C. (2001) *Keeping Students in Higher Education: successful practices and strategies for retention,* London: Kogan Page.

Munslow, A. (1997) *Deconstructing History*, London: Routledge.

Murray, K. and MacDonald, R. (1997) 'The disjunction between lecturers' conceptions of teaching and their claimed educational practice', *Higher Education*, 33: 331–49.

Nash, G., Jeffrey, J., Howe, J., Frederick, P., Davis, A. and Winkler, A. (1994) *The American People: creating a nation and a society*, New York: Longman.

National Center for History in the Schools (1996) *National Standards for History*, Los Angeles: University of California.

National Curriculum History Working Group (1994) 'National curriculum history working group final report', in H. Bourdillon (ed.) *Teaching History*, Buckingham: Open University.

Neumann, R., Parry, S. and Becher, T. (2002) 'Teaching and learning in their disciplinary contexts: a conceptual analysis', *Studies in Higher Education*, 27: 405–17.

Newton, D. (2000) *Teaching for Understanding: what it is and how to do it*, London: Routledge.

Newton, D. and Newton, L. (1998) 'Enculturation and understanding: some differences between sixth formers' and graduates' conceptions of understanding in history and science', *Teaching in Higher Education*, 3: 339–63.

Newton, D., Newton, L. and Oberski, I. (1998) 'Learning and conceptions of understanding in history and science: lecturers and new graduates compared', *Studies in Higher Education*, 23: 43–58.

Newton, J. (2000) 'Feeding the beast or improving quality', *Quality in Higher Education*, 6: 153–63.

Nicholls, D. (1992) 'Making history students enterprising: independent study at Manchester Polytechnic', *Studies in Higher Education*, 17: 67–80.

Nicholls, D. (1993) 'Using contracts in project placements', in J. Stephenson and M. Laycock (eds) *Using Learning Contracts in Higher Education*, London: Kogan Page.

Nicholls, D. (1994) 'Preparing student history teachers as subject co-ordinators', in L. Thorley and R. Gregory (eds) *Using Group-based Learning in Higher Education*, London: Kogan Page.

Nicholson, T. and Ellis, G. (2000) 'Assessing group work to develop collaborative learning', in A. Booth and P. Hyland (eds) *The Practice of University History Teaching*, Manchester: Manchester University Press.

Nickerson, R. (1985) 'Understanding understanding', *American Journal of Education*, 93: 201–39.

Nicol, D. (1997) 'Research on learning and higher education teaching', UCoSDA Briefing Paper Forty-Five.

Norton, L. and Crowley, C. (1995) 'Can students be helped to learn?: an evaluation of an approaches to learning programme for first year students', *Higher Education*, 19: 307–28.

Novick, P. (1988) *That Noble Dream: the objectivity question and the American historical profession*, Cambridge: Cambridge University Press.

Oberly, J. (1999) 'A comment on Daniel Trifan's "active learning: a critical examination"' in S. Gillespie (ed.) *Perspectives on Teaching Innovations: teaching to think historically*, Washington, DC: American Historical Association.

O'Malley, M. and Rosenzweig, R. (1997) 'Brave new world or blind alley? American history on the web', *Journal of American History*, 84: 132–55.

O'Neill, C. and Wright, A. (1993) *Recording Teaching Accomplishment: a Dalhousie guide to the teaching dossier*, Halifax, Nova Scotia: Office of Instructional Development, Dalhousie University.

Otter, S. (1992) *Learning Outcomes in Higher Education*, London: Unit for the Development of Higher Education.

Palmer, P. (1998) *The Courage to Teach: exploring the inner landscape of a teacher's life*, San Francisco: Jossey-Bass.

Paloff, R. and Pratt, K. (1999) *Building Learning Communities in Cyberspace: effective strategies for the online classroom*, San Francisco: Jossey-Bass.

Parlett, M. (1977) 'The department as a learning milieu', *Studies in Higher Education*, 2: 173–81.

Partington, G. (1980) *The Idea of a Historical Education*, Windsor: NFER Publishing.

Pascarella, E. and Terenzini, P. (1991) *How College Affects Students*, San Francisco: Jossey-Bass.

Pask, G. (1976) 'Styles and strategies of learning', *British Journal of Educational Psychology*, 46: 12–23.

REFERENCES

Pearce, R. (2000) 'History at University 2000', *History Today*, 50: 54–8.

Perry, W. (1970) *Forms of Intellectual and Ethical Development in the College Years: a scheme*, New York: Holt, Rinehart and Winston.

Peters, O. (1998) *Learning and Teaching in Distance Education: pedagogical analyses and interpretations in an international perspective*, London: Kogan Page.

Pleuger, G. (1997) *Undergraduate History Study: the guide to success*, Bedford: Semprigham.

Porter, J. (1999) 'Contextualizing learning and teaching: academics and the history curriculum of the future', *Innovations in Education and Training International*, 36: 205–18.

Potts, D. (1986) 'Paired learning: a workshop approach to a humanities course', in D. Bligh (ed.) *Teach Thinking by Discussion*, Guildford: Society for Research into Higher Education.

Potts, D. (1995) 'One-to-one learning', in D. Boud (ed.) *Developing Student Autonomy in Learning*, London: Kogan Page.

Pratt, D. (1992) 'Conceptions of teaching', *Adult Education Quarterly*, 42: 203–20.

Preston, G. (1996) 'Seminars for active learning', in A. Booth and P. Hyland (eds) *History in Higher Education*, London: Blackwell.

Price, M., O'Donovan, B. and Rust, C. (2001) 'Strategies to develop students' understanding of assessment criteria and processes', in C. Rust (ed.) *Improving Student Learning*, Oxford: Oxford Centre for Staff and Learning Development.

Prosser, M. and Trigwell, K. (1997) 'Perceptions of the teaching environment and its relationship to approaches to teaching', *British Journal of Educational Psychology*, 67: 25–35.

Prosser, M. and Trigwell, K. (1999) *Understanding Learning and Teaching*, Buckingham: Open University Press.

Quinlan, K. (1999) 'Commonalities and controversies in context: a study of academic historians' educational beliefs', *Teaching and Teacher Education*, 15: 447–63.

Quinlan, K. and Akerlind, G. (2000) 'Factors affecting departmental peer collaboration for faculty development: two cases in context', *Higher Education*, 40: 23–52.

Race, P. and Brown, S. (1993) *500 Tips for Tutors*, London: Kogan Page.

Ramsden, J. (1996) 'Teaching and learning through the visual media', in A. Booth and P. Hyland (eds) *History in Higher Education*, London: Blackwell.

Ramsden, P. (1979) 'Student learning and perceptions of the academic environment', *Higher Education*, 8: 411–28.

Ramsden, P. (1988) 'Context and strategy: situational influences on learning', in R. Schmeck (ed.) *Learning Strategies and Learning Styles*, New York: Plenum.

Ramsden, P. (1992) *Learning to Teach in Higher Education*, London: Routledge.

Ramsden, P. (1997) 'The context of learning in academic departments', in F. Marton, D. Hounsell and N. Entwistle (eds) *The Experience of Learning*, Edinburgh: Scottish Academic Press.

Ramsden, P. (1998) *Learning to Lead in Higher Education*, London: Routledge.

Reason, P. and Bradbury, H. (2001) *Handbook of Action Research: participative inquiry and practice*, London: Sage.

Reber, V. (1993) 'Teaching undergraduates to think like historians', in R. Blackey (ed.) *History Anew: innovations in the teaching of history*, Long Beach, CA: California State University Press.

Rice, E. (1992) 'Toward a broader conception of scholarship', in T. Whiston and R. Geiger (eds) *Research and Higher Education: the United Kingdom and the United States*, Buckingham: Open University Press.

Richardson, J. (1994) 'Mature students in higher education I: a literature survey on approaches to studying', *Studies in Higher Education*, 19: 309–25.

Richardson, J., Eysenck, M. and Warren Piper, D. (eds) (1987) *Student Learning: research in education and cognitive psychology*, Buckingham: Open University Press.

Roach, A. and Gunn, V. (2002) 'Teaching medieval towns: group exercises, individual presentations and self-assessment', *Innovations in Education and Teaching International*, 39: 196–204.

Roberts, B. (1992) 'Work-based learning: the B.A. hons. historical and political studies degree at Huddersfield Polytechnic', *PUSH Newsletter*, 3: 38–45.

Roberts, B. and Mycock, M. (1991) 'The experience of introducing work-based learning on an arts degree', *Journal of Further and Higher Education*, 15: 76–85.

Rosenzweig, R. (1995) 'So, what's new for Clio?', *Journal of American History*, 82: 1621–40.

Rowland, S. (2000) *The Enquiring University Teacher*, Buckingham: Open University Press.

Rowntree, D. (1979) *Assessing Students: how shall we know them?*, London: Harper and Row.

Rowntree, D. (1981) *Developing Courses for Students*, London: McGraw-Hill.

Salmon, G. (2000) *E-Moderating: the key to teaching and learning on-line*, London: Kogan Page.

Samuelowicz, K. and Bain, J. (1992) 'Conceptions of teaching held by teachers', *Higher Education*, 24: 93–112.

Samuelowicz, K. and Bain, J. (2001) 'Revisiting academics' beliefs about teaching and learning', *Higher Education*, 41: 299–325.

Schmeck, R. (ed.) (1988) *Learning Strategies and Learning Styles*, New York: Plenum.

Schon, D. (1983) *The Reflective Practitioner*, New York: Basic Books.

Schon, D. (1987) *Educating the Reflective Practitioner*, San Francisco: Jossey-Bass.

Schreiber, R. (1998) 'Indiana university history departments talk about history', *Perspectives*, 36: 27–8.

Schroeder, C. and Mable, P. (eds) (1994) *Realizing the Educational Potential of Residence Halls*, San Francisco: Jossey-Bass.

Seed, P. (1998) 'Teaching with the web: two approaches', *Perspectives*, 36: 9–12.

Shemilt, D. (1987) 'Adolescent ideas about evidence and methodology in history', in C. Portal (ed.) *The History Curriculum for Teachers*, Lewes: Falmer.

Sheppard, G. (1993) 'The sense of preparation: history students and high school/university articulation', *Canadian Social Studies*, 27: 107–10.

Sherry, M. (1994) 'We value teaching despite – and because of – its low status', *Journal of American History*, 81: 1051–4.

Shrock, A. and Shrock, R. (1994) 'Engaging the past', *Journal of American History*, 81: 1093–8.

Shulman, L. (1989) 'Towards a pedagogy of substance', *American Association for Higher Education Bulletin*, June: 8–13.

Shulman, L. (1993) 'Teaching as community property: putting an end to pedagogical solitude', *Change*, 25: 6–7.

Shulman, L. (1998) 'Course anatomy: the dissection and analysis of knowledge through teaching', in P. Hutchings (ed.) *The Course Portfolio*, Washington, DC: American Association for Higher Education.

Shulman, L. (1999) 'Taking learning seriously', *Change*, 31: 11–17.

Sicilia, D. (1998) 'Options and gopherholes: reconsidering choice in the technology-rich classroom', in D. Trinkle (ed.) *Writing, Teaching, and Researching History in the Electronic Age*, New York: M.E. Sharpe.

Smith, C. (1998) 'Can you do serious history on the web?', *Perspectives*, 36: 5–8..

Smyth, J. (1995) 'Developing socially critical educators', in D. Boud and N. Miller (eds) *Working with Experience: animating learning*, London: Routledge.

Snyder, B. (1971) *The Hidden Curriculum*, New York.

Soffer, R. (1994) *Discipline and Power: the university, history and the making of an English elite*, Stanford, CA: Stanford University Press.

Southgate, B. (1996) *History: what and why?*, London: Routledge.

Spaeth, D. (1996) 'Computer-assisted teaching and learning', in A. Booth and P. Hyland (eds) *History in Higher Education*, London: Blackwell.

Spaeth, D. and Cameron, S. (2000) 'Computers and resource-based history teaching: a UK perspective', *Computers and the Humanities*, 34: 325–43.

Stearns, P. (1993) *Meaning over Memory: recasting the teaching of culture and history*, Chapel Hill, NC: University of North Carolina Press.

Stearns, P. (1999) 'Teaching in transition in American higher education', paper presented at the History 2000 Conference, Bath, England.

Stearns, P. (2000) 'Getting specific about training in historical analysis: a case study in world history', in P. Stearns, P. Seixas and S. Wineburg (eds) *Knowing, Teaching and Learning History*, New York: New York University Press.

Stearns, P., Seixas, P. and Wineburg, S. (eds) (2000) *Knowing, Teaching and Learning History: national and international perspectives*, New York: New York University Press.

Stefani, L. (1997) 'Reflective learning in higher education', UCoSDA Briefing Paper Forty-Two.

Steffens, H. (1989) 'Collaborative learning in a history seminar', *History Teacher*, 22: 125–38.

Stenhouse, L. (1975) *An Introduction to Curriculum Research and Development*, London: Heinemann.

Stephenson, J. (ed.) (2001) *Teaching and Learning Online*, London: Kogan Page.

Stephenson, J. and Laycock, M. (eds) (1993) *Using Learning Contracts in Higher Education*, London: Kogan Page.

Stockton, S. (1995) 'Writing in history: narrating the subject of time', *Written Communication*, 12: 47–73.

Stovel, J. (1999) 'HELP – new tricks for old dogs', in S. Gillespie (ed.) *Perspectives on Teaching Innovations: teaching to think historically*, Washington, DC: American Historical Association.

Taylor, M. (1986) 'Learning for self-direction in the classroom: the pattern of a transition process', *Studies in Higher Education*, 11: 55–72.

Tennant, M. (1997) *Psychology and Adult Learning*, London: Routledge.

Thelen, D. (1994) 'The practice of American history', *Journal of American History*, 81: 933–60.

Thompson, P. (2000, 3rd edn) *The Voice of the Past: oral history*, Oxford: Oxford University Press.

Thompson, W. (2000) *What Happened to History?*, London: Pluto Press.

Thomson, A. (1998) *Undergraduate Life History Research Projects: approaches, issues and outcomes*, Brighton: University of Sussex.

Tillbrook, M. (2002) 'Content restricted and maturation retarded? Problems with the post-16 history curriculum', *Teaching History*, 109: 24–6.

Toohey, S. (1999) *Designing Courses for Higher Education*, Buckingham: Open University Press.

Topping, G. (1995) 'Why can't a woman be more like a man?', *Oxford Today*, 8: 24–7.

Tosh, J. (2000, 3rd edn) *The Pursuit of History: aims, methods and new directions in the study of history*, London: Palgrave.

Trifan, D. (1999) 'Active learning: a critical examination', in S. Gillespie (ed.) *Perspectives on Teaching Innovations: teaching to think historically*, Washington, DC: American Historical Association.

Trigwell, K. and Prosser, M. (1999) 'Changing approaches to teaching: a relational perspective', *Studies in Higher Education*, 21: 275–84.

Trigwell, K., Martin, E., Benjamin, J. and Prosser, M. (1999) 'Why and how can teaching be scholarly?', in C. Rust (ed.) *Improving Student Learning: improving student learning outcomes*, Oxford: Oxford Centre for Staff and Learning Development.

Trigwell, K., Martin, E., Benjamin, J. and Prosser, M. (2000) 'Scholarship of teaching: a model', *Higher Education Research and Development*, 19: 155–68.

Trinkle, D. (ed.) (1998) *Writing, Teaching, and Researching History in the Electronic Age*, New York: M.E. Sharpe.

Tripp, D. (1993) *Critical Incidents in Teaching: developing professional judgement*, London: Routledge.

Van Mentz, M. (1983) *The Effective Use of Role-Play: a handbook for teachers and trainers*, London: Kogan Page.

Van Mentz, M. (1992) 'Role-play without tears – some problems of using role play', *Simulations/Games for Learning*, 22: 2.

Voss, J. and Wiley, J. (2000) 'A case study in developing historical understanding via instruction: the importance of integrating text components and constructing arguments', in P. Stearns, P. Seixas and S. Wineburg (eds) *Knowing, Teaching and Learning History*, New York: New York University Press.

Walker, M. (ed.) (2001) *Reconstructing Professionalism in University Teaching*, Buckingham: Open University Press.

Warren, J. (1998) *The Past and Its Presenters*, London: Hodder and Stoughton.

Weimer, M. (1990) *Improving College Teaching*, San Francisco: Jossey-Bass.

Willcoxson, L. (1998) 'The impact of academics' learning and teaching preferences on their teaching practices: a pilot study', *Studies in Higher Education*, 23: 59–70.

Williams, R. and Davies, I. (1998) 'Interpretations of history: issues for teachers in the development of pupils' understanding', *History Teaching*, 91: 36–40.

Wilson, A. (1980) 'Structuring seminars: a technique to allow students to participate in the structuring of small group discussion', *Studies in Higher Education*, 5: 81–4.

Wilson, A. (ed.) (1993) *Rethinking Social History: English society 1570–1920 and its interpretation*, Manchester: Manchester University Press.

Wineburg, S. (1994) 'The cognitive representation of historical texts', in G. Leinhardt, I. Beck. and C. Stainton (eds) *Teaching and Learning in History*, Hillsdale, NJ: Lawrence Erlbaum.

REFERENCES

Wineburg, S. (2000) 'Making historical sense', in P. Stearns, P. Seixas and S. Wineburg (eds) *Knowing, Teaching and Learning History*, New York: New York University Press.

Wineburg, S. (2001) *Historical Thinking and Other Unnatural Acts: charting the future of teaching the past*, Philadelphia, PA: Temple University Press.

Winslow, B., Wiggins, K. and Carpio, M. (1998) 'Using multimedia computer technology to teach United States history', in D. Trinkle (ed.) *Writing, Teaching, and Researching History in the Electronic Age*, New York: M.E. Sharpe.

Winstanley, M. (1992) 'Group work in the humanities: history in the community, a case study', *Studies in Higher Education*, 17: 55–65.

Wisdom, J. and Gibbs, G. (eds) (1994) *Course Design for Resource Based Learning: humanities*, Oxford: Oxford Centre for Staff Development.

Wisker, G. (1997) 'Assessing for learning in English studies: some innovative practices', *Teaching in Higher Education*, 2: 123–39.

Wissenberg, A. (1996) 'TLTP history courseware consortium: a project report', *History and Computing*, 8: 46–7.

Witkin, H. (1976) 'Cognitive style in academic performance and in teacher–student relations', in S. Messick (ed.) *Individuality in Learning*, San Francisco: Jossey-Bass.

Wong, C., Day, J., Maxwell, S., and Meara, N. (1995) 'A multitrait-multimethod study of academic and social intelligence in college students', *Journal of Educational Psychology*, 87: 117–33.

Wrigley, C. (1980) *A. J. P. Taylor: a complete annotated bibliography and guide to his historical and other writings*, Brighton: Harvester Press.

Ylijoki, O.-H. (1994) 'Students' conceptions of teaching and learning', Paper presented at the Society for Research into Higher Education Conference, York.

Zuber-Skerritt, O. (1987) 'The integration of university student learning skills in undergraduate programmes', *Programmed Learning and Technology*, 24: 62–9.

Zuber-Skerritt, O. (1992) *Action Research in Higher Education: examples and reflections*, London: Kogan Page.

Zukas, M. and Malcolm, J. (1999) 'Pedagogies for lifelong learning: building bridges or building walls?, Paper presented at a global Internet colloquium on supporting lifelong learning, www.open.ac.uk/lifelong-learning/papers/index.html.

INDEX

INDEX

Schreiber, R. 3
Schroeder, C. 69
scientific historian 53, 54–5
secondary sources 19, 23, 25, 85,
    103–4, 119, 120
Seed, P. 122
self-assessment 120, 135, 136, 137,
    140, 141
self-awareness 25, 27, 78–80, 119, 136
self-confidence 7, 47, 118
self-esteem 7
self-expression 27
self-help groups 113
self-observation 155–9
self-reflection 11, 27, 78–9, 107, 135,
    146
self-reliance 118
seminars 8–9, 44, 60, 89, 91, 92–3,
    115, 131
serialist learning strategies 36
Shemilt, D. 16
Sheppard, G. 124
Sherry, M. 149
Shrock, A. 1, 8, 57
Shrock, R. 1, 8, 57
Shulman, L. 9, 151
Sicilia, D. 107, 121
silence 47, 48
simple audit 155
simulations 98–9
site visits 117–19
skills 4, 7, 14, 22–8, 71, 81–2, 84,
    123–6; -focused process-oriented
    approach 53, 55
Smith, K. 8
Smyth, J. 156
Snyder, B. 69
social class 46, 53, 96, 108
Soffer, R. 11, 26, 54, 133
Southgate, B. 27
Spaeth, D. 120, 121
spider diagram 95
Stalin, J. 18
Stearns, P. 16, 24, 55, 76, 124, 149, 151
Stefani, L. 106
Steffens, H. 114, 115
Stenhouse, L. 169
Stephenson, J. 119
Stockton, S. 145
stories 100–2

story writing 106–7
storyteller 53, 56, 165–6
Stovel, J. 103
    strategic approach 38
strategies, awareness of 10
Street, B. 146
structure 45, 72, 73, 80–5, 131
Structure of the Observed Learning
    Outcome 21
student activity, organizing and
    managing 61–2
Study Processes Questionnaire 141
study teams 113
study-skills programme 124–5
style of teaching 58
sub-groups 9, 97–8
Subject Benchmark Statement 23
Subject Centres 151
subject-focused study 85
subjectivity 47, 48
summative functions 129, 147
supervision 114
support 71
surface approach to learning 36–7, 38,
    49
survival keynote 94
Swain, G. 133
Swallow, B. 41
SWOT analysis 155

task 31, 134
Taylor, M. 18, 126
teachers, role of 41–3
teaching circles 165–7
Teaching and Learning Technology
    Programme 120
teaching methods 43–5, 69
teaching tasks 79
technical model 168
technology, new 119–23
Tennant, M. 31, 41
Terenzini, P. 31
Thelen, D. 1, 2, 52, 54, 150
themes 79
Theoharris, J. 4
theories of teaching and learning 20,
    58–64; facilitating student learning
    62–4; organizing and managing
    student activity 61–2; transmission
    59–61

201